ANSWERING
TO THE
LANGUAGE

Distinguished novelist and poet C. K. Stead is
also widely admired for his literary criticism,
particularly his classic study, *The New Poetic*.
Here he brings together 44 essays on a wide
range of literary topics, from Yeats and
Katherine Mansfield (on both of whom he is a
recognized authority) to Booker Prizewinners
Keri Hulme and Peter Carey. Always lively,
often provocative, *Answering to the Language* is a
collection of major significance for all those
interested in twentieth-century writing in
English.

Poetry
Whether the Will is Free
Crossing the Bar
Quesada
Walking Westward
Geographies
Poems of a Decade
Paris
Between

Fiction
Smith's Dream
Five for the Symbol
All Visitors Ashore
The Death of the Body
Sister Hollywood

Criticism
The New Poetic
In the Glass Case
Pound, Yeats, Eliot, & the Modernist Movement

Edited
New Zealand Short Stories Second Series
Measure for Measure: a Casebook
Letters & Journals of Katherine Mansfield
Collected Stories of Maurice Duggan

ANSWERING TO THE LANGUAGE

Essays on Modern Writers

C. K. STEAD

AUCKLAND UNIVERSITY PRESS

First published 1989
Auckland University Press
University of Auckland
Private Bag, Auckland

ISBN 1 86940 038 0

Typeset by Sabagraphics Ltd
Printed by SRM Production Services

Publication is assisted by the New Zealand Literary Fund
of the Queen Elizabeth II Arts Council.

ACKNOWLEDGEMENTS

My thanks are due to the editors who asked me to write for (in the
U.K.) the *London Magazine*, the *London Review of Books*, the *New
Statesman*, *PN Review*, and the *Times Literary Supplement*; (in Australia)
AUMLLA, the *Sydney Morning Herald*, and *Scripsi*; (in Canada) *Ariel*,
and the *Yeats/Eliot Review*; (in Germany) *Akzente*; (in France)
Libération; (in New Zealand) the *Press*, the *Dominion, Islands, Landfall*,
the *NZ Listener*, *Metro*, and *Rambling Jack*. Thanks also to publishers
who commissioned work reprinted here — the Athlone Press, Croom
Helm, and Vanderbilt University Press; and to my hosts at the Yeats
Summer School, Sligo, the Princess Grace Irish Library, Monte Carlo,
the University of Liège, the University of Victoria, B.C., Harvard
University, New York University, and the University of California at
Los Angeles. A special acknowledgement goes to my editors at
Auckland University Press, first Dennis McEldowney and now
Elizabeth Caffin.

C.K.S.

CONTENTS

INTRODUCTION:
AT THE GRAVES OF YEATS

In August 1986, I went as one of the lecturers to the Yeats Summer School in Sligo, Ireland. Every morning at breakfast in the Silver Swan Hotel I sat looking down at the shallow fast-flowing river that rushes over rocks, between stone walls, under stone bridges, from Lake Innisfree through Sligo town and on past the quays to the Atlantic. More than twenty years after publishing a chapter in *The New Poetic* on Yeats I was in the Yeats countryside for the first time. On a hot Sunday I set out to walk from Sligo to the Yeats grave in Drumcliff Churchyard. It might have been four miles each way — I'm not sure, but it seemed a long walk in the heat. Just before reaching the churchyard I found a little isolated store where I bought a can of cold drink and a small bar of chocolate.

The grave as I recall it was not far from the church door. There was a line of tall trees, beyond which, across fields, you could see Ben Bulben.

> Under bare Ben Bulben's head
> In Drumcliff Churchyard Yeats is laid.

Standing there I had a moment of intense well-being which at first I mistook for something literary. Then I recognized it as my body's grateful response to chocolate and chilled lemonade. I thought how differently I would have felt if, as a young and ardent admirer, I had stood there; and I remembered the feelings I had had in the 1950s standing looking at the bare white cross on a Welsh hillside which at that time was all that marked the grave of Dylan Thomas.

There is loss in this change — this aging; but I'm sure there is gain as well. Once the power of Yeats's poetry was its own justification, and it evoked a corresponding reverence. Now, incantation is not enough. In some of the essays in this collection I make demands of the poems

9

that might have seemed needless or impertinent twenty-five years ago. To some readers they will seem needless or impertinent now. I don't think there is a way of determining that the critic then or the critic now is 'right'. Though they are the same person, and in agreement that Yeats is a great poet, they are also two different critics making different demands. Criticism is never right or wrong but only more or less persuasive. We don't say Dr Johnson is one of the major critics in English because we consider him to be right (any fool can be that), but because he articulated one possible critical point of view in a way that makes us understand it and feel the presence of the man who held to it. Academic criticism often fails because it does not carry with it — in fact works to exclude — the personality of the critic. Who is responsible for these bodiless opinions? Even if we agree we may be bored.

So the man who wrote the essays, lectures, and reviews collected here is and is not the critic who wrote a many-times-reprinted piece on 'Easter 1916'. He is prepared, even in his fifties, to walk miles to visit the grave of a great poet. But when he looks down on that epitaph carved at the poet's 'command',

> Cast a cold eye
> On life, on death.
> Horseman, pass by!

he thinks, enjoying his lemonade, *What* horseman? Why did Yeats not write 'Motorist, pass by!'? Because, of course, such an injection of reality would have interfered with the rhetoric of the occasion. Yeats was the kind of poet who could not leave even his obsequies to others.

But circumstances intervened. Yeats died in 1939, not in Ireland but in Roquebrune on the French Mediterranean coast. Less than a year after my Drumcliff visit I was standing at his 'other' grave — or rather, before the stone in Roquebrune cemetery commemorating his first interment, which lasted six years until the ending of the Second World War made it possible for his bones to be brought home on an Irish warship and his instructions for burial carried out to the letter. With me were his son and daughter, now in their sixties, and two dozen of the most eminent authorities on his life and work. We had been invited by the Princess Grace Memorial Library in Monte Carlo to hold a seminar on his poetry; and on a Sunday at the end of it we made our visit. Somewhere in everyone's mind there must have been the widely discussed story that a mistake was made at the time of the disinterment, and that it was not the coffin of Yeats that was removed from Roquebrune to Drumcliff. In fact our seminar had received assurances from the local mayor that his records convinced him no such mistake could have been made.

However well- or ill-grounded, the story, like many such, is unprovable and unkillable. Yeats, possessor of a wicked Irish sense of humour, would have enjoyed it (and I once heard that his brother Jack, the painter, was its source); but it seems to me it mocks the deliberateness, the artifice, the solemnity, of Yeats's own well-laid plans for his burial, and of that epitaph with its 'Horseman, pass by!'

While we stood there enjoying the wonderful views of steep rocky slopes, headlands, and blue bays, I was aware also of two lines of big black undertaker ants marching in and out of a crack in one of the tombs which, because of the steep terrain, are cemented above ground. Whether the bones shipped home were those of Yeats or another, they must certainly have been stripped clean long before Ireland received them — bones suitable for emblematic purposes; and that, perhaps, is appropriate. Yeats is the poet who cries out 'Another emblem there!' as a swan flies over. The priority of symbol over fact in much of his work may be the aspect with which I find myself most at odds. I am the first to acknowledge the complexity of what we call 'reality'; but at heart I am, for all the difficulties such a position involves, a realist before all else. With a sort of Johnsonian literalness I feel that 'Horseman, pass by!' is a suitable injunction only in a time and place where there are horsemen. To refuse the reality, or ignore it, seems to me as much an impropriety as these reflections of mine upon the bones of the poet will seem to those who think the presence or absence of actual horsemen a mere detail and not worth quibbling over.

After the visit to Roquebrune cemetery we descended by bus to visit the ruins of the Hôtel Idéal Séjour where Yeats died. Work had begun on converting it — I think to modern apartments. But the shell remained as it must have been in the 1930s; and we walked about in the garden at the back where Anne and Michael Yeats had played as children. Michael (now a Senator of Ireland and I think a Member of the European Parliament) pointed out which trees had grown up, what buildings were new, and how the view down to the bay had changed. And here I began to experience the feelings I might have expected to feel on that walk to Drumcliff. The old hotel seemed like a stage-set for one of Yeats's last plays. I felt the ghostly presence of the old poet, dying there, attended by his wife, and the ghosts of the two children, subjects of poems which seem to bear no relation to their living presences, who on earlier, happier visits had played in this Mediterranean garden. My imagination was engaged, not by the full Yeatsian rhetoric, but by the human drama. But would the reality have so moved me if I had not first been stirred by the rhetoric?

Yeats himself articulates the problem:

> The rhetorician would deceive his neighbours,
> The sentimentalist himself; while art
> Is but a vision of reality.

11

That 'but', an Irishism for 'only', is something we may grow weary of in Yeats, but there it is cunningly placed. Art is 'only' a vision of reality! Not a picture of it, but a vision. It is reality as seen by one person, the artist.

Science can measure reality. Cameras can photograph it. Only art can arrest it. What we want from literature is both the shock of recognition — to be shown what confirms our experience; and also the shock of difference — to be shown it as someone not ourselves perceived it. If I complain sometimes of the Yeatsian artifice (and Yeats is chosen only to illustrate a critical point), it is because what is different in his vision is sometimes permitted to invade and impose itself on the reality. To put it another way, the conflict between personal and impersonal is sometimes less than equal.

Different genres of literature deal with different areas of reality. If my own interests over the years, both as writer and critic, have extended to include fiction, that I suppose is because what I have called the human drama is more generously served by it. There are some things which only fiction can do — some kinds of representation, especially of simultaneous inner and outer, which the impurity of the genre allows, and which are excluded from poetry. Conversely there are things only possible in poetry; and when I come back to poetry, either as writer or critic, I always recover my sense that it is the senior, because the most demanding, literary art.

All literature is grounded in language and in observation. Imagination, exalted by the Romantic movement, was never a vehicle of escape from reality but rather a mode of entry. It was 'sympathetic'. And under 'observation' must be included not merely close and accurate noting of detail and circumstance but also, in works of any amplitude, an awareness of society at large, of politics, of intellectual cross-currents. From time to time the writer finds himself, as in my third section, 'arguing with the zeitgeist'.

But the writer's first and last responsibility is to the language, word by word, phrase by phrase, sentence by sentence — to the sense, to the sound, to the sound-and-sense in orchestration. The language, because it belongs to us all, seems almost to have a life of its own. Sometimes it may even seem that if we pay it enough attention, serve it diligently enough, everything else will be done for us. The work will discover its own direction and meanings, as if by a kind of natural magic.

Of the languages that lie back along the genetic track before it reached me, three have been shed in favour of the fourth, English. Perhaps some shadows, some faint patterns of the others remain. All I can feel is gratitude for the marvellous, rich, sinuous, linguistic instrument, so widely dispersed and various in its local uses, which it has been my good fortune to grow up with. It is hard to imagine Yeats lamenting that aspect of his country's history that made him a poet in the English language. As a writer in Gaelic he would have been no less talented; but he would have inherited a more limited and limiting tradition, and a language with no general currency. The same is true of writers of Maori descent who know little or nothing of their native language and who write only in English.

It is unfashionable these days to talk about the common reader. We are told by modern literary theorists that no such animal exists — that we all, whether conscious of it or not, have specialist interests when we read, and that we bring to the text particular doctrinaire assumptions. There may be half a truth in that. But as I have argued in my first essay, 'Poetry', if there is a specialist in every common reader there is also a common reader in every specialist, and it is to that person I address myself. For that reason I think there is no important difference in tone, in vocabulary, or in the demands they make, between my academic papers and my reviews for journals. I am not interested in arcane dialogue. I would like, where possible, to be understood.

ONE

POETRY

POETRY

The Concise Oxford Dictionary's first definition of 'poetry' is 'art or work of the poet'. Its first definition of a poet is 'writer of poems'. Two pages back a plumber is 'workman who fits and repairs water pipes'; and plumbing is 'plumber's work'.

The differences between the two ways of defining are subtle but important. It's clear 'plumber's work' is usually done by a plumber, but may be done by a home handyman. On the other hand, 'poetry' can only be produced by a poet. Poetry is evidence of the condition of being a poet. But more, there is that definite article: not 'a poet' but 'the poet', which suggests a more special and singular identity. The capacity to be 'poet' is something inborn. In this sense it is almost possible to imagine a 'poet' who has never written a poem.

So the Concise Oxford's second definition of poetry is 'elevated expression of elevated thought or feeling in metrical or rhythmical form'; and its second definition of poet is 'writer in verse, esp. one possessing high powers of imagination, expression, etc.'. 'Elevated . . . elevated . . . high': the poet clearly belongs on some kind of pinnacle or pedestal. He and his work are lifted above the common. In earlier times he has been credited with mystical or magical powers, capable of making crops grow or rain to fall. He has been charged with celebrating weddings and victories, with lamenting defeats and deaths, and with committing to memorable form the history of family, clan or kingdom. He has been the channel of collective feeling, the packager of myth, wisdom and history. He has had about him something of the priest and something of the oracle. He has had commerce with the Muse and been receiver and transmitter of the divine breath. His symbols have included the aeolian harp, played upon by the winds of inspiration, and the winged horse, Pegasus, whose hoof striking the ground on Mt Olympus brought forth the Hippocrene fountain.

17

Not much of all this remains clearly present in modern notions of the poet; yet, faintly, it all remains. The words 'poet' and 'poetry' may appear neutral until you turn out the light, when they will be seen still to glow in the dark like hot coals. When the fashion in twentieth-century literature turned against the more extravagant claims for the poet's art inherited from the Romantic movement, the words 'poet' and 'poetry' were given a rest. 'Poetry' became 'verse', and 'poets' 'practitioners'. This was the period when anthologies had titles like *The Faber Book of Modern Verse* (1936), *The Oxford Book of Modern Verse* (1936), *The Penguin Book of English Romantic Verse* (1968), and so on. And in the writings of F. R. Leavis and the *Scrutiny* group especially, but also in the work of many other critics during the 1930s, '40s and '50s, authors of poems were almost always 'practitioners', seldom 'poets'. The words 'poet' and 'poetry' could not be neutralized simply by giving them a neutral context. They brought with them grand claims and magical associations. If literature was to be rid of that baggage, the words had to be set aside. But as the words have come back, so have the associations, which were probably in any case never effectively shed.

There are a number of reasons for this curious power that resides in the idea of poetry, and hence in the word. One is that language more than anything else is what distinguishes us as a species, and poetry has been generally conceded to be the most comprehensive and demanding use, or manifestation, of language. Language represents power in society. There are other forms power can take, from brute force through to the most modern operations of science and technology. But populations are still influenced and ultimately controlled by the word. Not by poems, it's true, but in language resides the ordering of human affairs; and though the poet is no longer the rhetorician and public bard, the sense that he has special understanding of that source of power earns a deference which you may choose to see as superstitious, but which is nonetheless real. It must surely be some sense of this fact which led Shelley to claim that poets were the unacknowledged legislators of the world.

Of course it must be acknowledged that for any and every function which is practical and specific, poetry is unsatisfactory. Messages and information are best conveyed in prose; plans for buildings, roads, bridges, in design sketches and specifications. Science and mathematics have their own languages. So has modern philosophy. As human skills have become more specialized, the function of poetry has contracted, and so it, too, has become more specialized. One no longer looks to a poet to teach history, or ethics, or the management of crops — all of which in the past have been conveyed 'in metrical or rhythmical form'. As these purposes have vanished from poetry, what has been left has not been a weakened brew but a stronger and more arcane spirit. The object of the poem, as T. S. Eliot saw it, was to be 'poetry, and not another thing'. The object of all those kinds of language which have a specific function is to serve that function. When it is served — the message understood, the information conveyed, the alarm sounded, the reward delivered — that is the end of the matter. Such language is there to be used — and (Valéry suggests) *used up*. The purpose of literary language in general, and most particularly of that kind of literary language we call poetry, is to survive any particular use. In fact language becomes poetry when it is comprehensive enough to attain to a life of its own beyond any single function.

There used to be an argument between aesthetes and moralists about what was the proper aim and object of poetry. Traditionally, poetry was enjoyed. It gave pleasure. It represented beautiful things and was itself beautiful. This was the decorative aspect of the art of poetry. On the other hand there was always the feeling that when this side became overemphasized, poetry lost some of its power, its weight, its (in Matthew Arnold's phrase) 'high seriousness'. So against its aesthetic function was its moral one. Poetry had to delight but also to instruct. In fact its aesthetic function, from this point of view, was hardly more than a sugar coating so that the pill of morality would be effortlessly swallowed.

The argument has swung back and forth, with now one side now the other seeming to have the upper hand. Since the time of the Romantic movement Keats has been held up as the great exemplar of the poetry of aestheticism — though even then it was not quite beauty for beauty's sake but beauty for the sake of the truth it bodied forth. The great public poets of the nineteenth century, on the other hand, and especially Tennyson, were read as moralists. This may not have been quite fair to them; but along with the pleasures and profits of a large audience, which Tennyson enjoyed, went disadvantages not suffered by those poets who have had 'fit audience though few'. Chief among those disadvantages was that a large audience, when there is one, asks that poetry should speak for causes beyond itself. It is not permitted to be 'poetry, and not another thing'.

So in the late years of the nineteenth century there was a reaction against poetry-as-morality — the Art for Art's Sake movement, which had a brief heyday and then died in the cold blast of scandal emanating from the trial of Oscar Wilde.

All such arguments are inevitably crude, since the antagonists tend to answer one another rather than to look clearly at the object of dispute which lies between them. Those who argue for morality are invariably arguing for a particular morality; while the 'aesthete' is often arguing against that morality rather than for poetry. Poetry becomes like the child in a custody case between warring parents — not permitted to have its own identity, but claimed by each as a possession.

Wordsworth said the poet was 'a Man speaking to Men'. It doesn't at first sight seem to match the exalted notion of the poet we have been considering. But Wordsworth goes on to make clear that those human qualities which are general as distinct from those which make a person a professional, or a specialist, will be unusually highly developed in the poet; and that the person to whom the poet speaks will be addressed 'not as a lawyer, a physician, a mariner, an astronomer, or a natural philosopher, but as a Man'. Here we have the notion of the Common Reader in a form which I think answers the objections of modern literary theorists who have argued that no such animal exists — that we are all 'specialist' readers, with special interests, commitments, and (whether recognized or not) ideological bases. Wordsworth's statement does not deny that we are none of us innocent readers. What it insists is that beneath our special interests and ideological or theoretical commitments lies the innocent ground of our humanity. It is not that the Common Reader is one person and the specialist another. It is that in every specialist there is also a Common Reader, and this is the 'Man' to whom the poetry addresses itself. This seems to me unarguably true. There is a special kind of neutrality about poetic language. As soon as it begins to argue, to cajole, to insist, the sense that we are reading a poem diminishes. Of course poets can write political or 'committed' verses, and these will sometimes (not always) survive as poems. But when they do, that is because their statement seems to exist in inverted commas. They dramatize the passion of commitment. As soon as reasoning replaces passion and dramatization in such writing, the sense that this is a poem vanishes. It is this latter kind of writing that twentieth-century criticism has tended to call 'rhetoric', using the word not in its older sense of a set of learnable skills with language, but pejoratively. 'We make of the quarrel with others rhetoric', says W. B. Yeats; 'of the quarrel with ourselves, poetry.'

There are elements of craft skill with poetry as with all the arts; but what seems to be implied when we distinguish between an art and a craft is that learned skills will not be enough — there must be that inborn potential as well. And because poetry is an art with a long history, the poet must inherit the tradition through the medium of those who have gone before. Not that the poet must have read assiduously back through the ages (though it will be none the worse for him if he has); but rather that there is a flow-on effect — a kind of apostolic succession. All past poetry is present in the poetry of the present. The poet (especially the young poet) reads rather in the way the body breathes, drawing life from what has gone before as from an atmosphere. The poet's individual talent is not sufficient to account for poetry. Only those who have acquired, by however selective a method, that sense of a living tradition flowing through poetry from age to age into the present, will carry the tradition forward.

It is true that the history of poetry is full of schools, wars, and youthful rebellions. The Romantic poets rebelled against the Augustans; Modernists rebelled against the great figures of the nineteenth century. In France rebellion is almost required — Romantics against Classicists, Parnassians against Romantics, Symbolists against Parnassians, Modernists against Symbolists, and so on. But where rebellion occurs, the flow-on effect is never less marked, and sometimes more. There is no need for rebellion where what has gone before has had no effect. It is because, in literature as in society at large, the French are such traditionalists that they have such need of rebellion.

So far I have moved around my subject in general without attempting to say what is and what is not poetry. In the popular mind — that's to say among people who don't normally read poetry — a poem is distinguishable by the fact that it is broken up into lines which usually rhyme and have some metrical pattern. Poetry is manifest in its form. Even before modern poets began to abandon regular forms, this notion was less than satisfactory. It must always have been apparent that you could write out a statement that would satisfy the formal requirements of a sonnet, or of any other verse form, without achieving poetry; while conversely, passages of prose — in the King James *Bible*, or *Moby Dick*, or *Wuthering Heights*, to take only three very obvious examples — were so heightened, and so powerful in their effect, that no reader would want to quarrel with the suggestion that they were poetry. Poetry then, almost by definition, is a quality, not a form; though to this you may add, if your disposition is strongly conservative, that the quality 'poetry' does not alone make a poem, and that a poem occurs only when that quality finds itself in conjunction with one or another of the traditional forms.

But there seems little point in insisting upon limits which poets themselves have set aside. 'Free verse', 'open form', 'field' poems, poems in prose, 'open' sonnets — though these developments certainly don't rule out the use of traditional forms, rhyme-schemes and metres, they do tend to make any rigorous observance of old measures seem like an exercise in literary pastiche — just as modern music written in the style of Mozart, however brilliant, would seem more a stylistic exercise than the composition of new and original music.

What I think we have to say is that a poem will have form, but that *the form which matters* (and this will be true even of, say, a traditional sonnet) is the one which is unique to that poem; and that a poem is a piece of writing in any form which manifests throughout, and in its unity, the quality of poetry. We have to say further, that the quality of poetry will be achieved from time to time in compositions which, by intention (a novel) or failure (some of Ezra Pound's *Cantos*) do not amount as a whole to poems. And we have to recognize that often in the present day, readers and critics find the fragmentary but brilliant

21

flashes of gold in the seam of rock of greater human and even semantic interest than the extracted and crafted ore. This is neither to be regretted nor applauded; it is simply a fact — an important fact — of literary life in our time.

Of course that begs the question of what is the quality of poetry. But we can (once again) walk around it, attempting to describe if not to define. That something is to be seen as 'poetry' will depend on a consensus of readers over a period of time.

Poems exhibit in their writing some quality — force, intensity, density, texture, incandescence — which makes them exceptional. The language seems to have a life beyond its most obvious function, which is to 'mean'. Reading it is an experience demanding and receiving more of the reader than is the case with a non-poetic text. But all of that is true of most texts which are literary as distinct from those texts which are not. So we have, really, a spectrum of literary texts from the least to the most intense, from the least to the most densely textured, from the least to the most semantically active and alive with a talent for composition, and somewhere along that spectrum we pass into the realm of 'poetry'. Traditional forms have given an illusion of marking a clear dividing line between the one and the other, but all it signals really is an intention on the part of the writer. The distinction of poetry, as we've observed already, resides more in a quality of language than in a measurable form.

One of its commonest features is said to be imagery — and I will come back to that, in part to agree, in part to question. But I think perhaps less challengeable as an inevitable feature of poetic language is economy, and this is so even in a writer like Shakespeare, where at a glance what we appear to have is linguistic opulence, words in excess of the needs of the statement. We are told frequently that economy is a stylistic virtue; that 'brevity is the soul of wit' — and so on. If that is so (and I think it is) it must be for a better reason than that generations of teachers and critics have said so. And the reason is probably relatively simple. If all of whatever was intended in twelve words — evocation, meaning, emotion, aural and visual effect — can be conveyed in eight, then those eight words, because they are working harder, doing more, will seem more active, energetic, muscular, radioactive (any one of a number of metaphors will make the point) than the twelve doing the same work. And this has the paradoxical effect of making us more rather than less aware of language as language. The language does its work; but it exists also for its own sake and in its own right. When that happens we begin to feel the action of poetry.

Many of the most obvious and exhilarating examples of this in English are found in Shakespeare. In *Antony and Cleopatra* Caesar reflects on the fickleness of the populace who want a leader only before they have him and after they lose him:

It hath been taught us from the primal state
That he which is was wish'd until he were;
And the ebb'd man, ne'er lov'd till ne'er worth love,
Comes dear'd, by being lack'd.

The lines say what the dramatic moment requires them to say, but in a way so peculiar and compacted that to anyone sensitive to language the words have a life much more memorable than their meaning alone will account for. But then, as if to double up on the effect, the speech offers an image of the fickleness of the crowd ('this common body') moving with the 'tide' like a 'flag' (said by the Shakespeare commentaries to be an iris, as indeed it is — but can we not equally read it as a flag in the more obvious sense?) in a stream —

This common body
Like to a vagabond flag upon a stream
Goes to and back, lackeying the varying tide
To rot itself with motion.

Here again it is not simply the 'meaning' that accounts for the 'poetry'; but neither alone does the image, though the image is beautiful and succinctly apposite. Again there is a sense of energy springing out of economy; and also a music in the way the words echo and half-imitate one another's sounds — 'vagabond flag upon'; 'back, lack . . .'; 'lackeying the varying . . .'. The life of the language is so intense it not only serves meaning, it also stands apart from meaning.

One of the most interesting examples, or series of examples, illustrating a failure by later poets to recognize what it is in Shakespeare's poetry that accounts for its linguistic richness is to be found in the many nineteenth-century poetic dramas which attempt to imitate him. Most (with the possible exception of two of Byron's plays) make the mistake of adding 'imagery' more and more lavishly to the basic statement. That imagery is decoration laid on rather than something growing inevitably out of the drama. The language is static and the effect artificial. The lines seem to call attention to themselves rather than to express a character or a situation. They are 'poetic' in the bad sense.

In the present century, although a great deal of thought has been given to the nature, status and function of the poetic image, the emphasis of Modernist and post-Modern poets on spoken language — an emphasis made more than ever possible by the freeing-up of poetic forms — has reduced the predominance of imagery as a prime element in poetic language. It used to be said (citing Aristotle) that the use of metaphor was a measure of genius, and that a simile was only a weak metaphor, lacking the courage of its convictions. Today it is at least as plausible to reverse the proposition and argue that a metaphor is only a simile

23

laying claim to an exactness it doesn't possess; and that poetic imagery can too easily become a short-cut. When in doubt that you are achieving 'poetry', lay on some images! In such cases imagery becomes only another artificiality, a form of 'poetic diction' — what Wordsworth called, in a withering phrase, a 'family language of poets'.

In saying this I don't mean to suggest that metaphor, with all its subtle variations that are usually gathered under the general heading of the poetic image, has had its day. But for the moment, current stylistic practice seems more often than not to suggest that the uniquely 'poetic' element in language lies elsewhere.

Much, perhaps most, poetry works by one or another form of analogy. There is almost always an air of mysteriousness or obscurity at some level. But imagery is not the only way by which language can be made to mean more than it says, or say more than it means. Sometimes the whole poem may seem to suggest, or stand for, a subject nowhere stated in the text, as in William Carlos Williams's famous

> so much depends
> upon
>
> a red wheel
> barrow
>
> glazed with rain
> water
>
> beside the white
> chickens.

No imagery there; and *why* so much depends upon the wheelbarrow, *what* depends upon it, the poet has not permitted himself to say. What he has ensured is that we have experienced it; and over that primary experience he has in effect hung a sign saying 'This is important'. The colour, the shapes, the shine, the contrasts — these are prior to thought and outlast it. Williams's 'The Red Wheelbarrow' is probably a poem against intellect — or one that puts the intellect in its place; but if it is, we as readers must not merely assent — we must make it so.

Then there are times when the whole poem may seem to contain its opposite, as in Wordsworth's strange lines about the death of Lucy:

> No motion has she now, no force
> She neither hears nor sees;
> Rolled round in earth's diurnal course
> With rocks, and stones, and trees

where the 'force' and 'motion' of the second pair of lines seem at least in part to belong to Lucy, who is said to lack them, but for whom the whole natural world has become a single eternally revolving vault.

Ever since the French Symbolists enunciated it as a principle, there has been a recognition among modern poets that, whether by accident or design, some of the best effects in poetry are achieved by a kind of openness which suggests more than it says, leaving the reader free to engage with the language and discover, or impose, 'meaning'. Poems mean many different things to different readers. Some readings may be wrong because they are perverse, silly, or ignore something of prime importance; but many different readings may be right, because one half of any reading is the reader. If one reading alone is unambiguously and unchallengeably right, we may say we are not dealing with a poetic text. It is this fact which renders so many 'definitive' academic readings, dismissive of all others, inevitably absurd.

The Romantic poets quarrelled with their Augustan predecessors about what was called 'poetic diction' — whether there was or was not a restricted language appropriate to poetry. The attempt was to get rid of literary conventions and get back closer to the living language. As Romantic poetry itself became, through the nineteenth century, a set of conventions there was yet another rebellion in the name of spoken language — that of the twentieth-century Modernists.

Throughout this period there has also been an ever-greater insistence upon particularity, concretion, in poetic language. For Dr Johnson, as for most literary theorists and poets of the eighteenth century, the purpose of poetry was to offer, in verse as near to impeccable as could be, general truths. As the faith in general truths has diminished, so the insistence upon the mysteriousness and at the same time the particularity of poetry has increased. Poetry deals in the concrete, not in abstract ideas, which belong to philosophy and other forms of prose discourse. 'No ideas but in things' William Carlos Williams insists — a statement nicely matched by his wheelbarrow poem. And even poets like W. H. Auden and Philip Larkin who were, or became, relatively conservative in their attitude to poetic form, and who seem at times to versify abstract ideas, are really dramatizers of a position rather than its proponents. Along with the 'idea' in their poems goes the dramatized persona, its upholder, to whom various readers are free variously to respond.

Language refers, 'means', denotes, points to what exists outside and beyond itself. On the other hand language has a texture of its own. It has sound, literally; and metaphorically it has colour, taste, smell, and feel. It also evokes sense impressions through meaning. It forms itself — or is formed — into grammatical structures which have symmetry and can have beauty independent of the meanings and references which they also create. In the breaking or unusual compression of the normal decorums of syntax, language can enact personality, muscularity, restlessness, anxiety. By imposing itself upon the breathing of the reader it can have a direct physical effect matching that upon mind and imagination. There is in fact such complex potential in the operations of language that it is almost impossible to be simultaneously conscious of all the things a rich poetic text is doing at any one moment. We may receive the whole operation in a single experience; and we may go back and take it apart, making ourselves conscious of all that it contained. What I think is not possible is to receive the full impression and be fully conscious of it at the same time - any more than it is possible to watch a movie and at the same time be aware of it frame by frame.

How then is such a complex operation achieved by the poet? It happens, it seems, most often by a kind of speeding up of mental processes, and it is this, I suppose, which poets have traditionally called 'inspiration'. Because in this kind of writing something is achieved that could not be produced by means of fully conscious and controlled effort, poets have tended to describe the experience magically — the feeling, for example, of being 'breathed through' by the divine spirit, or possessed by the Muse. T. S. Eliot once called it demonic possession, describing his experience in completing the final section of *The Waste Land*. Of course not all poetry is 'inspired'. Among twentieth-century poets, both W. B. Yeats and Dylan Thomas laboured their poems through many painful drafts. But one way or another an exceptional text seems to require an exceptional state of being. It is not something to be achieved simply by acts of will; and poets develop ways with themselves of achieving the necessary condition. This means in turn that poetry is a highly personal art, and one that calls not merely for invention but for that higher faculty which the Romantics called imagination.

Yet it has been traditionally thought of as a mimetic art — an art which 'imitates', or holds a mirror up to nature. Both these views — the personal and the mimetic — are surely correct. When the sense of a particular viewer disappears — when, as Yeats says, the poet vanished into the quicksilver at the back of the mirror — our desire that the view should be particular, peculiar, personal, in fact unique, may go unsatisfied. On the other hand (and this may happen if poetry goes too far in the direction of a surreal or fantastic vision, or in the case of a poet like John Ashbery whose grammar parodies many meanings but denies all of them any warrant) when the poet insists so much upon the uniqueness of his vision that we begin to lose all sense of a common world shared by reader and writer, then equally, if the poetry is not sustained by some quirk of fashion, or as that fashion passes, the call will be for more mirror and less imagining. These are poles between which the poetic pendulum inevitably and always swings.

From these opposite and necessary ends of the argument come the two seeming contradictory but really reconcilable truisms about poetry: that it deals in truth ('The true poets must be truthful', Wilfred Owen said), and that it deals in falsity ('the truest poetry is the most feigning', Shakespeare has the Clown say in *As You Like It*). Plato's position, at least in *The Republic*, is rather odd, in that he castigates — in fact casts out — the poets, not for excesses of imagination but because their mimesis is of the real world which is necessarily itself only an image of the Ideal. Poetry is a copy of a copy and the poet is punished for his fidelity to (in Wallace Stevens's phrase) 'things as they are'.

Matthew Arnold's view was that poetry would gradually take over a large part of the ground occupied by religion. T. S. Eliot mocked Arnold for this; but if we can broaden the term poetry and include all the arts, then it could be said that Arnold's prediction has been proved right. The practice of formal religion in Western society has declined in the past hundred years, while for a sizeable section of the population (though still perhaps a minority) the arts — music, literature, painting, theatre, one or all of these — represent man's highest intellectual and spiritual achievements and are the source of anything from relaxation and superior entertainment through to enlightenment and exaltation.

On the other hand, since Arnold's time the public for poetry has seemed to decline markedly, and its dissemination has in a significant degree become part of the function of university English Departments. Though it might be argued that no one who cares about poetry could do other than welcome this development, and even that English studies have saved poetry from extinction, there is room for a good deal of doubt. Academics have more and more seemed to be the possessors of the necessary keys of entry to a mysterious and difficult art; and at the same time, by 'teaching' poetry and examining students on their reading of it, they have invaded, and in many cases laid waste to, what perhaps ought to be an inviolable private domain. Poetry has become an area of specialist knowledge, like physics or higher mathematics, and teachers in schools seem less and less willing to treat it as a natural part of a general curriculum. So where it appears university studies have helped poetry, they may also have done it harm.

There must also be a question as to whether the decline in a potential audience for poetry since the nineteenth century is as absolute as it appears. Dylan Thomas, much of whose work was so obscure it seemed unimaginable that it could ever be popular, had a huge following on both sides of the Atlantic in the early 1950s. T. S. Eliot in a different, more decorous way, must have achieved very considerable sales over a lifetime. In America Allen Ginsberg in the 1960s and 1970s revived the figure of the popular public bard. In London in 1965 a poetry reading which included Ginsberg on the programme filled the Albert Hall and many were turned away. Yet that was also the period when John Betjeman, a totally different kind of poet, was becoming a household name. More recently in Britain, Craig Raine, poet and poetry editor at Eliot's old

27

firm Faber and Faber, has again given poetry a public face. In fact it is probably wrong to think of 'the public' for poetry. There are a number of publics for it, different and overlapping.

Meanwhile current critical theory has made what might be seen as the latest attempt to deprive those words 'poet' and 'poetry' of the power we began by discussing. It tells us that the poet is irrelevant — indeed in some sense non-existent; and that there is not a 'poem' but a 'text'. When reader and text are joined, the poem comes into being, uniquely. Thus the text itself in its unread state is less important than what is made of it when it is read — and there is no hierarchy of texts.

This view, which within its limits makes perfectly good sense, is usually presented as a kind of liberation — a rebellion against the authority of all the academic criticism and commentary which stands in the way of every fresh new reading. So it may be; but it is also a rebellion of the academic against the authority of literature. If both poet and poem are denied primary importance, then the critic has written himself into the position of primacy. The significant creative skill passes from poet to reader, and is demonstrated in what the critic makes of the text.

Poetry, however, is so intrinsic and inevitable an upshot of linguistic life and consciousness, it will surely survive in one form or another, whatever happens to it in the marketplace, and in the minds and writings of those who are its critics and theorists.

STENDHAL'S MIRROR AND YEATS'S LOOKING-GLASS: A RECONSIDERATION OF *THE TOWER*

In Donald Davie's still marvellously readable, challenging, and rewarding book, *Articulate Energy*, W. B. Yeats appears from time to time as the modern poet who, almost alone, holds to the 'conscious mind's intelligible structure' [1] against the chaotic 'realism' of the Modernists — a realism that for Davie is signalled by the breakdown of traditional syntax. The poet who (as Yeats liked to put it) withdraws into the quicksilver at the back of the mirror, merely reflecting the chaos that lies about him, is abandoning one of the sacred duties of art — to impose order. In *The Tower* we see the Yeatsian order imposed in two separate but related ways. These poems can be described as 'philosophical'. That's to say their 'thinking' is apparently orderly, purposeful, and of a generalizing nature. And the poet's deliberation is also apparent in the forms he uses. These poems are demonstrations of craft-skill in the very highest degree. No one who has tried to write poetry — or perhaps I should say no one who grew up writing poetry at a time when everyone experimented with verse forms — can be indifferent to this aspect of the later Yeats; and it is especially evident in the three verse sequences, 'The Tower', 'Meditations in Time of Civil War', and 'Nineteen Hundred and Nineteen'.

Yet these are also highly subjective poems. The persona and the poet are always close and often indistinguishable. Yeats's response when he reread the whole collection was surprise at what he saw as the revelation of his own bitterness. Here speaks the 'sixty-year-old smiling public man', a man troubled by the 'absurdity' of

This was first given as a lecture to the Yeats Summer School, Sligo, Ireland, in August 1986; then to the English Department, University of California at Los Angeles, April 1987. It appeared, revised, in *On Modern Poetry: Essays Presented to Donald Davie*, ed. Vareen Bell and Laurence Lerner, Nashville, Tenn., 1988.

29

                        — this caricature,
        Decrepit age that has been tied to me
        As to a dog's tail;

a poet wondering whether he should

            bid the Muse go pack,
        Choose Plato and Plotinus for a friend
        Until imagination, ear and eye,
        Can be content with argument and deal
        In abstract things.

Yeats is present in the volume as the man who has loved and lost Maud
Gonne and who continues to remember that loss with varied and powerful
emotions; as a husband late in life and father of young children; as a
man who has taken up residence, or summer residence, in a tower situated
in countryside he has already made his own in poetry; as a man recording
and commenting on a violent phase in Irish political history; as a man
anxious about the future of Western civilization; as a man trying to
order his mind while he comes to terms with the onset of old age and
what it means. And it's not just that the man, Yeats, is in the poems;
he's in them as poet, asking (for example) in verse whether he should
stop writing verse. This is a twentieth-century version of Wordsworth's
'egotistical sublime'. If one grows tired of anything in Yeats, it's likely
to be the first person singular.

    Yeats often expressed dissatisfaction with the realist tradition, citing
Stendhal's description of a novel as 'a mirror dawdling down a lane'.
He rejected most modern fiction because he felt it satisfied Stendhal's
requirement. But what if the alternative to Stendhal's objective,
perambulating mirror should be merely the poet staring into his own?
Part of my argument will be that the poet in Yeats was at war with
the philosopher. It was the philosopher who resented and rejected
Stendhal's realist mirror, but the poet had need of it if he wasn't to
go wildly astray in total subjectivity.

    Yeats's System (as he called it), set out in the book he called A Vision,
might be seen as an attempt to break out of the Berkeleyan solipsism.
It was, at least, a broadening of the view, giving pseudo-scientific
patterning to the movements of history, the rise and fall of civilizations,
and even to the changing fortunes of individual men and women, by
relating them to the mathematical precision of the stars and planets.

    The apparent objectivity of all this (leaving aside the question of its
truth, or its value) is undermined by wild rhetorical assertions of total
subjectivity — as in part III of 'The Tower' for example:

        I mock Plotinus' thought
        And cry in Plato's teeth,

> Death and life were not
> Till man made up the whole,
> Made lock, stock and barrel
> Out of his bitter soul,
> Aye, sun and moon and star, all,
> And further add to that
> That, being dead, we rise,
> Dream and so create
> Translunar Paradise.

(I will come back to those lines.) Or the lines from 'Blood and the Moon' about Berkeley:

> And God-appointed Berkeley that proved all things a
>   dream,
> That this pragmatical, preposterous pig of a world, its
>   farrow that so solid seem,
> Must vanish on the instant if mind but change its
>   theme.

Nevertheless, within that subjectivity, or Berkeleyan solipsism, the poet's view could be large or small. The prison of the self could be ample or confining; and in the years in which the poems of *The Tower* were written, Yeats went all out for amplitude. So he could be disappointed lover, or Irish republican, or paterfamilias, on a larger stage. Or he could very occasionally absent himself altogether in favour of 'history'. One such occasion, signified by the absence of the first person singular, is the poem 'Leda and the Swan':

> A sudden blow: the great wings beating still
> Above the staggering girl, her thighs caressed
> By the dark webs, her nape caught in his bill,
> He holds her helpless breast upon his breast.
>
> How can those terrified vague fingers push
> The feathered glory from her loosening thighs?
> And how can body, laid in that white rush,
> But feel the strange heart beating where it lies?
>
> A shudder in the loins engenders there
> The broken wall, the burning roof and tower
> And Agamemnon dead.
>   Being so caught up,
> So mastered by the brute blood of the air,
> Did she put on his knowledge with his power
> Before the indifferent beak could let her drop?

Yeats, as I've said, is absent from the poem, except that his fingerprints are everywhere. The form, however, is unusual. It's a sonnet. I can think of one other Yeatsian sonnet — 'While I from that reed-throated whisperer' at the end of *Responsibilities*, which has a much more extraordinary and sinuous syntax, and which, being a personal statement, seems to belong to its form. What's odd about 'Leda and Swan' is that Yeats drops the first person singular but uses the form that seems most to call for it — the sonnet being traditionally a personal expression of love or piety.

Nevertheless, formal constraints always brought the best out of him as a poet. 'Difficulty is our plough', he told Margot Ruddock;[2] it gets us 'down under the surface'. The 'difficulty' in this poem was to compress an action exactly into the octave, and its implications into the sestet.

Zeus as swan rapes Leda — that is described in the octave with a curious, almost cold precision, part pictorial, part dramatic, part psychological. The problem for me — and I don't believe I can be unusual in this — is that in the mythology the form the god takes for this invasion of the human universe is that of a bird; and what Yeats's poem does is to bring the mythological event up close, making it so real, or plausible, it becomes very nearly *de*-mythologized.

Birds were important to Yeats. Like Maud Gonne, he kept many in cages. They were caged in his poems, too, as emblems. ('Another emblem there!' as a swan goes over in one of the Coole Park poems.) Zeus in disguise is not the only swan in *The Tower*, and certainly not the only bird. Along with the swans go crows, daws, peacocks, water hens, moorhens, hawks, owls, starlings, parrots, and nightingales; then there are unspecified 'wild birds and caged birds', 'passing birds', 'birds of the air'. There are also phoenixes; there are the 'brazen hawks' and 'the innumerable clanging wings that have put out the moon' in 'The Tower'; and there is that famous golden bird Yeats was to become when he had shaken off his mortal dress. And when he wanted to present himself negatively, he chose a scarecrow for image — something that frightens the birds from their song.

The soul is likened to a swan in one of these poems. But in the sonnet Zeus as swan is decidedly not incorporeal. He's a very birdy god — an almost believable avian rapist, worthy of Alfred Hitchcock. The physical details — Leda's 'thighs caressed/ By the dark webs', her 'terrified vague fingers' that try to push the 'feathered glory' away, her 'loosening thighs', her body 'laid in that white rush' — these can be almost repellent, or absurd, or distasteful exactly in the degree to which Yeats's skill has made them real.

But if by the end of the octave the mind of a reader can be delicately poised between admiration and distaste, the opening two and a half lines of the sestet must, I think, swing the balance entirely in the poem's favour. They are among the great lines of modern poetry, and they tend to gather to them all that's positive in one's response to the octave and neutralize all the latent negatives:

> A shudder in the loins engenders there
> The broken wall, the burning roof and tower
> And Agamemnon dead.

This is Ezra Pound's method of the' luminous detail' — so little standing for so much — and it probably derives directly from the opening lines of Canto IV:

> Palace in smoky light,
> Troy but a heap of smouldering boundary stones.

The sonnet moves now to its conclusion, which takes the form of a question — not the strongest way to finish a poem, but the form is sustained perfectly, and any slight downturn in energy can be justified (if it needs justification) as a kind of postcoital lowering.

Modern criticism has learned partly from dealing with Yeats that a purist insistence that the text in isolation must yield up all its meaning won't do. It doesn't help to complain about it — it's simply a fact that all the poem 'means' is not in the text. The fullness of its meaning is found in reading other Yeats poems, and in reading his prose work. So we find 'Leda and the Swan' has a place in the book called *A Vision*, where it heads a section called 'Dove or Swan'. There Yeats tells us:

I imagine the annunciation that founded Greece as made to Leda, remembering that they showed in a Spartan temple, strung up to the roof as a holy relic, an unhatched egg of hers; and that from one of her eggs came Love and from the other War.

Eggs came from the rape. One produced Helen of Troy. They also produced those two huge abstractions of which Helen is symbol or focal point — Love and War.

Yeats's use of the word 'annunciation' signals the pattern he is constructing: new civilizations are initiated by divine intervention. Leda is to the Graeco-Roman culture what the Virgin is to the Christian. In each case the god implants the seed of the new in the mortal body of a woman. What is born lasts two thousand years. Our own civilization is about to end. As Yeats has it in 'The Second Coming' (another poem ending in a question):

> And what rough beast, its hour come round at last,
> Slouches towards Bethlehem to be born?

If you are at all of a (Dr) Johnsonian and literal disposition, as I am, you have to keep reminding yourself that all this is intellectual and symbolic. One is not required to struggle toward literal belief, nor even, I think, to whole-hearted suspension of disbelief in the rape of Leda

33

by a feathered Zeus. One must, in fact, see through the feathers to the abstract idea — that the new civilization, simply *because* it's new, must appear to the old in the guise of rapist and destroyer. Leda is victim in the poem; she is being invaded by the new and therefore the unknown. In its power there may be a kind of glory (both words occur in the poem), but she tries vainly to push it away. This brutal quality of historical inevitability was something that fascinated Yeats. To itself the Rough Beast of the future may be beautiful; to us it will appear with 'a gaze blank and pitiless as the sun'.

I suggested that in its attention to detail the poem seems to go dangerously close to de-mythologizing its subject and thus rendering it absurd. Once our extended reading has put the idea back into the event, the poem is protected against our literalness. But solving one problem can immediately produce another. Yvor Winters complains as follows:

If we are to take the high rhetoric of the poem seriously, we must really believe that sexual union is a kind of mystical experience, that history proceeds in cycles of two thousand years each, and that the rape of Leda inaugurated a new cycle . . . But no one save Yeats has ever believed these things, and we are not sure that Yeats really believed them.[3]

Although Winters is often unfair to Yeats and misrepresents him by overstatement, there is an element of truth in this objection that I think it's wrong to dismiss out of hand. A kind of 'high rhetoric', to use Winters's phrase, *is* carrying us along over some very strange intellectual territory.

My response is first to acknowledge that I can't take Yeats's 'System' seriously. But I'm prepared in some degree to entertain it, as one entertains a fiction. His history is, if you like, his narrative structure — a narrative in which the characters are half-human, half-abstract. I suppose this has always been the case in poetry that dealt with mythological figures. What is new here is the degree of self-consciousness. It's as if Yeats has produced both a primitive mythology and a modern commentary on it.

Yeats called the spiritual presences who spoke to him through the mediumship of his wife, his Unknown Instructors. When he offered to give up the rest of his life to expounding the truths they were conveying, they replied, 'No. We have come to give you metaphors for poetry'. But if the metaphors were for poetry, what was the poetry for? Not, evidently, simply a vehicle for these arcane truths — or Yeats's offer to expound them would have been accepted. How then do we answer Winters if he argues that we either take Yeats's 'silly ideas' (as he calls them) literally or condemn the poetry to a self-enclosed, self-referential function — metaphors for the sake of poetry, poetry for the sake of itself?

I think one can argue that the psychological truth of these poems resides in the notion of historical inevitability, and that's something one can accept without getting tangled up in details of gyres and cones and two-thousand-year cycles. As we age and the world ceases to be the one we were born into, history appears more and more as an unwelcome force. It alters the rules of lifemanship we grew up with; it changes the look of everything that established our notion of normality; and worse, it reminds us that we will shortly be removed altogether from the scene. Leda and the Swan can be seen, each of them, as part of the human psyche as it comes to terms with time and change. One represents an onrushing eagerness to embrace the future — to establish (in the famous concluding line of another modern sonnet) 'new styles of architecture, a change of heart'.[4] The other resists, fears, experiences horror, or what has been called lately 'the shock of the new', but is forced to recognize necessity.

And history as rapist is what makes the underlying psychology of this apparently impersonal sonnet engage and interlock with that of the personal, first-person poems of *The Tower*, where Yeats laments what time has done to his body, and resolves to prepare his mind, or his soul, for what remains of life. A man learns historical necessity by the decline of his own powers.

The sonnet concludes with a question: 'Did she put on his knowledge with his power . . . ?' If you look at three variously representative critics of Yeats — Yvor Winters, Richard Ellmann, and Helen Vendler[5] — you will find they don't agree at all on what to make of this question, and that perhaps signals a weakness. Ideally, I think, such an emphatic poem as this is should not end on something that produces uncertainty. Nevertheless, I have to say that when I look long and hard at the poem, the meaning at that point doesn't seem to me unclear.

The two key words in the question are 'knowledge' and 'power'. The god's power has been displayed in the poem. If his knowledge is also there, it must be knowledge of the future he's engendering:

> The broken wall, the burning roof and tower
> And Agamemnon dead.

Did Leda also see into the future at the moment of consummation? That I think is the question the poem asks but doesn't answer.[6] But again (if that is what the question means) it connects the poem with Yeats himself as a victim of time. In old age *he* has had a vision of the future. In another of his favourite dicta, 'It is only at the moment of darkness that the owl of Minerva descends.' Wisdom arrives too late to be of use.

The Tower as a collection (to go back to the beginning) opens with 'Sailing to Byzantium'. Here the 'I' who speaks is not quite the literal Yeats, a persona, but very close indeed to the real man. In marvellously packed lines he evokes the natural world of time and change, of procreation and death, in which he feels himself to be nothing but a scarecrow; he bids that world farewell and prays to be purged of his physical existence in 'God's holy fire':

> Consume my heart away; sick with desire
> And fastened to a dying animal
> It knows not what it is; and gather me
> Into the artifice of eternity.

In the final stanza he declares that after purging in the holy fire he will become a golden bird singing to lords and ladies of Byzantium of past, present, and future. Does he mean that after death he will become his poetry? It seems so — except that we all know Yeats believed not only in the soul's immortality but also in strange and various reincarnations. Perhaps he did want to be a golden bird. As so often in Yeats, the statement may seem equivocal. If we lean on it too literally, it will say, 'Ease off. I'm only a metaphor.' But the moment we lessen our pressure on its meaning it begins again to strut about and put on airs like a *real* statement.

But what stays powerfully with the reader is not the final stanza but those opening images of teeming nature, and then the astonishing force and directness of the self-characterization: 'sick with desire/ And fastened to a dying animal'. It's an image that makes most confessional poetry of the 1960s look pale.

Immediately after 'Sailing to Byzantium' comes the title poem, 'The Tower', and it opens with lines that seem to follow directly from the preceding poem:

> O heart, O troubled heart — this caricature,
> Decrepit age that has been tied to me
> As to a dog's tail.

He goes on to assert that his imagination is more 'Excited, passionate, fantastical' than ever, and his ear and eye more alert, yet they ('imagination, ear and eye' are repeated) must give up poetry and be content with philosophy — 'Choose Plato and Plotinus for a friend'.

There is a puzzle in this. If imagination is active and ear and eye alert, why must poetry be given away? In the end it isn't. Plato and Plotinus are sent packing and poetry seems to reassert itself, but why should the question have arisen? This poem was written in Yeats's sixtieth year. He was in reasonably good health (he had in fact thirteen years to live). He was at the height of his fame and of his powers; he was a Nobel Prize winner, an Irish senator, a family man, and (most important) he was writing more authoritatively than ever. So what was the source of this insistence on age and incompetence?

It was undoubtedly connected with sex, perhaps specifically with sexual performance. 'Sick with desire' seems to make that clear, as does a letter to Olivia Shakespear in which he says some of the poems of *The Tower* were written in a mood 'between spiritual excitement and sexual torture'. The torment came, no doubt, partly from a sense of, or a fear of, declining sexual competence, and from the very widely held belief (or perhaps one should say the very common *recognition*) of a link between sexuality and creativity. So when he says he must 'Choose Plato and Plotinus for a friend', the word 'friend' half-suggests, as it often does in Yeats, 'lover'.

All this is familiar enough, I suppose, in the history of art and literature. But in the case of Yeats there was the additional recognition of how much he had denied himself in his youth, and how that denial had sprung from a romantic conception of the spiritual bond between himself and Maud Gonne — a bond she had treated with indifference. In the later years of his life his early years of self-imposed celibacy seemed to weigh on him sometimes, as if it had all been a folly and a waste.

In the opening poem of the sequence called 'A Man Young and Old' — a poem called 'First Love' — the young man believes the woman he loves has 'A heart of flesh and blood'; but when he lays his hand on her breast, he finds 'a heart of stone'. This is reminiscent of the 'hearts with one purpose alone' in 'Easter 1916' that are 'enchanted to a stone'; and it contrasts surprisingly with what Leda experiences, raped by the Swan who is a god, or even an abstract idea, but whose 'strange heart' she feels beating. Maud Gonne had become abstract, more idea than woman; conversely, the ideas that had come to Yeats through the mediumship of his wife seemed to possess not merely wisdom, but flesh and blood.

In a letter written at the time these poems were being composed Yeats tells Olivia Shakespear — his mistress of those early years when his passion for Maud was still at its height — that he had come on two early photographs of her (Olivia). He has been struck by her beauty, and by the fact that he took so little of what she offered. And he says, 'One looks back to one's youth as to a cup that a mad man dying of thirst left half-tasted.'⁷ This in turn becomes one of the poems of 'A Man Young and Old':

> A crazy man that found a cup
> When all but dead of thirst,
> Hardly dared to wet his mouth
> Imagining, moon-accursed,
> That another mouthful
> And his beating heart would burst.
> October last I found it too
> But found it dry as bone,
> And for that reason am I crazed
> And my sleep is gone.

'The Tower', as we've seen, begins and ends with personal declarations — part I asking what the aging man is to do with himself, part III making his public/poetic last will and testament and committing his soul to school itself finally in the great traditions of art and literature. In between comes part II, a curious, apparently leisurely, not consistently well-turned perambulation around the countryside of Ballylee — thirteen eight-line stanzas invoking real and mythological characters associated with the region. We meet the aristocratic Mrs French; the beautiful peasant girl Mary Hynes; the blind poet Raftery who made Mary into his Helen as Yeats did with Maud; the local men who were driven mad by Mary's beauty, or by Raftery's songs of her beauty; then there's the man-at-arms and his troop who once occupied the tower; and finally Hanrahan, Yeats's own fictional creation.

Toward the end of this section the poet calls together the ghosts of these various characters because he has a question to put to them — in fact he has announced in the very first stanza of part II that he is going to ask them something. The question when it comes in stanza 11 is this:

> Did all old men and women, rich and poor,
> Who trod upon these rocks or passed this door,
> Whether in public or in secret rage
> As I do now against old age?

It seems a curiously empty question after such a build-up; and almost at once, without waiting for an answer, Yeats dismisses them all, except Hanrahan:

> Go therefore; but leave Hanrahan,
> For I need all his mighty memories.

And now comes the heart of part II, which makes all the rest of it seem like a beating about the bush, or a strategy of obfuscation — because Hanrahan, the one fictional character, appears to be another of those disguises for Yeats himself. He's addressed as 'Old lecher with a love on every wind'; and in the final stanza he's asked

> Does the imagination dwell the most
> Upon a woman won or woman lost?
> If on the lost, admit you turned aside
> From a great labyrinth out of pride,
> Cowardice, some silly over-subtle thought
> Or anything called conscience once;
> And that if memory recur, the sun's
> Under eclipse and the day blotted out.

This is the real question — the question behind the question — and the answer is clear enough: imagination dwells more on the woman lost than the woman won. Here for the first time — I think for the only time — Yeats sees his failure with Maud as being of his own making. She rejected him, of course. But he accepted the rejection, complied with it, built a mythology around it, made out of it something like a profession and a career. The old man, in the strength and confidence of his maturity, sees the young man's acceptance of defeat as something springing from cowardice, conscience, pride and, he says, as if for a moment he has become Yvor Winters, 'silly over-subtle thought'. So when memory recurs, it brings darkness, gloom, despondency.

It's not a particularly well-turned stanza. But to my ear it comes in some ways nearer to the feel of truth than almost anything else Yeats wrote on the subject of Maud Gonne. It's an important moment in his poetry — a brave denial of such a large part of the rhetorical and emotional structure of what he had written previously on the subject.

When I first read 'The Tower' as a young man (this was in the 1950s, and of course I'm referring to a number of readings), the whole poem seemed to gather in strength toward the final section, and especially toward the marvellous closing lines — 'Now shall I make my soul / Compelling it to study', and so on — and I don't think I gave much thought to how Yeats got there. But if I am to apply the kind of rigour that Donald Davie's criticism has taught us to bring to such matters, how can I overlook the fact that Yeats gets there via that final stanza of part II which seems to question the whole Maud-mythology and everything that goes along with it? And doesn't that moment of realism and self-reproach provide at least one measure — a very important one — by which what follows must stand or fall?

Pride, cowardice, and an over-subtlety that he allowed himself to call conscience — these, Yeats acknowledges, more than Maud herself, were what stood in the way; and these in turn permitted the romantic self-denial, the heroic celibacy, the elevation of Maud into an Irish Helen. Now the 'Old lecher with a love on every wind', blown about by alternating gusts of exaltation and bitterness, acknowledges the folly of it.

Pride is the first of the faults acknowledged. But in part III it's as if he forgets his moment of truth, or sets it aside. His pride is what he bequeaths to the young; and pride is the first quality of the people he claims as his own:

> Pride like that of the morn
> When the headlong light is loose,
> Or that of the fabulous horn,
> Or that of the sudden shower
> When all streams are dry,
> Or that of the hour
> When the swan must fix his eye
> Upon a fading gleam

Float out upon a long
Last glittering reach of stream
And there sing his last song.

How can any sensitive reader be immune to the beauty of that? But how can I (once I've thought of it) avoid asking in what way pride is *like* early morning light, or *like* the horn of plenty, or *like* a sudden shower of rain, or *like* the hour when the swan dies? Whatever pride is *like* apart from itself, it seems to me it's not like any of these things. And of course the swan there is not a swan at all but W. B. Yeats taking his cue from Zeus and wearing feathers. The swan singing his last song is the poet writing his last verses.

Next we turn to his faith, and it's as if the renewal of pride has licensed a new intellectual extravagance, beyond anything we've seen from Yeats up to this point:

And I declare my faith:
I mock Plotinus' thought
And cry in Plato's teeth,
Death and life were not
Till man made up the whole,
Made lock, stock and barrel
Out of his bitter soul,
Aye, sun and moon and star, all,
And further add to that
That, being dead, we rise,
Dream and so create
Translunar Paradise.

I've read some pretty flushed defences of those lines. The best is probably Ellmann's. It's not good enough, Ellmann says, to object that these lines are 'philosophical nonsense'. In that way Ellmann contrives to acknowledge that they *are* 'philosophical nonsense' but to insist it doesn't matter. The lines are, he goes on, 'a dramatic cry of defiance against those who would denigrate man or subject him to abstractions like death, life, heaven or hell, God, Plotinus's One, Plato's Good or eternal ideas'.[8]

I'm all for rescuing humanity from its own self-terrorizing abstractions — including, if you like, God, heaven, and hell. But how are we rescued from death by the mere assertion that we ourselves invented it? If for just a moment you can stretch your credulity to the limit and accept that all that Yeats names — everything in fact — is invented by the human imagination, how then are the facts of human life altered? If we invented birth and death, we're still therefore born, and we still die. And if we've invented something called 'Translunar Paradise' (which suggests to me something like a transcendental fun-park), I'm not sure that means — even to Yeats — that we *have* it, or *go* there.

Is it possible to see the lines as heroic? I suppose it must be, and that's what they aim to be. If I were in a mood to make an entirely positive summary of the poem, it would go something like this: The 'Old lecher', 'derided by' age, which is 'a sort of battered kettle at the heel', acknowledges that youth was wasted in romantic dreams, refuses to lament, asserts his pride, declares his faith in the poetic imagination and in the Anglo-Irish stock from which he comes, and determines to go forward boldly as a poet, not retreat into philosophy — though he will at the same time school his soul in indifference and so prepare it for death.

Locked up in 'The Tower' there is very obviously a modern confessional poem asking to be let out. If it had been, what would it have said? Perhaps that the opening of the gates of sex late in life can lead to an excess of desire, as if to make up for all that has been missed. That with this discovery of appetite has come renewed energy and strength. That the suppression of appetite has been a suppression of one's full powers, disguised as sensitivity and scrupulousness. That the loved object could indeed have been won, and thus rendered more real, less abstract, more ordinary, if those powers had been released earlier. Now, released late, they are served by a body that has begun to fail. Age would be less terrible if youth had not been sacrificed to heroic dreams.

Some of that — I think a good deal of it — is in the poem, half-buried, half-uncovered, half-confronted, and then all swept aside by a marvellously theatrical conclusion that revives the dream more forcefully than ever. The sensitive pride of youth is acknowledged and blamed; but then a new, bold, nonchalant, elderly pride is asserted in its place. The folly of youth is admitted, but then a more extravagant folly is celebrated. It's as if Yeats will challenge the facts of life and death by a display of heroic will. I enjoy the challenge. But I also know that the facts of life and death won't be bullied; and I think in this poem Yeats fails to face them. Gesture has replaced thought; or the bold gesture has replaced the timid one. Yeats invokes the blind poets Homer and Raftery, and that's perhaps appropriate. He is blind himself in this poem, because in the end he shuts his eyes.

If by rhetoric in the modern pejorative sense that Yeats himself used we mean an eloquence that is in some degree empty, language in excess of what is being said, then 'The Tower' is for me rhetorical, and I prefer 'Nineteen Hundred and Nineteen', a less masterful, less seductive poem, but one that does, I think, look bravely at the facts of the world we occupy.

In 'Sailing to Byzantium' Yeats prayed to be gathered into 'the artifice of eternity' where he would become a golden bird. Eternity was an artifice because, as 'The Tower' asserts, it and everything else is created by the mind of man. In both poems Yeats seems to be twisting about in a web of recognition and counter-assertion. The recognition is that death is absolute and that the traditional palliatives are false — invented by the mind of man. The counter-assertion is that it is one of the glories of the human mind to create the reality it desires. Eternity may be an artifice, but that's no reason why Yeats should not enter it singing and become a golden bird. The problem is perhaps the old one of those who send God off the field of play and immediately bring on a substitute. If the imagination becomes God, everything it creates must be real, and in fact there is nothing it doesn't create. That seems to be Yeats's philosophical position — one that stands, I suppose, as an assertion, or rude gesture, against alternative realist philosophies.

The world view presented in the poem 'Nineteen Hundred and Nineteen' is very bleak, and it contains no compensating assertions of the power of the poetic imagination, or the heroic will, to make things better. It begins by looking squarely at the fact that the traditional notion of the eternity of art is an illusion.

> Many ingenious lovely things are gone
> That seemed sheer miracle to the multitude.

Even the great Athenian sculptures didn't survive. Nor did the great peace of the nineteenth century, which was thought to have rendered armies merely decorative.

> Now days are dragon-ridden, and the nightmare
> Rides upon sleep.

Later sections of the poem acknowledge that the dreams of youth have not been fulfilled, that an apt image of modern public life is 'the weasel's twist, the weasel's tooth', and that mockery is what the time seems most readily and pertinently to call forth. Finally comes an apocalyptic vision of the future, one in accordance with Yeats's idea that our era must soon come to a violent end.

My approval of 'Nineteen Hundred and Nineteen' as against 'The Tower' doesn't come from a temperamental pessimism or an appetite for large negatives. But this poem, although parts of it draw heavily on the historical overview of *A Vision*, has about it so much less of the Yeatsian bluster and so much more of what one senses to be hard, even harsh, reality. That engagement with realities gives the language more solid work to do. It gives a more compacted poetic texture, a greater linguistic density. What I'm saying here, I think, is not just something about 'style'. It's something about 'philosophy' (in the broadest sense) as well, and how the two interact and express each other. When Yeats allows the realist in himself more room, when he gives a little more attention and credence to Stendhal's perambulating mirror and a little less to the Berkeleyan looking-glass, then there is correspondingly more grit, or salt, and less wind in his style. And perhaps what makes *The*

Tower as a whole the marvellous book it is, is not the philosophy, not the heroics, not the vision, but the solid background of Irish place and circumstance that Yeats was too good a poet ever to abandon.

But something else in 'Nineteen Hundred and Nineteen' helps to give it a sense of balance and of truth. Section 2 calls up an image of Loie Fuller's Chinese dancers — that memory as an image of the movement of history. What, seen close up, is violence and destruction — days that are dragon-ridden — from the perspective of eternity is a graceful dance. Loie Fuller's dancers also made a dragon, but it was 'a floating ribbon of cloth'.

> All men are dancers and their tread
> Goes to the barbarous clangour of a gong.

If this is a statement of faith — that there is, after all, some coherence, some pattern, even beauty in what happens in the world at large — it's a faith that is modest in scope and doesn't conflict with the negatives. The clangour of the gong is 'barbarous'; nevertheless, the movements are a dance.

The image of the dance brings us finally to 'Among School Children', which is one of the great Yeats poems. It stands in much the same relation to 'Leda and the Swan' as 'A Prayer for my Daughter' does to 'The Second Coming' — the personal, even domestic statement as against the impersonal, symbolic one.

I offer two observations: first, that in all but its conclusion this poem is simpler than the commentaries suggest. Its subject — like 'Sailing to Byzantium' and 'The Tower' — is simply and consistently *age*. Yeats's diary entry for 14 March 1926, reads:

Topic for poem — School children and the thought that [life] will waste them perhaps that no possible life can fulfill our dreams or even their teacher's hope. Bring in the old thought that life prepares for what never happens.[9]

My second point is that insofar as it's a difficult poem the difficulty can't be entirely overcome or explained away. The poem makes a huge and uncharacteristic leap into its final stanza, but that leap makes it a great poem.

The poem is about a visit to a school. Children make the 'sixty-year-old smiling public man' more than ever conscious of his age. His image of himself is again the scarecrow, making the children, by shadowy implication, birds — 'those dying generations at their song', which he sails away from in 'Sailing to Byzantium'. Here he tries by smiling to be a '*comfortable* scarecrow'. In his mind he has the image of Maud, daughter of the Swan — of Zeus in fact, because he equates her with Helen. Maud's once 'Ledaean body' is now wasted like his own, her face

> Hollow of cheek as though it drank the wind
> And took a mess of shadows for its meat.

What mother of one of these children, he wonders, would think it all worthwhile if she could see her child in old age. He thinks of the great philosophers — Plato, Aristotle, Pythagoras. By the time their fame was achieved they were like him, 'Old clothes upon old sticks to scare a bird'.[10]

So far the poem is elegant, benign, its tone beautifully balanced. It is what Yeats called it — his' curse on old age' — but a mellow, wry accommodating curse.

But in stanza 7 the complexities set in:

> Both nuns and mothers worship images,
> But those the candles light are not as those
> That animate a mother's reveries,
> But keep a marble or a bronze repose.
> And yet they too break hearts — O Presences
> That passion, piety or affection knows,
> And that all heavenly glory symbolise —
> O self-born mockers of man's enterprise.

'Both nuns and mothers worship images'. He's at a Catholic school, being shown around by a nun, so the thought has its feet on the ground of the poem. But what are the images both nuns and mothers worship? To the fond mother the child is not simply itself. It is also an image of what it may become, and in this the child is to the mother what the statue of Christ or the Virgin is to the nun — a symbol and a focus of hope for the future. And the young lover too once worshipped a 'Ledaean body', an image rather than a woman. These worshipped images represent hope. They invoke a future. The notion of 'heavenly glory' is only a more grandiose version of the lover's dream of consummation and the mother's dreams for her child. They are 'self-born mockers of man's enterprise' because they are trapped in time. The imagined consummations — of religion, of love, of family life — lie always somewhere ahead. Tomorrow never comes. Or, as Yeats says in that note sketching the idea for the poem, life prepares us for what never happens. Desire looks forward, and imagination — that imagination he has been celebrating in this book — is its servant. But it is in the present that life is lived; and it's the present that those desires cloud. Life passes in a wishful haze, and we wake — if we wake at all — to find ourselves wise old scarecrows. Once again, 'It is only at the hour of darkness that the owl of Minerva descends'.

And so we take a leap into the final stanza, which is a sort of visionary resolution:

Labour is blossoming or dancing where
The body is not bruised to pleasure soul,
Nor beauty born out of its own despair,
Nor blear-eyed wisdom out of midnight oil.
O chestnut-tree, great-rooted blossomer,
Are you the leaf, the blossom or the bole?
O body swayed to music, O brightening glance,
How can we know the dancer from the dance?

Here labour is no longer *hard* labour; it blossoms or it dances 'naturally',
effortlessly. Here beauty and wisdom occur without pain or effort. And
the two images of this marvellous ease and naturalness are the chestnut
tree and the dancer. The tree doesn't imagine a future, and neither does
the dancer. One blossoms, the other dances, and both are integrated,
whole, unified, and beautiful.

Keats says somewhere (also using the image of a tree): 'If poetry come
not as naturally as the leaves to the tree it might as well not come
at all.' That Zen-ish attitude to poetic composition is quite alien to the
Yeatsian deliberation and labour; yet here at the end of 'Among School
Children' Yeats seems to celebrate a similar notion of natural, unforced,
easeful flowering or burgeoning. In fact it seems to me that the poem
by a kind of inner logic has forced Yeats to reverse the direction of
thought that is characteristic of most of the poems of *The Tower*. Instead
of aspiring beyond the world toward 'Translunar Paradise' or some new
incarnation, aspiring to leave the world of 'dying generations' to become
a golden bird singing in an immortal city, Yeats finds his images of
perfection — dancer and tree — in the mortal world and in nature.

I say the poem forced him to this because if you think about it, how
could it be otherwise, given the stanzas that go before? Byzantium and
the golden bird of art are only Yeatsian variants of those images that
nuns, lovers, and mothers worship. They too are 'self-born mockers of
man's enterprise'. The extraordinary thing is that, after a long hesitation
in the process of composition, Yeats had the courage to follow that logic
and to make what seems like a blind leap into the final stanza — a
leap that, at least philosophically, very nearly cancels out all the poems
that go before; and it's the courage of that leap that produces the curious
exaltation in the closing lines. The way out of the trap of time is neither
backward into memory nor forward into desire. It is in the moment
itself. It is in being, not in becoming.

When I stand back from what I've been saying about these poems,
the implications are something like this: I judge the poems as *poems*. That's
to say I'm a person expert in a poetic tradition, and through that, in
language — and to the best of my ability I judge the poem as a linguistic
event. But strengths and weaknesses in language reveal something that
can be expressed in terms of 'philosophy' or of a world view. What

45

I discover in *The Tower* is, I think, that the poems are in some degree at war with the poet. They resist some of the things he asks them to do. Another way of putting this is to say that the poet in Yeats is at war with the philosopher, or that the language of poetry contradicts the language of philosophy. Or again, that some of the things Yeats wants to believe don't stand up when put to the test of poetic language. He can force them through in rhetorical gusts; but when the cloud clears, the world is unchanged. He sees that it's unchanged, and his language reflects what he sees. The report of Stendhal's mirror conflicts with that of Berkeley's looking-glass. Yeats the man might have preferred Berkeley and the freedom to dream; but Stendhal's mirror wouldn't go away. It went on dawdling along its lane, showing him what he called 'this pragmatical, preposterous pig of a world', and because of that the realist he disliked so much finds in the best of his poems an equal voice, or even at times gets the upper hand.

YEATS THE EUROPEAN

I suppose everyone preparing a paper for this conference must have given a long thought to the word 'European'. Or perhaps not. A European (whatever that might be) — a resident of Europe — might give less thought to it than an American; and I think an American might give it less thought than a New Zealander.

Am I a European? Am I more or less European than W. B. Yeats? What is Europe? What are its boundaries? Is it a racial category, or a geographical one? Or again, is it cultural?

I was born and brought up in New Zealand. Racially I am European, and I suppose culturally — though geographical removal begins to have a bearing on culture, and the official (and therefore not entirely truthful) description of New Zealand is that it is a bi-cultural society. Neither of my parents ever crossed the equator into the Northern Hemisphere; and although I have crossed it many times it has always been with the intention of crossing back again after a given period.

On the other hand one of my great-uncles was killed in France in the 1914-18 war and must be buried here; and an uncle was wounded and captured in Crete in the 1939-45 war and spent a number of years in a German prisoner-of-war camp. Does New Zealand's eager participation in Britain's recent wars make it more European than Ireland? Or could one turn the argument around and say that Ireland, a Catholic country, retained links with continental Europe which Protestant England severed? But how would that argument affect Yeats, who was of Protestant stock?

Here is another (slightly contentious) way of looking at the subject. In 1922, when Catholic Ireland finally succeeded in severing its ties with

A paper read at a conference held at the Princess Grace Memorial Irish Library, Monte Carlo, May 1987, on the theme of 'Yeats the European'.

Britain — or, if you prefer, succeeded in throwing off the British yoke — Irish people became aliens in Britain. But Northern Ireland remained part of the United Kingdom. Workers from the Republic continued to be allowed free access to find employment in Britain. Tourism and trade continued; and the English appetite for dairy products was as important to Ireland as to New Zealand. The BBC was listened to, and more recently watched, in Ireland. And now that Ireland has joined the European Community the two are part of a larger political bonding. One could argue that in some degree Ireland has never ceased to be part of the United Kingdom; that its freedom, when it came, was more symbolic than real. The dominant language was English, not Irish, and remains so. If Yeats is a great European poet he is great in the English language; and if the language were Irish, the sense of 'Europeanness' would be less, if only because it would be inaccessible.

I have introduced these random and perhaps rather idiosyncratic questions and comments in order to subvert as far as I can what might seem to be the purpose or hope underlying the title given this conference: Yeats the European. It suggests an invitation for us all to nod wisely and agree that though Yeats was a great poet, and Irish, he was not just a great Irish poet; he was also a great European. There's a sense in which this is true. How could it be otherwise? But the truism seems to me so obvious, it must be more interesting to challege it than to affirm it.

With these general remarks in mind I'm going to discuss now the poem Yeats called 'Nineteen Hundred and Nineteen'. I may have to do a wide circle around the subject of the 'Europeanness' of Yeats, but by the end, or before the end, we will have come back to it.

Thomas Whitaker, in his reading of the poem,[1] tells us that 'the title of "Nineteen Hundred and Nineteen", reminds us of the Black-and-Tan terrorising of the Irish countryside'. I'm not sure who is indicated by Whitaker's 'us'. Yeats scholars, I suppose, we who learn, and mislearn, Irish history by studying Yeats. And I have no precise knowledge of what, if anything, that date would immediately signify to most Irish readers. It does seem however that Yeats wanted to use the Black and Tan brutalities as his example of the breakdown of an old order. We know that the stanza about the mother murdered by 'drunken soldiery' describes a Black and Tan atrocity (mentioned also in Lady Gregory's journal).[2] But we don't know this from the poem; and whether we can agree with Whitaker that it is somehow indicated by the date appears doubtful. This is something I will come back to.

Let's look first at the overall movement of the poem; because it is not primarily *about* its occasion. Another instance of violence might have been chosen. The poem is about impermanence. It is, for most of its length, an anguished acknowledgement that nothing endures — not even art. And the anguish comes from the recognition by the poet that he has pursued an illusion of permanence — that in some degree he is still pursuing it. His activity and achievements have been in the sphere of time, and because of that, time will do its work on them.

The Tower as a collection is remarkable for the way it sustains and extends certain Yeatsian truisms and dogmas; and more remarkable for the way in moments of stress it throws them overboard. Yeats can be seen hanging on to his romantic devotion to Maud Gonne; but part II of the poem he called 'The Tower' can be read as a bitter rejection of that devotion — as if it had been a waste of youth and of life. In 'Sailing to Byzantium' he bids farewell to the world of 'dying generations' in favour of the undying world of art. But then, in the last stanza of 'Among School Children', that very Yeatsian proposition is suddenly reversed. Art is rejected in favour of nature, eternity in favour of time. The notion of an eternal beauty, represented in 'Sailing to Byzantium' by the image of the golden bird of art, becomes another of those 'self-born mockers of man's enterprise', while the images of perfection — dancer and tree — are taken from the mutable world, the region of mortality.

Finally there is Yeats's valuation of politics as something time-bound and inferior compared to art, which partakes of eternity. This has been throughout his career surely the most consistently sustained dogma of the Yeatsian value system; and perhaps its consistency explains why no one seems to have noticed the extraordinary reversal that occurs in 'Nineteen Hundred and Nineteen'. It's not that politics is suddenly valued. It's that art is put on a level with it. After a life of insisting that art is superior to the political mode he suddenly stands back and sees them both as temporal — equally subject to time — equally illusory.

So we begin with the great works of the ancient world which are gone. They seemed 'sheer miracle' — protected against time and change — but that was an illusion. And from art in stanza 1 we move to politics in stanzas 2 and 3. The great artifact of nineteenth-century Europe was not artistic but political and social — peace, stability, law, and with them a belief in Progress. All that has gone. Violence has broken out again. If we can face the reality (the poet tells us), it is that nothing — neither the work of great artist nor that of great statesman — has power to endure.

> no work can stand
> . . .
> No honour leave its mighty monument.

The despair which this induces in the poem is odd, and distinctly subjective. It comes not so much from the pity that nothing is stable and enduring, as from the fact that the poet is identifying with those whose great work will not last.

> no work can stand
> Whether health, wealth or peace of mind were spent
> On master work of intellect or hand.

Not too well hidden there inside the public eloquence is a private and familiar Yeatsian lament against the nature of things. *He* has spent health, wealth and peace of mind; he has worked to make these wonderful poems and now, late in life, he faces the thought that if time destroyed the work of the great Athenians, it will certainly destroy his. 'Man is in love and loves what vanishes.' The only comfort is that

> all triumph would
> But break upon his ghostly solitude

— and we need to wait to section III of the poem to be quite sure what that means.

But now in section II there is a reconciling image — a very beautiful and important one. The nights of terror in section I are 'dragon-ridden' — the dragon represents the return of violence; or as Yeats says in a letter, 'the return of evil'.[3] In section II Yeats remembers Loie Fuller's Chinese dancers in Paris floating a ribbon of cloth so that it seemed a dragon. That is likened to the 'Platonic year' — the astrological cycle bringing change, destruction and renewal. In the aspect of eternity — *sub specie aeternitatis* — there is order in all things.

> All men are dancers and their tread
> Goes to the barbarous clangour of a gong.

The clangour is barbarous. Things are destroyed. But there is an order, a dance. Individual works are destroyed, but they come and go within the greater work of eternity. To create individual works is to try to stand out against the flow. One is not fortunate to have any success in this attempt, because it distracts the soul from its true work, which is to be absorbed into the larger order of things.

> A man in his own secret meditation
> Is lost amid the labyrinth that he has made
> In art or politics.

There again art and politics are surprisingly put together, and of no use in soul-making — because (as we learn from the lines that follow) after death the soul tends to cling to its bad earthly habits, artistic or political. The more we succeed in the world the more ill-prepared we are for what is to follow. Success develops the ego and the ego won't readily give up the ghost. It won't go out gracefully. Like other poems that would be collected in *The Tower* volume, this one is partly about man's preparation for death.

Whether the poem requires us to accept that the soul persists after death is unclear, as it often is in Yeats, I suppose because he believed and disbelieved at different levels of mind. In the opening of section III the soul's *life* is described as a 'brief gleam' — 'Before that brief gleam of its life be gone'. And in the last stanza the soul as swan leaps into a heaven which is 'desolate' —

> The swan has leaped into the desolate heaven:
> That image can bring wildness, bring a rage
> To end all things, to end
> What my laborious life imagined, even
> The half-imagined, the half-written page;
> O but we dreamed to mend
> Whatever mischief seemed
> To afflict mankind, but now
> That winds of winter blow
> Learn that we were crack-pated when we dreamed.

Is the despair total here? Does it come from the feeling that the soul too must die — that it has nowhere to go — that 'heaven' is 'desolate'? Or does it come only from the recognition that the world must be left and that time will destroy our achievements? Whichever way Yeats meant it — if it was clear to himself what he meant — there's no doubt that he is suffering once again that recurring sense of having wasted a life in literary labour — 'this sedentary trade', as he calls it elsewhere — rather than having lived it to the full in action. The phrase 'my laborious life' harks back to that line about spending 'health, wealth and peace of mind' on master-works which time will treat with the same indifference it has shown to the sculptures of Phidias. Now politician and poet merge into one. Both had the same good intentions, though the means were different:

> O but we dreamed to mend
> Whatever mischief seemed
> To afflict mankind. . . .

Death approaches, the winds of winter are blowing, and he knows that dream was 'crack-pated'. Everything moves in its due cycle, despite our efforts and our naive notions that we can promote 'Progress'. The latest turn of the wheel is bringing new violence and horror into the world. Honour and truth have become empty words:

> We, who seven years ago
> Talked of honour and of truth,
> Shriek with pleasure if we show
> The weasel's twist, the weasel's tooth.

So what is left but mockery? Section V mocks in turn the great, the

51

wise, the good, and finally turns on itself, mocking the poet who has nothing left to offer but mockery. In the nihilism of the poem's concluding sections we come clear of questioning and into a direct expression of the poet's current mood of despair. As Harold Bloom says, 'self-mockery in Yeats is always a sure gate to poetic splendour'.[4]

And so the poem concludes as 'The Tower' does also, with visionary lines representing the destruction of an old order. Out of the 'tumult of images' and the 'labyrinth of the wind' lurches the 'insolent fiend' Robert Artisson, 'his great eyes without thought / Under the shadow of stupid straw-pale locks' — a figure at once mindless, sexual and anarchic. Both in the section on mockery, and in this final vision of destruction, there is a kind of exaltation, as if Yeats is glad at last to have freed himself both of optimism and of analytic discourse. If Samson has to die, he's glad he has at least the power to go out in the grand manner. And because there is a kind of joy in the contemplation of destruction, the conclusion renders section II of the poem, with its image of the dragon of cloth and the universal dance, more central than ever.

In its general sweep, then, this was not — and is not — specifically an Irish poem. In fact Yeats first called it 'Thoughts Upon the Present State of the World'. It was published with that title in the *Dial* in September 1921 and again in the *London Mercury* in November. It retained that title when it appeared in a little collection called *Seven Poems and a Fragment* in 1922, and didn't receive the title 'Nineteen Hundred and Nineteen' until it appeared in *The Tower* in 1928. In that collection it received not only its present title, but also the date 1919 at the end of the text — and it's on that authority, I suppose, that Professor Jeffares and others date it as having been written in that year. But it was not written in 1919, and could not have been. As Jeffares tells us, the lines about the Black and Tan murder derive from an incident also described in Lady Gregory's journal; and that journal entry shows that the event occurred in November 1920.[5] Further, in letters written in April 1921 Yeats mentions that he is writing the poem. On 9 April he writes to Olivia Shakespear that he has written two sections; a day later to Lady Gregory that he is writing the third.[6] But there is an odd discrepancy. In the letter to Olivia Shakespear he tells her

I am writing a series of poems ('thoughts on the present state of the world' or some such name). I have written two and there may be many more. They are not philosophical but simple and passionate, a lamentation over lost peace and lost hope.

To Lady Gregory a day later he writes, 'I am writing a series of poems about the present state of things in Ireland and am now in the middle of the third.' To Mrs Shakespear in London, poems about the present state of the world; to Lady Gregory in Ballylee, poems on the state of things in Ireland. Is the difference significant? I think it is. I think it represents Yeats's curiously ambiguous position as between England and Ireland. But if the text is to sanction one of these descriptions, then clearly the one to Mrs Shakespear — which became the title until he changed it in 1928 — is much more accurate. This is not a poem *about* Ireland. It is a poem about the state of the world — the European world — as Yeats saw it at that time.

So I come to the question of his changing the title and altering the date. Why did he not only rename the poem 'Nineteen Hundred and Nineteen', but give it that date at the end of the text, when in fact it was written in 1921?

Before I noticed this discrepancy I thought the poem — which I've always admired — had one curious weakness. Stanzas 2 and 3 of section I so clearly describe, from a distinctly British point of view, the great peace and stability of the latter half of the nineteenth century. The event which destroyed that tranquil order was the Great War of 1914–18. But Yeats doesn't write about that war in the poem — and that seems to leave a curious hiatus. We leap from those sweeping images summing up a whole era — the optimism, the faith in Progress, the durable peace, the dependable law and stable order — not to a European war but to a parochial incident, the accidental shooting of an Irish mother at her door by drunken soldiers. I don't mean to minimize the horror. Such a killing is awful wherever and however it occurs. But incidents of that kind had happened at intervals everywhere in the Empire, and sometimes in Europe, throughout the great peace which the previous stanzas describe. In fact massacres occurred, and wars which, though short, were nasty and brutish. (There was one in New Zealand in the 1860s.) If an era had come to an end the Great War was the event that marked its conclusion. Why does Yeats not say so?

It is, I think, because he has no satisfactory perspective on that war — or at least can't allow himself one publicly. What he wished said about it publicly he had put into the mouth of Major Robert Gregory:

> Those that I fight I do not hate,
> Those that I guard I do not love;
> My country is Kiltartan Cross,
> My countrymen Kiltartan's poor,
> No likely end could bring them loss
> Or leave them happier than before.
> Nor law, nor duty bade me fight,
> Nor public men, nor cheering crowds,
> A lonely impulse of delight
> Drove to this tumult in the clouds.

'An Irish Airman Foresees his Death' is among the most perfectly turned of Yeats's short poems but it's doubtful whether it represents what

Gregory's feelings would have been about the war he died in; and I'm sure it doesn't truly represent Yeats's either. He was not indifferent to the outcome. Certainly he didn't want to see Britain defeated by Germany. But the complexities of internal politics in Ireland did not permit him to say so.[7] There could be no acknowledgement anywhere in his poetry that he favoured the British as against the German cause; and no acknowledgement of that war as an event whose magnitude and consequences dwarfed everything happening in Ireland. To admit that would among other things have seemed to offer an excuse to the British for the severity with which they had dealt with the 1916 uprising.

Yet Yeats knew perfectly well the relative scale of things as it must appear to European eyes. In preparing a speech for the opening of the Tailteann Games in 1924 he wrote:

A fortnight before the great war a friend of mine was standing beside an English member of Parliament watching a Review in one of the London Parks. My friend said as the troops marched past 'It is a fine sight.' And the Member of Parliament answered 'It is a fine sight, but it is nothing else, there will never be another war.' There will never be another war, that was our opium dream.[8]

That is the same thought we find in the poem — but here it's clear, as it's not in the poem, that it was the 1914-18 war which brought an end to the era of peace and order. In the same 1924 speech Yeats seems to welcome the onset of a new era of violence and violently imposed order. And, remembering that his audience will be international, he writes the acknowledgement that is lacking in the poem: 'I see about me the representatives of nations which have suffered incomparably more than we have, more than we may ever suffer. Our few months of war and civil war must seem in their eyes but a light burden.'[9]

I repeat, seen close to, the killing of the woman in 'Nineteen Hundred and Nineteen' is a horrendous event. But seen as an event in the kind of panoramic spectacle that precedes it, it is relatively insignificant. The switch from a European perspective to a parochial Irish one creates what I've suggested is the poem's one serious fault — that hiatus between stanzas 2 and 4 of section I. And the same problem is reflected in the two descriptions of the poem — to Mrs Shakespear in London, a poem about the state of the world; to Lady Gregory in Ireland, a poem about the present state of Ireland.

So it appeared in England and America first, in periodicals, as 'Thoughts upon the Present State of the World'; and it retained that title in the little 1922 collection, *Seven Poems and a Fragment*. But when Yeats came to put together his 1928 collection, he altered the title, and, as if to emphasize it, dated the text 1919.

I don't pretend to be able to answer with certainty why the date 1919 was chosen; but I do reject one suggestion put to me after this paper was first delivered, that it was simply a matter of forgetfulness. A date at the foot of a text might well be wrong simply through carelessness; but a date as *title* means that the year chosen signifies something particular.

Many commentaries[10] take the year as simply signifying the Black and Tan terror, and that was my own first assumption. I'm assured however that no Black and Tan troops were deployed until the early months of 1920;[11] and certainly 1920 was the year when the particular killing described in section I occurred. On the other hand 1919 is the year when the post-war Irish troubles, leading finally to independence, began.

But Yeats's view of history at this time, and in this poem, is not just Irish. It is European. By 1919 the fear for some, excitement for others, of the 1917 Bolshevik revolution was extending its influence through Europe. A Communist International was founded in that year; and Yeats was nervous that the nationalist struggle in Ireland might begin to take the form of a socialist revolution. This was also the year of the Versailles treaty which it had been vainly hoped might include some consideration of Ireland's claim for self-determination.

For Yeats personally 1919 was significant because it was the year in which he became at last a father, and his excitement mixed with apprehension can be felt in 'A Prayer for my Daughter' and 'The Second Coming', both written in that year. And all of this, for him, was given a 'philosophical' context by his thinking towards *A Vision*. This year (if I understand these matters correctly) saw the world, in Phase 22, beginning to move back from 'antithetical' (aristocratic) towards the primary (democratic) darkness in which the cycle began, and out of which the new cycle of history would be violently born.

One can see that 'Thoughts upon the Present State of the World' was an unsatisfactory title for the poem in the 1928 volume, unless the text were dated. He was not, after all, writing about the state of the world in 1928. But why was the original title not kept and the true date, 1921, put at the foot of the text? If that had been done there would not have been the problem which now occurs in section IV:

> We who seven years ago
> Talked of honour and of truth,
> Shriek with pleasure if we show
> The weasel's twist, the weasel's tooth.

Seven years ago in 1921, when the poem was written, takes us back to 1914 and the outbreak of the European war, which was no doubt what he meant when he wrote it. Seven years back from 1919 takes us to 1912 and nothing in particular.[12]

I offer speculation at this point, not confident assertion; and it seems more important to have raised the question of the dating and title than to pretend to answer it finally. But I have in mind that some essential conflict is represented here between Irish Yeats and Yeats the European. In a letter written to George Russell in the crucial year, 1919, Yeats speaks of Ireland's 'lunatic faculty of going against everything it believes England to affirm'. And he adds in a postscript: 'Do you remember a European question on which Ireland did not at once take the opposite side to England? — well, that kills all thought and encourages the most miserable form of mob rhetoric.'[13]

What is monumentally missing from 'Nineteen Hundred and Nineteen', though it also lurks there shadowy and undeclared, is the Great War — just as the most notable gap in Yeats's *Oxford Book of Modern Verse* is the result of his refusal to include the English poets of that war. For Yeats and the Irish Republicans it was England's war, not Ireland's; and if Robert Gregory fought and died in it that was his business and had nothing to do with England, Germany, politics, or morality. 'A lonely impulse of delight, Drove to this tumult . . .' Gregory's nobility as an aristocrat and artist were displayed there; while the English war poets, making mirrors of their minds, consumed with pity for the men under their command ('the poetry is in the pity', Owen had said), lacked 'tragic joy' and turned the war into something philosophically meaningless: 'some blunderer has driven his car on to the wrong side of the road — that is all.'[14]

Here, as elsewhere in Yeats, one feels the short Irish view to be at odds with the long European one. On the one hand 'Nineteen Hundred and Nineteen' is saying 'We Irish were promised Home Rule when the war was concluded and got instead the Black and Tans'; on the other it is saying 'Europe thought it had order, peace, law and progress for all time but now the new phase of history brings violence and terror back into the world'. Those are two orders of discourse, one political, the other historical-philosophical, and it is not easy to reconcile them within a single poem. It is this problem, I suspect, which leads to Yeats's fiddling with title and date. My suggestion is, then, that Yeats is sometimes, inevitably, guilty of the Irish 'lunatic faculty' he describes in his letter to George Russell. His Irish fix on, or fixation with, England, distorts the wider European focus. It is in this sense that he can sometimes seem *parochial* Irish, causing his greatness as a European to waver.

POUND

The Poetic Achievement of Ezra Pound, by Michael Alexander (1979)
Ezra Pound and the Pisan Cantos, by Anthony Woodward (1980)
Ezra Pound and the Cantos: A Record of Struggle, by Wendy Stallard Flory (1980)
End to Torment: A Memoir of Ezra Pound by H.D., edited by Norman Holmes Pearson and Michael King (1980)

In 1949 when a panel of his fellow poets (including T. S. Eliot, Robert Lowell, Elizabeth Bishop, W. H. Auden, and Allen Tate) awarded Ezra Pound the Bollingen Prize for The Pisan Cantos there was an immediate and angry public debate. The reaction is not surprising and might have been worse had the texts of Pound's wartime broadcasts over Rome radio been publicly available. What is surprising is that the award was made to him and that thirty years later is appears to have been thoroughly deserved. Pound's broadcasts contained naked anti-semitism and economic balderdash. His support for Mussolini in Italy was unwavering, even after the defeat. Canto 74 opens with 'the tragedy' of the death of Mussolini who in the course of the sequence is bracketed with Manes, the Albigenses, and Pound himself, as heretic martyrs. In Canto 84, written during October 1945, Pound not only honours the memory of Mussolini ('Il Capo') and various dead Fascist ministers, but salutes the traitor premiers, Laval and Quisling, as they go to face their respective firing squads.

The anti-semitism had got into some of the Cantos written during the 1930s — those historical compilations with occasional eruptions of myth and of 'beauty' which were really a sort of educational guidebook for the reform of the West. But there is none of it, so far as I can recall, or very little, in the Pisan sequence. There is some grumbling about usury; but for the most part Pound's politics exist there as 'the dream' (opening line) which has collapsed with the fall of Facist Italy; and the lack of any recantation, the firm if covert assertions of continuing loyalty (giving the date Fascist style, for example, 'Pisa, in 23rd year of the effort'), which in 1945 might have marked him as incorrigible, at this distance seem, even to one who deplores the side he had chosen, acts of courage. Of all the things which make Pound extraordinary not the least is that he is a great writer — the only one writing in English — who lived through and recorded what it felt like to be defeated in the Second World War.

I concentrate for the moment on *The Pisan Cantos* because that seems to me, as it does to Anthony Woodward, Pound's 'greatest achievement'. Everything that had begun to go wrong with *The Cantos* — their obsessive, one-dimensional quality in that forced march the reader takes through Cantos 52 to 71 — is righted at Pisa; and if literature in English has things to thank the U.S. Army for, one, surely, must be the fact that when they captured Pound in 1945 and held him prisoner for six months near Pisa (awaiting his recall to Washington where he had been indicted for treason), they deprived him of most of those books he had got into the habit of ransacking for 'material', and thus forced him to rely on what was retained, and to that extent processed, in his remarkable head. The Pisan sequence is in many ways more difficult than anything which precedes it. Its movement is so much the random movement of the mind, from distant memory to close observation, from reading to reflection, and through a great range of feeling — anger, despair, love, regret, remorse, amusement, in rapid transition. But there is the man's situation in the Detention Centre compound as point of focus; and there is a marvellous particularity, and a unifying tone that is humane and accepting.

Pound received his award and then was very largely forgotten except as the extraordinary entrepreneur of literature who had discovered Joyce and Eliot. It was on his protegé (always loyal, it should be said) 'Possum' Eliot that the post-war world especially showered its blessings — many honorary doctorates, the Order of Merit, the Nobel Prize. Eliot was celebrated, studied, written about, endlessly cited (Delmore Schwartz wrote in 1949 of 'the literary dictatorship of T. S. Eliot'), while Pound, released in 1958 after thirteen years' confinement, soon lapsed into the silences which are his final Cantos.

Two separate facts kept his reputation alive, however. One was that the best of the post-war poets in America, of varying persuasions and schools, all owed something to Pound in general and to the Pisan sequence in particular. Black Mountain, the Beats, the New York School, 'confessional' poets like Lowell and Berryman — none of them is imaginable in their various experiments and excellences without the precedent of Pound. And second, there were a few devoted but enormously able scholars, most notably Hugh Kenner, but also (and strangely, considering his origins in the neo-Augustan 'Movement' of the fifties) Donald Davie, who kept the subject respectable, the interest alive.

Michael Alexander suggests that 'indifference and bafflement are today more common than hostility', and that may be so. But there has been some excellent work done on Pound recently — Leon Surette's *A Light from Eleusis*, Richard Sieburth's *Instigations*, and now Alexander's manageably-sized study of the whole corpus of the poetry, and Woodward's of *The Pisan Cantos*. My feeling is that Pound's stock is rising, and that one reason for this is that time is helping us all to get over the enormous hurdle of his anti-semitism and his monetary obsessions — helping us to recognize that these were part of the madness of the time, and that the best of Pound preceded and survived the 1930s and the war, when the worst of his follies occurred.

Anyone writing about Pound's place in literary history must at some point think of throwing him into the scales against Yeats and Eliot. Alexander and Woodward are both brave enough to allow us a glimpse of themselves doing it. Alexander writes 'Indeed [Pound's] writing is so frequently touched with greatness that only Yeats and Eliot seem of a clearly superior order among contemporaries.' I can't help wondering whether there is not a failure of courage in that, a wish to reassure, to appear 'reasonable'. It may be one of those statements more tactical than honest, which a critic afterwards wonders why he made. If Alexander really means it he must have very good books to write about Yeats and Eliot.

Woodward approaches the comparison by means of negatives:

Each of the three poets had his endemic flaws as an artist, a flaw rooted in temperament and hence in life; Eliot's a cerebral monotony, Yeats' a too conscious eloquence, Pound's an allusive incoherence. Each had his exalted poetic flights, and of the three I myself find Pound's the most moving.

That is very well said — and not least the last sentence. In the end one ought to be able to recognize the various arguments for advancing any of the three above the others. Only the critic's feelings as he reads will determine which of those arguments is the one he wants to employ or to listen to.

My feeling is that as social conventions, and conventions of language with them, free up, open out, give us more air to breathe, more space in which to move, Pound's work seems less bizarre and strange, more alive, while Eliot's seems to shrink and wither behind its collar and tie. Eliot's early clerkishness was an anti-romantic gesture, a new freedom. His later clerkishness was something quite different — a retreat. *The*

Waste Land is a great poem by two authors, Eliot primarily, but also Pound. *Four Quartets* is almost exactly contemporary with *The Pisan Cantos*, and the latter work is the measure of its lack of linguistic vitality.

Yeats, unlike Eliot, has a range comparable with Pound's, and it would be easy to construct an argument in his favour. In fact the two poets do it for us, Yeats congratulating himself in his very last poems on having brought 'something to perfection', Pound coming out of his silences only to say 'my errors and wrecks lie about me', and 'I cannot make it cohere'. My own feeling about this comparison is that it cannot be divorced from my sense of the *usefulness* of Pound to the continuation of poetry itself. Yeats is one of those great and wonderful figures fixed in the past, in history. The problems he faced, both linguistic and 'philosophical', are not those which a poet faces in the 1980s, and consequently his practice, while being exemplary in general, can have no particular application. Pound, by comparison, was living, linguistically at least, in our present before it had quite arrived. In addition I would be inclined to say that Pound's dislike of the Middle Eastern monotheisms, which he thought fostered moral fanaticism, and his attempt to revive some sense of the older and multiple deities that belonged to the soil of Europe, still has more point and relevance than Yeats's magic, or, indeed, Eliot's.

There is a puzzle about Pound which critics deal with in varying ways. It concerns the 'personal' element in his work. This brings us back particularly to *The Pisan Cantos*, which are often said to be more successful than earlier Cantos because here at last Pound, first person singular, emerges from behind the screen. Hugh Kenner in *The Pound Era* describes the form of *The Pisan Cantos* as 'free-running monologue'. Leon Surette says their success depends on 'the introduction of a single speaking voice'. Alexander describes them as 'a directly autobiographical record' and says the 'continous primary effect' is of 'conversation'. And Woodward writes: 'In *The Pisan Cantos* the poet's own self, having been largely absorbed into mask, pastiche and translation in earlier Cantos, for the first time appears on stage.' All this is true and not true, and the sense in which it is not true is important.

Pound and his circumstances in the detention camp are at the centre of *The Pisan Cantos* and this is a change from previous Cantos. As well as the governing sensibility which has always been there, his are now the experiencing senses, the observing eye, the recording ear, the remembering mind. There is even from time to time the first person singular pronoun ('I have been hard as youth 60 years'), though as often as not it is in a foreign language ('Les larmes que j'ai créées m'inondent'). But as soon as one reads the sequence alongside passages from Wordsworth's *The Prelude*, or some of Yeats's first person poems, or even a passage from *Four Quartets* like the one beginning 'So here I am in the middle way, having spent twenty years . . .', one is forced to recognize

how fleeting that 'I' is in Pound, how extensively it is avoided. It is
not just a matter of grammar. Pound is at the centre but he refuses
to construct a 'personality' or a 'mask'.

> Saw but the eyes and stance between the eyes
> colour, diastasis,
>   careless or unaware it had not the
> whole tent's room

Who saw? It was Pound of course; but the grammar asserts that it is
not who saw, but rather the seeing, and what was seen, that is important.
If after reading the sequence one is disposed to credit Pound with courage,
fortitude, resilience, that is not because he presents himself in detail and
in a good light but because he, and his suffering where it shows, are
a small item on a very large canvas.

Critical tact, therefore, is called for, if one is not to misrepresent
the personal element in Pound's poetry — and both Alexander and
Woodward possess it. Wendy Stallard Flory does not. Her argument
is that Pound's *Cantos* is a poem 'of an intermediate genre' between a
hero-epic like the *Odyssey* and an autobiographical epic like *The Prelude*.
Pound 'initially was determined to keep himself out of his [poem] as
much as possible'. He didn't altogether succeed in this, and the best of
his early Cantos are the most personal. Finally with *The Pisan Cantos*
Pound 'stands forth in full view'. Flory's method will therefore be to
relate the poem to the man's biography, which she says (strangely) will
offer a 'broader perspective'.

I have no particular complaint with what she finds more and less
successful in the *Cantos*, only with her simple-minded explanations of
how things succeed or fail and what they signify. Of Canto 39 she writes

At first we see the poet in his home setting, at Olga Rudge's apartment at Sant'
Ambrogio, but he is in an unsettled state of mind and the opening word of
the Canto forewarns us of this: 'Desolate is the roof where the cat sat . . .'

That this should get into a book published by Yale University Press is
an example, I suppose, of what can happen when academics talk politely
to one another about literary matters without being answerable to a
larger world, a general readership, something that might be called
'common sense'. For the fact is (and any sensible reader will know it)
we do *not* see 'the poet' anywhere in Canto 39, nor Olga Rudge's apartment
at Sant' Ambrogio. 'Research' (or just reading) may lead us to suppose,
on firm but not conclusive evidence, that Pound visualized the setting
of Circe's Ingle in Canto 39 in terms of Olga Rudge's house at Sant'
Ambrogio — but that is quite another matter. It is a matter of interest;
but it does not justify what Flory has written.

Once she has her method established and her nose down, Flory keeps going until she comes to the end. Resourceful as a scholar, she is insensitive to poetry and has nothing general to say beyond the immediate task, point by point. Woodward, by contrast, is remarkable for his ability to draw general critical reflections out of particular instances. His book is perhaps more muted, less energetic in its prose, than its subject deserves; but it is the closest and best study to date of what is probably the most admired section of Pound's *Cantos*. Alexander's book has similar merits and must, I think, replace Donald Davie's first book on Pound (*Ezra Pound Poet as Sculptor*) as the best broad survey of all the poetry. None of these books of course has the scope or importance of Kenner's *The Pound Era*.

End to Torment contains a diary/memoir by the poet H.D. written during 1958 when Pound was about to be released. It seems to have been undertaken more for therapeutic reasons than anything else. It recalls her love affair (if that is the right description of their adolescent attachment) with Ezra. Very little is remembered 'in fact' but that little is surrounded with a huge aureole of tremulous emotion. Sympathy is called for, but I feel myself shrinking away from H.D.'s neuroticism. Perhaps Pound did too.

Pound's poems written to her at this time (1905) — 'Hilda's Book' — are reprinted along with H.D.'s memoir. Pound described his early verses, when Faber reprinted some of them in the 1960s, as 'stale cream puffs' and that description isn't too unfair, though the best of them, done to a recipe from the early Yeats, show the young poet's skill. These were always cream puffs, but they weren't always stale.

ELIOT, ARNOLD, AND THE
ENGLISH POETIC TRADITION

The important critic is the person who is absorbed in the present problems of art, and who wishes to bring the forces of the past to bear upon the solution of these problems. *The Sacred Wood*

Every renewal of the sense of possibility within an art depends on a corresponding reappraisal of its history. Such a reappraisal was offered by T. S. Eliot in his essays written during the second and third decades of this century. Eliot in effect changed our perspective on English literary history, and the influence of his essays was so strong and so widespread that by 1950 it was scarcely possible for a critic to embark on any aspect of English poetry from 1600 to the modern period without at some point touching on, being influenced by, or at least dissenting from, something that stemmed from Eliot.

The critical orthodoxy which Eliot replaced was that of Matthew Arnold — the late Arnold of *Essays in Criticism Second Series*, which was in its turn very largely an orderly reassertion of the basic principles of English Romanticism. Arnold had begun as something of a rebel against the great figures of the early years of his century; at least he had wanted to mark out for himself as a poet a space where he would not be overshadowed by them; and perhaps more particularly (like Eliot after him) to distinguish himself from their degenerate heirs, his now forgotten contemporaries. Hence the elements of 'classicism' in his early criticism. But Arnold was to find his place finally, not as a rebel against the great Romantics, but as the most persuasive latterday spokesman for their poetry and for the tradition they had invoked to support it. The reputations of Wordsworth and Byron in particular, and also of Gray and Milton, were given new

The Literary Criticism of T. S. Eliot: New Essays, ed. David Newton-de Molina, London, 1977.

support by Arnold, while the obloquy into which Dryden and Pope had fallen since 1798 was confirmed.

Arnold's influence was long lasting. In 1933 Eliot wrote: 'Examination of the criticism of our time leads me to believe that we are still in the Arnold period.'[1] In 1941 Allen Tate wrote: 'Arnold is still the great critical influence in the universities, and it is perhaps not an exaggeration of his influence to say that debased Arnold is still the main stream of popular appreciation of poetry.'[2] To this I can add my own testimony, for what it is worth. In the fifth and sixth forms in New Zealand in the late 1940s — a time when some little literary history was still taught in New Zealand schools — I learned that Pope and Dryden were classics of our prose and that Wordsworth was the third great English poet after Shakespeare and Milton. I did not hear much about Arnold, but the judgements were couched in terms I now recognize as his. When I enrolled at Auckland University College in 1951 I learned an entirely new version of English literary history, and I learned that it was Eliot's.

These versions of history are at times so overpowering, so all-pervasive, and so bound up not only with the criticism of poetry but with the practice of it as well, that it can be difficult to see them with any degree of detachment. My purpose here is to try to see afresh the historical orthodoxy Eliot established, which means in part to see it against the background of the orthodoxy it replaced.

The most famous sentences which fixed in the minds of his contemporaries, and of several generations succeeding him, at least the negative aspect of Arnold's view of the literary history of England, are those about 'Dryden, Pope, and all their school', whose poetry was 'conceived and composed in their wits', whereas 'genuine poetry is conceived and composed in the soul'. Theirs was the language of prose, not of poetry, and it was Gray's misfortune, and the explanation of why 'he never spoke out', that he was 'a born poet' who 'fell upon an age of prose'.[3]

There are some sentences Arnold wrote in 1881 which fix this view in a broader historical frame:

We had far better than the poetry of the eighteenth century before that century arrived, we have had better since it departed . . . We do well to place our pride in the Elizabethan age and Shakespeare, as the Greeks placed theirs in Homer. We did well to return in the present century to the poetry of that older age for illumination and inspiration, and to put aside, in great measure, the poetry and poets intervening between Milton and Wordsworth. Milton, in whom our great poetic age expired, was the last of the immortals . . . The glory of English literature is in poetry, and in poetry the strength of the eighteenth century does not lie.[4]

Arnold had a hierarchical mind and his English hierarchy was headed by Shakespeare, Milton and Wordsworth in that order. Milton, though second to Shakespeare, was superior to him in 'sureness of perfect style'. He was 'the one artist of the highest rank in the great style whom we have'.[5] Wordsworth lacked style, but he had 'fidelity', he had *'life'* (the italics are Arnold's and not once but many times), and he taught us 'joy'.[6] To these three poets may be added the others to whom Arnold assigned their various and relative places; and the hierarchy is expanded to include European as well as English poets.

One structure of Arnold's criticism, therefore, might be represented as a simple tennis-club ladder. But another (and here he resembles Eliot in the structure if not in the details of interpretation) is the historical curve, representing a high point in Shakespeare, only a very slight drop to Milton, a sharp dip into the eighteenth century, and an upward curve with the arrival of Wordsworth. The downward curve in poetry, however, is accompanied by an upward one in the quality of prose.

This is the view we have learned at least to reject, if not positively to despise. For my purposes at this point, however, it should be considered neither right nor wrong but simply one way of seeing, which Eliot replaced by another.

Eliot's principal statements on this subject occur in his essay on the Metaphysical poets and put forward a theory which explains literary developments in terms of what might be called a piece of historical psychology. In the seventeenth century 'something . . . happened to the mind of England', a 'dissociation of sensibility . . . from which we have never recovered'. The result was a decline in the quality of poetry, for while 'the language became more refined, the feeling became more crude'. Whereas in the best of the Metaphysical poets and Jacobean dramatists we find 'a direct sensuous apprehension of thought or recreation of thought into feeling', in the poets who succeed them feeling and thought are progressively more and more dissociated. By the time we get to the nineteenth century we find poets think and feel 'by fits'. One or two passages in Shelley and Keats reveal 'traces of a struggle towards unification of sensibility. But Keats and Shelley died and Tennyson and Browning ruminated.'[7]

This 'dissociation of sensibility' was in the first version of the essay in question said to be 'due to', in the later version 'aggravated by',[8] the influence of Milton and Dryden. 'Each of these men performed certain poetic functions so magnificently well that the magnitude of the effect concealed the absence of others' — and by turning to the essay 'Andrew Marvell', published in the same year, we may find what functions each performed.

Early in the Marvell essay Eliot writes: 'Out of that high style developed from Marlowe through Jonson . . . the seventeenth century separated two qualities: wit and magniloquence.'[9] 'Wit' here suggests Dryden, 'magniloquence' Milton — and this is confirmed eight pages on: 'Dryden was great in wit, as Milton in magniloquence'; but Dryden by isolating wit and Milton by dispensing with it, 'may perhaps have injured the language'.[10]

Eliot's history, then, is like Arnold's in representing a decline in English poetry after a high point reached in the late sixteenth–early seventeenth centuries. But for Eliot the decline begins a little earlier (in Milton) and continues longer into the Romantics and beyond. If there is recovery at all (and there are clear hints of this), it is in the poetry Eliot himself and Pound were writing in the years following the First World War. The nature of the decline, or its causes, are also differently described. Whereas Arnold sees a decline in eighteenth-century poetry caused by poets composing in their 'wits' instead of in their 'soul', Eliot sees an unfortunate separation of the faculties we may suppose 'wits' and 'soul' to represent — a separation of 'intellect' and 'feeling'; but he adds that where such a separation occurred, the greater damage to the poetic tradition was done by the poetry of 'soul' (Milton's 'magniloquence') than by the poetry of the 'wits' (Dryden's 'wit').

Some years after he first set forth this view Eliot reiterated it, emphasizing again the superiority of Dryden over Milton as an influence on the poetry that followed:

I have said elsewhere that the living English which was Shakespeare's became split up into two components one of which was exploited by Milton and the other by Dryden. Of the two, I still think Dryden's development the healthier, because it was Dryden who preserved, so far as it was preserved at all, the tradition of conversational language in poetry: and I might add that it seems to me easier to get back to healthy language from Dryden than it is to get back to it from Milton.[11]

In 1920 *The Sacred Wood* appeared, establishing Eliot as an important new critical voice. A year later he wrote the three essays enunciating the view of literary history which was to become *our* view — 'The Metaphysical Poets', 'Andrew Marvell', and 'John Dryden'. The three essays appeared together under the title *Homage to John Dryden* in 1924, and it is surely their influence in succeeding decades which put the Metaphysical poets and Jacobean dramatists at the centre of academic studies of English literature, made the study of Dryden (and by extension of Pope) respectable, and set up at least some barriers to the appreciation of Milton and of what Eliot called 'the popular and pretentious verse of the Romantic Poets and their successors'.[12] 'The line of wit', as F. R. Leavis calls it, is essentially Eliot's line; and Leavis, like every other major modern critic, could trace his development back to a source in Eliot's early criticism, and in particular to those three essays.

Yet the essays contain their own half-concealed uncertainties and disclaimers. Though they appear finally to bury Arnold, Arnold still speaks in them; and it is this point I wish now to turn my attention to.

The essay on Marvell defines more clearly the 'wit' of poetry that has not suffered the 'dissociation of sensibility'; and at the same time, because the comparison is in part with Dryden, it shows how the beginnings of that 'dissociation' place limits on Dryden's achievements. Marvell is not a great poet, as Milton and Dryden are, but he is a 'classic'. 'There is . . . an equipoise, a balance and proportion of tones, which, while it cannot raise Marvell to the level of Dryden or Milton, extorts an approval which these poets do not receive from us.'[13] His wit is 'an alliance of levity with seriousness (whereby seriousness is intensified)',[14] whereas in Dryden 'wit becomes almost fun, and thereby loses some contact with reality'.[15]

What troubles Eliot is a lack of 'seriousness' ('high seriousness' Arnold would have called it) in Dryden — and he makes the same point a few years later when he says that Dryden's satire is 'in the modern sense humorous and witty' but that it lacks 'the proper wit of poetry'.[16]

In the essay on Dryden Eliot quotes (misquotes, in fact) Arnold saying that the poetry of Dryden and Pope 'is conceived and composed in their wits, genuine poetry is conceived in the soul' and rebukes him for it.[17] 'Dryden', Eliot insists, 'is one of the tests of a catholic appreciation of poetry'[18] — and he goes on to try and correct the view of Dryden that had been fashionable in the nineteenth century and was, no doubt, still current in 1921. But late in the essay Eliot concedes two points against Dryden: first, that he had 'a commonplace mind'; second, that although Dryden's words 'state immensely', 'their suggestiveness is often nothing'. Eliot goes on: 'The question, which has certainly been waiting, may justly be asked: whether, without this which Dryden lacks, verse can be poetry?'[19]

Having put the question, however, Eliot retreats from it and does not answer. 'What is man to decide what poetry is?' he asks. He proceeds to quote and to praise Dryden's elegy on Oldham. And he concludes: '[Dryden] remains one of those who have set standards for English verse which it is desperate to ignore' — verse, not poetry, and it is Eliot himself who has made the distinction.

Dryden had 'a commonplace mind', he 'lacked . . . a large and unique view of life; he lacked insight, he lacked profundity',[20] his poetry lacked verbal 'suggestiveness': it is, on close inspection, strange 'homage' that is offered to Dryden in the book of that title. The qualifications are consistent, of course with Eliot's view that Milton and Dryden together represent the two halves of the divided, or dividing, English sensibility — that they mark the moment at which 'the English mind altered'.[21] But this undertone seems remarkably close to Arnold, from whom the essay ostensibly parted company — Arnold who was always willing to concede that Dryden was a 'master in letters', a man of 'admirable talent', 'a man, on all sides, of such energetic and genial power', but whose 'verse' lacks 'high seriousness', lacks 'poetic largeness, freedom, insight, benignity' and whose language is essentially the language of prose.[22]

There is, then, at least some common ground between Eliot and Arnold on the subject of Dryden. What of Milton? We are most likely to remember that Eliot said 'Milton writes English like a dead language',[23] while Arnold said that in the matter of style Milton is superior even to Shakespeare — 'the one artist of the highest rank in the great style whom we have'.[24] But to discover in more detail what Arnold thought of Milton, and of Milton's epic, we have to go back a few years before the essay 'Milton' (which was no more than an address delivered at the unveiling of a memorial window) to one called 'A French Critic on Milton', where Arnold asserts equally firmly that Milton 'is our great artist in style, our one first-rate master in the grand style',[25] but allows the French critic, Scherer, to say for him, or to support him in saying, what is unsatisfactory in Milton.

Milton the man is 'unamiable'; 'his want of sweetness of temper, of the Shakespearean largeness and indulgence, are undeniable'.[26] Much of *Paradise Lost* awakens merely 'languid interest'.[27] Indeed its subject 'has no special force or effectiveness'.[28] In substance it is 'a false poem, a grotesque poem, a tiresome poem',[29] yet in style it is 'the very essence of poetry'. Milton's 'power both of diction and of rhythm is unsurpassable'.[30]

Why then is Milton important? It is because, in an age when few readers learn at first hand the greatness of style of the best of Latin and Greek literature, his poetry, in its 'flawless perfection of . . . rhythm and diction'[31] gives us the sense of that ancient greatness, recreates it in our own tongue, and thus acts as a bulwark against 'the Anglo-Saxon contagion, all the flood of Anglo-Saxon commonness'.[32]

Is not Arnold saying what Eliot says — that 'Milton writes English like a dead language' — but saying it approvingly? In the case of Milton, as in that of Dryden, Arnold and Eliot are nearer agreement than appears at first sight to be the case. Neither likes Milton the man, nor the substance of Milton's epic. Both see him chiefly in terms of style. The differences in what they choose to emphasize and to value depend, not on a difference of seeing, but on what each feels the needs of the present moment to be. And ten years after his first essay on Milton Eliot is prepared to acknowledge that even to a poet of the twentieth century Milton may, after all, be useful:

. . . it is his ability to give a perfect and unique pattern to every paragraph . . . and his ability to work in larger musical units than any other poet — that is to me the most conclusive evidence of Milton's supreme mastery. The peculiar feeling, almost a physical sensation of a breathless leap, communicated by Milton's long periods, and by his alone, is impossible to procure from rhymed verse. Indeed, this mastery is more conclusive evidence of his intellectual power, than is his grasp of any *ideas* that he borrowed or invented.[3]

Arnold's later essays restated and confirmed the view of English literary history that had served as the foundation of what we now recognize as the Romantic revolution in English poetry. Eliot put forward a new view which served the Modernist revolution. Neither of these men were literary historians. They were critics, not scholars; and like all great critics before them, they were poet-critics. It is not in fact the literary historian who can radically alter our perspective on literary history. He sees too many exceptions to commit himself to the broad sweep; and his evaluations are usually tentative and always relative. You need to have some clear notion of how poetry of the past will bear upon the poetic practice of the present before you can say confidently that one kind of poetry is a more vital force than another. The literary historian's tasks most often prove to be menial. He follows behind the major critic, confirming, completing, complaining, correcting.

It is difficult to be sure how much Arnold or Eliot knew in depth and in detail about the eighteenth century (on which both had a good deal to say and in which neither was primarily interested); but it is certain that the instinct for generalizing usefully from relatively small areas of reading and knowledge was highly developed in both of them. One cannot be sure, for example, whether either of them quite recognized that in the mid eighteenth century poets were committing themselves to one or another of two styles (which meant in effect to a total poetic stance) by acknowledging Milton and Spenser on the one hand, or Dryden and Pope on the other, as their great forebears.[34] Yet with or without this knowledge, both Arnold and Eliot inherited the terms of the argument, Arnold favouring Milton, Eliot committing himself to Dryden. For Arnold the difference between Milton and Dryden, between 'genuine poetry' and the poetry of 'an age of prose', was to be located in its genesis — its source in the 'wits' or the 'soul' of the poet. True poetry was in some sense a poetry of 'inspiration', which the 'unamiable' Milton could produce and the 'genial' Dryden could not. I have tried to show elsewhere[35] that Eliot, for all his presentation of himself as anti-Romantic, understood these 'Romantic' distinctions perfectly well from his own experience of writing poetry. Poetry which drew a part of its strength from 'below the levels of consciousness' offered resonances of meaning and of music which more consciously crafted verse could not match: hence the lack of 'suggestiveness' in Dryden's words; hence too, perhaps, the lack of a fundamental 'seriousness' in his wit.

But for Eliot there was another consideration — that of diction; and it is this which accounts for the pre-eminence given to Dryden over Milton in Eliot's criticism. It was one of the tenets of the Pound-Eliot revolution that poetry ought to have the virtues of good prose, and that it should be free to employ vernacular language and to work into its texture the music of contemporary speech. It was in this respect that it seemed to Eliot in the 1936 Milton essay 'easier to get back to healthy language from Dryden than . . . from Milton', because 'it was Dryden who preserved, so far as it was preserved at all, the tradition of conversational language in poetry':

Milton does . . . represent poetry at the extreme limit from prose; and it was one of our tenets that verse should have the virtues of prose, that diction should become assimilated to cultivated contemporary speech, before aspiring to the elevation of poetry . . . And the study of Milton could be of no help here: it was only a hindrance.[36]

The problem of 'poetic diction' is complex and can only be touched upon here. In the eighteenth century Gray believed that 'the language of the age' was 'never the language of poetry'.[37] Johnson censured Gray for this — for having 'thought his language more poetical as it was more remote from common use',[38] and censured Milton's diction in the same terms;[39] yet Johnson also complained of Shakespeare using words which had been made 'low by the occasions to which they [were] applied, or the general character of them who use them'.[40] Wordsworth in his Preface to the *Lyrical Ballads* announced a new poetry that would employ 'the real language of men',[41] and insisted that 'there neither is, nor can be, any essential difference between the language of prose and metrical composition'.[42] Arnold appreciated and praised this 'perfect plainness'[43] of Wordsworth's, yet condemned Dryden and Pope as poets of 'an age of *prose*', elevated the ornate Gray above them, and described Milton as the greatest master of style in the language. In Eliot's essay on Dryden we can see this history of confusion and misunderstanding continuing when he quotes Hazlitt saying 'Dryden and Pope are the great masters of the artificial style of poetry in our language as . . . Chaucer, Spenser, Shakespeare and Milton . . . [are] of the natural'; and Eliot comments on the 'absurdity' of this 'contrast of Milton, our greatest master of the artificial style, with Dryden, whose *style* . . . is in a high degree natural'.[44]

What is surprising perhaps is not the misunderstandings (deliberate or otherwise) but the continuity of the debate and the consistency of its terms. There is, of course (and this is what Eliot implies), an element of contradiction in the Romantic movement declaring itself to be in revolt against artificiality while maintaining Milton at the centre of the English poetic tradition. Yet the contradiction is more apparent than real. There are different kinds of 'artificiality'. There is the artificiality of decorum — the total decorum Johnson stood for, of which a plain (but not 'low') poetic diction was merely a part. And there was the other, more particular, and purely literary artificiality — that of the Miltonic style, the Miltonic high sentence, which was only one of several means used by poets in the mid eighteenth century (Collins, Gray, and others) in their attempts to penetrate beneath the polished surfaces of wit and propriety. In this sense Wordsworth's 'simple' poetry can be seen as another weapon, a powerful new agent *joining forces with* Gray's and Collins's most complex odes, to break down that total decorum of which Johnson was the last great spokesman. It was not 'the real language of men' Wordsworth wished to represent so much as their real *passions*. And if the Miltonic music as it revived in the eighteenth century had served a purpose it was that of permitting the poet once again to express a passionate commitment to his subject and to his own role as poet, which Dryden's and Pope's worldly couplets seemed to preclude:

> Cold is Cadwallo's tongue,
> That hush'd the stormy main:
> Brave Urien sleeps upon his craggy bed.[45]

This is (to employ Eliot's terms again) the 'magniloquence' of Milton revived in an age of 'wit'; it has (to employ Arnold's term) the Miltonic 'movement'; and it was because of this quality of passionate, committed, bardic utterance that the nineteenth century (and Arnold) could see Gray as a true poet, and Dryden and Pope, for all their relatively plain diction, as 'artificial'.

If what Eliot had to say about Milton and Dryden had been at the centre of his criticism it could not have had quite the effect that it did. But by pushing the Metaphysicals to the centre and inviting us to see that as their rightful place, he brought about a critical revolution. He did not discover the Metaphysicals. His article on them was a review of a selection of their poems by Sir Herbert Grierson — evidence of an interest which already existed. But Eliot made very large claims for these poets, claims which were both new and difficult to refute, and in writing about them he put them into a framework of three centuries of English poetry. Here, at its best, in the best poems of Donne and Marvell (and in some of the Jacobean dramatists) was a poetry of wit which was not merely analytical but passionate as well. The poet was not engaged in rending others but in rendering himself, or a mask of himself. Why the ears of English readers had been closed so long to the music of Metaphysical poetry would be difficult to decide; but it is certain that Eliot taught twentieth-century readers to hear it, and in doing so significantly altered our conception of the possibilities of poetry in the language. The lyrical and beautiful became less interesting than the dramatic and authentic. The poet capable of committing his passion to the hilt without losing a precise sense of the nature of that passion, including its defects and absurdities, commanded more respect than the poet who, in the full flood of rhetorical confidence, could be seen, by a slight twist of the reader's perspective, as the victim of his own feelings. What was to be admired in Marvell, for example, was 'not cynicism' but 'a constant inspection and criticism of experience . . . a recognition, implicit in the expression of every experience, of other kinds of experience which are possible'.[46] 'Irony', 'ambiguity', 'paradox', though not terms Eliot himself used very much, followed naturally upon his criticism as terms of approbation.

Eliot is at his best in writing about these poets, and at his most genuine. He is less satisfactory in the criticism of later ages, partly perhaps because he gets entangled in the terms of an old debate, and because he seems to take sides less from the promptings of innocent critical feeling than from a sense of how his statements will bear upon the literary politics of the moment. In his Preface to *Homage to John Dryden*, for example, he writes:

I have long felt that the poetry of the seventeenth and eighteenth centuries, even much of that of inferior inspiration, possesses an elegance and a dignity absent from the popular and pretentious verse of the Romantic Poets and their successors.

A few years earlier he had written:

Because we have never learned to criticize Keats, Shelley and Wordsworth (poets of assured though modest merit), Keats, Shelley and Wordsworth punish us from their graves with the annual scourge of the Georgian Anthology.[47]

In each of these statements (and in many more like them) we can see that Eliot's primary target is his contemporary enemies, the Georgian poets and critics, but that he strikes at them through the great Romantics, whose heirs they claim to be. For this reason Eliot never comes properly to terms with the Romantic movement. At the end of his essay on Marvell he admits that 'wit' of the kind he has been discussing is 'irrelevant' to the best poems of Wordsworth, Shelley and Keats; but he never extends the terms of his own criticism to take in or appreciate the best of their poetry. Consequently the expansion of our sense of poetic possibilities which his criticism offers in one area is achieved at the cost of contraction in another.

In *The Use of Poetry and the Use of Criticism*, a series of lectures given at Harvard in 1932-3, Eliot proposed to make a survey of the relation of criticism to poetry from the Elizabethan age to the twentieth century. Such a survey might have been expected to offer some clarification and expansion of his already stated view of the history of three centuries of English poetry, and to bring the Romantic movement into clearer definition within the overall picture. In the chapter on Dryden the idea of a 'dissociation of sensibility' seems to be reaffirmed:

It is not so much the intellect, but something superior to intellect, which went for a long time into eclipse; and this luminary, by whatever name we may call it, has not yet wholly issued from its secular obnubilation. The age of Dryden was still a great age, though beginning to suffer a death of the spirit, as the coarsening of its verse rhythms shows . . .

In the succeeding chapters, however, Eliot does not make full use of the opportunity to 'place' the Romantics. He is elusive, even defensive, seeming to recognize the special claims that might be made in particular for Wordsworth, but perhaps finding it still undesirable, in terms of the politics of contemporary poetry and criticism, to acknowledge them: '. . . much of the poetry of Wordsworth and Coleridge', he writes, 'is just as turgid and artificial and elegant as any eighteenth century die-hard could wish' (p. 72) — thus trapping himself into writing about the eighteenth century in pejorative terms that would have suited Arnold, and into acknowledging that there is some, at least, of the poetry of Wordsworth and Coleridge, to which these terms do not apply. Then, surprisingly, he writes a few pages later:

In Wordsworth and Coleridge we find not merely a variety of interests, even passionate interests; it is all one passion expressed through them all: poetry was for them the expression of a totality of unified interests . . . (p. 81)

— a statement which strongly suggests some kind of 'unified sensibility'. But at the end of the chapter there is this:

What I see, in the history of English poetry, is . . . the splitting up of personality. If we say that one of these partial personalities which may develop in a national mind is that which manifested itself in the period between Dryden and Johnson, then what we have to do is to re-integrate it . . . (pp. 84-5)

In the chapters which follow we are told that Wordsworth and Shelley are guilty of an 'abuse of poetry' (p. 89) in that they use poetry as a vehicle for ideas rather than using ideas to make poetry. Keats, on the other hand, did not abuse poetry in this way. Nor was he guilty of any 'withdrawal' in not propagating ideas: 'he was merely about his business' (p. 102) — the business of making poetry. This much is consistent with Eliot's argument, in other essays of the same period, that the poet's use of language has to be clearly distinguished from that of the philosopher or 'thinker'.[48] The philosopher makes the language serve his thought or idea; the poet makes an idea serve his poetry; and the Romantics, or at least Wordsworth and Shelley, 'abused' poetry by making it serve rather than use ideas. In the case of Wordsworth this may not matter too much; but in Shelley's case it sets up a barrier, because Shelley's ideas were 'ideas of adolescence' (p. 89) 'bolted whole and never assimilated' (p. 92).

One might have thought that Eliot would have found common ground with Arnold here. But when he comes to Arnold it is only to repeat what he said a few years earlier[49] — that Arnold was partly to blame for the decadence of the 1890s. Though Wordsworth's use of poetry as a vehicle for ideas was an 'abuse', nevertheless Arnold is condemned for inviting readers to set Wordsworth's 'philosophy' aside. Arnold had written of Wordsworth: 'His poetry is the reality, his philosophy the illusion', adding that one day we might learn to make this proposition general and to say 'Poetry is the reality, philosophy the illusion.' Eliot describes this as 'a striking, dangerous and subversive assertion' (p. 113).

It is no more 'striking, dangerous and subversive' than several assertions on the same subject made by Eliot himself;[50] and Arnold's essay on Wordsworth (one of his best if carefully and sympathetically read) rejects only the extravagant claims of 'the Wordsworthians' that their hero's poetry should be read for its 'scientific system of thought'. But one can see the line of Eliot's thinking. 'For Wordsworth and for Shelley poetry was a vehicle for one kind of philosophy or another'; this was bad, but at least 'the philosophy was something believed in' (p. 113). For Arnold the 'poetry' is not merely a thing in itself, distinct from the religion and philosophy it may be said to 'contain'; it becomes a *substitute* for religion and philosophy — it 'supersedes both' (p. 113); and it is this elevation of poetry which Eliot cannot accept and which seems to him to lead to some of the excesses of aestheticism.

Once again one notices the complications of an argument that takes place across decades and generations. Arnold, who was aware of the drift towards aestheticism, and who tried to counter it (in the essay on Keats, for example, or in the passage on Leopardi in the Byron essay) by arguing that style is not enough, that it must be accompanied by an adequate interpretation of life, is here found guilty of promoting aestheticism by giving poetry too high a place and by asking too much of it.

For the purpose of this essay I have been concerned almost exclusively with Eliot's early criticism. His later criticism, though it is full of interest and has many virtues, lacks the programme and consequently the coherence of the earlier. It is less decided, less emphatic, more demure, less original. It has no particular point of view other than that of the reasonable man of letters. It is not broadly influential in the way the early criticism was. The Eliot who has remained a force in modern criticism is the Eliot of those early essays.

Thus in putting Eliot's influential criticism alongside, or against the backdrop of, Arnold's, it is a matter of putting early Eliot against late Arnold. Arnold found his way gradually towards the general view articulated most clearly in *Essays in Criticism, Second Series*, which remained influential — almost 'standard' — long after his death. Eliot articulated the new general view when he was still relatively young, and lived long enough to look back on it and comment on it (while it continued to have its effect) almost as if it had been produced by someone else.

The men who have come to be recognized as the great critics in English — Sidney, Dryden, Johnson, Coleridge, Arnold, Eliot — have been poets and their criticism has related almost exclusively to poetry and poetic drama. Each of them, at least since Dryden, has offered or implied a view of the development of English poetry — a view which accounted for the poetry of the critic's own age, and which was so broad as to be at once compelling and unsatisfactory. They are views which cannot properly be thought of as 'right' or 'wrong' but only as more or less persuasive, more or less serviceable in focusing the expectations of readers and the ambitions of poets upon the practice of poetry in the present age.

Arnold's position in relation to his age was not unlike Johnson's, in that he reformulated a view of English literature which had been established before him and which was already in some degree being challenged. Eliot's position was nearer to that of Wordsworth (the Wordsworth of the Preface to the *Lyrical Ballads*) — making way for something new in poetry, something apparently revolutionary, yet for which the ground was already well prepared. Thus Eliot's criticism animates a new poetry as Arnold's does not. Chiefly, of course, it animates his own, and in particular *The Waste Land*.

I have argued elsewhere[51] that *The Waste Land* has to be seen, not as the work of an anti-Romantic, but as a poem whose antecedents are unmistakably Romantic; and that a great deal of Eliot's criticism, particularly as it bears upon the important question of poetic composition, is likewise Romantic, despite its eye-catching anti-Romantic declarations and neo-classical catch-phrases. Eliot wore the ribbons of one party while in the secrecy of the polling booth compulsively voting for the other. But he tried very hard to believe himself to be a witty poet and to act as if he had inherited the neo-classical 'line of wit' rather than the soul music of Romanticism. He wrote homage to John Dryden, but, as we have seen, his doubts about Dryden crept in. He praised the Metaphysicals, but for their passionate wit, not for wit alone. He complained of Milton and found him unamiable, but knew perfectly well (as shown by the quotation above about the 'almost . . . physical sensation of a breathless leap communicated by Milton's long periods') how central Milton's musical qualities were to the strongest elements in the English poetic tradtion. And this conflict in Eliot, discernible in his criticism, is now clearly revealed in the manuscripts of *The Waste Land*.

Even a casual glance at Mrs Valerie Eliot's edition of *The Waste Land* manuscripts shows that the poem in its draft form was quite different from the poem we have come to know as probably the greatest single item in the history of the Modernist movement in poetry. In its early stages the poem was an uneven, often indifferent, attempt at a neo-

Augustan satire (much of it in heroic couplets), in which the predominating voice was too personal for comfort, its feeling of superiority and disgust too naked, over-riding the deeper and more humane notes of lyricism and despair.

How those early drafts were transformed into the poem we know has been traced by Professor Hugh Kenner,[52] who sees their possible beginning in Eliot's writing of the review which became his essay on Dryden. 'To enjoy Dryden', Eliot wrote hopefully in that essay, 'means to pass beyond the limitations of the nineteenth century into a new freedom' — and Professor Kenner sees Dryden's presence in the earliest conception of the poem, and in particular in the first version of the 'The Fire Sermon'. In the course of the revisions, however 'all identifiable trace of Dryden vanished . . . Also gone was the long opening of "The Fire Sermon" which had imitated Pope. Of this there was nothing left at all, not a line and there was no way to tell that the whole central section of Eliot's long poem had moved through modes of Augustan imitation.'[53] Thus the poem's original conception bore little relation to the identity and form it finally acquired; and the whole composition lacked shape and direction until pulled together at a late stage by the writing of 'What the Thunder Said', which had 'little . . . to do with what seems to have been the poem's working plan. "What the Thunder Said" was virtually a piece of automatic writing. Eliot more than once testified that he wrote it almost at a sitting . . . and the rapid handwriting of the holograph . . . bears him out. False starts and second thoughts are few, and later retouching was insignificant.'[54]

The Waste Land, then, was 'reconceived from the wreckage of a different conception'.[55] In the extraordinary, exciting, and complex process by which not one creative mind but two went to work on the original material and transformed it, the centre of the poem had shifted from 'the urban panorama refracted through Augustan styles' to 'the urban apocalypse, the great city dissolved into a desert where voices sang from exhausted wells'. In this transformation was achieved 'the visionary unity that has fascinated two generations of readers'.[56]

Now let us consider for a moment Eliot's position as poet and critic during the years with which I have been chiefly concerned — the months immediately following the First World War. Born in the year of Arnold's death, Eliot read the Romantics avidly as an adolescent but felt he had outgrown them with his young manhood. The conventions of Romanticism, in their several forms, had been debased and diluted by repetition and by the end of the first decade of the century the landscape seemed as cluttered with indifferent neo-Romantics as it seems now cluttered with indifferent neo-Modernists. Eliot was looking for 'a new freedom' and thought perhaps he had found it, or a way to it, in 'the line of wit'. Acerbity appealed especially, because it was a way of setting himself apart from the sentimentalism and weak lyricism of so many of his contemporaries.

In the writing of *The Waste Land* Augustan imitation gave Eliot at least material — a start, an impulse, something like a plan, and in due course lines of verse — to work on. After that it was a matter of creative instinct, his own abetted by Pound's, pruning, expunging, shifting the fragments about and spawning new ones, the excitement of shaping the poem itself creating the impulse for further writing, until in due course the unforeseeable because entirely new masterpiece was born.

What was Eliot to make of what he had done? He was bound to be conscious of what had happened consciously, and uncertain about the rest — and what had been conscious, and remained so, was some sense of a debt to 'the line of wit', and a belief that his poetry came forth in reaction against something that could be called Romanticism. In some ways Eliot was less well placed to see what he had done than we are fifty years later — just as Coleridge, among the prevailing literary conventions of his time, was incapable of recognizing that 'Kubla Khan' was a finished poem and not a fragment. The *Waste Land* must have seemed as strange to Eliot as it was to seem to its first readers — strange, yet compelling. In presenting it to the public Eliot nervously added the now famous notes, which in turn encouraged a generation of critics to treat the work as a conscious and orderly construction whose hidden 'meaning' could be unlocked with aids like Jessie Weston and Sir James Frazer. In fact the poem was something quite different. Fragmentary in form yet also complete and self-sufficient, it was essentially a musical structure, playing upon certain themes and motifs taken, many of them, from a context of ideas, but not used as such in the poetry.

That Eliot in *The Waste Land* was more truly the heir of the Romantic movement than his Georgian contemporaries who laid claim to the inheritance is something I suspect many more critics would now be willing to recognize than was the case ten or fifteen years ago. The Augustan tradition — in particular the tradition of mock-heroic satire that passed from Dryden to Pope — maintained its surfaces at all costs. It was the poetry of a determined because precarious social sanity. It was beneath those surfaces that Romantic poetry in its finer moments successfully probed. The probing was instinctive and the results often obscure and fragmentary, like the salvaging of something from the ocean — and Eliot's recurrent image of things brought up, transformed, from the depths is central to his writing at this time. In composing *The Waste Land* he created a mock-heroic surface and then broke it, plunging beneath to sources of feeling which lay deeper. In this process he lived out his own neo-Romantic revolt against his own neo-classicism.

The form of the poem which resulted is organic. It grows from within, dictated by its own materials and history. Elements of the original satire remain, but these are (in both senses) *contained* within the total form. They are part of the total consciousness, but they are subdued by a larger charity, just as their couplets are subdued by a form which is larger, more expansive, more generous.

'Modernism', like *The Waste Land*, defined itself not according to this or that programme or plan but only as it came into being. It inherited everything that was revolutionary in Romanticism, yet it was no dead repetition of Romantic themes and surfaces. But if it was to understand itself it needed to understand Romanticism, and it is here that its critical consciousness can be seen in retrospect to have been inadequate.

I come back now to Matthew Arnold, and to Eliot's criticism seen alongside Arnold's. Eliot called his first book of criticism *The Sacred Wood*, taking his title, no doubt, from the first pages of Sir James Frazer's *The Golden Bough*, which describe an ancient ritual whereby a priest occupies a sacred wood as long as he can kill or drive off any contender for his priesthood. But whoever kills the priest assumes the role himself until he in turn is murdered. 'The post which he held by this precarious tenure carried with it the title of king.'[57] It is difficult to see what else Eliot could have meant by this title than that, as critic, or as critic and poet, he was entering the sacred wood in order to challenge the reigning priest; and if that is the case the title can be seen in retrospect as an oblique yet daring declaration of an intent that was in due course carried out. If the old priest, Arnold, 'died', it was Eliot who 'killed' him; and if Eliot no longer breathes, as he once did, in virtually every piece of criticism written on the subject of poetry in England, no full-scale contender for his priesthood has yet made an effective challenge.

Sustaining the metaphor for a moment one may add, however, that none of the old priests really 'dies'. They form, rather, a 'familiar compound ghost' with whom the new priest conducts his dialogues. Arnold in some degree still speaks in Eliot; and some of the questions he asks remain to be answered.

What is confusing and makes any attempt to sort out the historical strands at once difficult and interesting in this particular case is that in some significant respects Arnold is more 'modern' than Eliot. Arnold's criticism did not, and could not, animate a new poetry. It did not animate his own. It was, much of it, an unhappy substitute for the poetry he would like to have written. His essay on Gray is partly an essay on himself — a man who did not write more because he could not, and who could not because he was born at the wrong time: '. . . a man born in 1759 could profit by that renewing of men's minds of which the great historical manifestation was the French Revolution . . . If Gray . . . had been just thirty years old when the French Revolution broke out, he would have shown, probably, productiveness and animation in plenty.'

I think it is safe to say that Eliot could never have written such sentences. He could not have seen the French Revolution as 'the great historical manifestation' of a 'renewing of men's minds'. When he looked back it was with the nostalgia of the reactionary temperament to a time before 'something happened to the mind of England'. Yet Eliot lived to demostrate Arnold's point, that a true poet, even one of deeply conservative temperament, could be animated by the spirit of his time if the time was right for the appearance of something new. Eliot set out in *The Waste Land* to imitate Dryden and Pope and castigate his age, but without quite knowing what he was about he passed beyond his satiric intention into a new depth and a new freedom; and in this transformation of the neo-Augustan satire into the neo-Romantic visionary poem, Eliot offered a strange practical corroboration of the most central, and the most contentious, of Arnold's critical statements. 'Their poetry', to repeat what Arnold wrote of Dryden and Pope, 'was conceived and composed in their wits; true poetry is conceived in the soul.' Arnold's terms, if they are less than satisfactory, remain intelligible. *The Waste Land* was conceived in the wits but it was composed in the soul.

Thus a study of Eliot's poetry can lead one to precisely the same kinds of questions that arise from placing alongside one another Arnold's and Eliot's respective statements on the history of English poetry, and it is appropriate now to return where we began. Once one has recognized, for example, the tentativeness of Eliot's 'homage' to Dryden, and the lack of any developed criticism of Pope, it becomes apparent that no major critic since Johnson has spoken unequivocally for these figures whom Arnold described as 'classics of our prose'. Can Arnold's criticism, then, be said to have been effectively answered? Can it be answered? Or does the combination of satiric substance and couplet form place such restrictions on the range of feeling that such poetry is, even when written by masters like Dryden and Pope, of a second order? Is the couplet itself, which breaks the flowing verse sentence that characterizes Shakespeare, Milton and Wordsworth at their best, alien to the finest of the English genius in poetry? And on the other front, does not Eliot's failure to come clearly to terms with the Romantic poets leave Arnold's late assertions on their behalf — in particular that they revived a greatness lost after Milton — still *critically* unchallenged?

These are large questions — so large as to seem impertinent. It is my point that they are questions raised but not answered by re-reading Eliot's criticism against the background of Arnold's. Eliot's most original contribution lay in what he had to say about the Metaphysicals and about the verse of the Jacobean dramatists. But this is something *added on* to the traditional appreciation of English poetry, without quite answering the questions raised in the late eighteenth century or rebutting the assertions made in the nineteenth.

The problems which the Romantic poets were the first to confront head on remain. Science, technology, the fact, continue to advance at the expense of the mythologies on which poetry was traditionally founded. But while the mythologies recede literally, their imaginative truth becomes more and more essential to the preservation of our humanity. We grow nearer to, not further from, an understanding of Keats's 'I know nothing but the truth of imagination and the holiness of the heart's affections'.

Modernism inherited, by whatever by-paths and indirections, the Romantic commitment to the 'truth of imagination', adding new claims for the freedom of poetry to range widely and to create boldly in the search for that truth. Yet because in clearing the ground it had to skirmish with an indifferent poetry that already identified itself with the Romantic tradition, the Modernist movement perhaps lost the proper sense of its own inheritance. At least it seems to me that if there is to be a criticism capable of animating the genuinely new in poetry today, it must look once again to those areas of English poetry — and chiefly the Romantic area — which Eliot's most influential criticism failed to look at squarely. And in this task it may prove that there is still something to be learned from Arnold.

Note
Since writing this essay I have made a much more thorough and detailed study of the composition of *The Waste Land*, which will be found in Chapter Four of, and an Appendix to, my *Pound, Yeats, Eliot & the Modernist Movement*, London & New Brunswick, 1986. In that study I disagree with Professor Kenner about the order in which the parts of the poem were composed. But the general point, derived here from Kenner, stands — that in the course of composition, neo-Augustan satiric elements were almost entirely shed in favour of a poem grounded in the inheritance of European Romanticism.

ELIOT: UNDER THE INFLUENCE

Eliot's Compound Ghost: Influence and Confluence, by Leonard Unger (1981)

This is principally a book about sources and influences in Eliot's poetry; or more precisely, about echoes. It is an attempt to trace, and re-trace the various voices of past writers that can be heard within the nevertheless individual voice that is the poet Eliot's. We have heard about many of these before; others are new, or at least the role and importance assigned to them are new. F. H. Bradley, Browning, Lewis Carroll, Coleridge, Conrad, Dante, Gray, Henry James, James Joyce, Keats, Laforgue, Lawrence, Marvell, Milton, Shakespeare, Arthur Symons, Tennyson, James Thomson, Wilde, and Yeats are among the voices. But it is to Edward Fitzgerald, in particular to his version of *Omar Khayyam,* and to his (and Pater's) biographer A. C. Benson, that Professor Unger returns most often.

Some of the passages through which these voices are said to echo are indeed intricate and maze-like. There is, for example, from Fitzgerald's translation of a play by Calderón, a speech quoted by A. C. Benson in his Fitzgerald biography which, Unger argues, is echoed in 'A Game of Chess'. But this speech has no exact parallel in the Calderón play. It has been invented by Fitzgerald, echoing Milton, who in turn may be echoing Spenser, and read by Eliot not in Fitzgerald but in Benson.

Scholarship, like History, has many contrived corridors. It deceives with whispering ambitions and guides us by vanities. Professor Unger is clear and helpful in his general remarks on the nature and processes of literary influence. He is convincing when arguing, for example, the general case that Eliot was influenced early and permanently by Fitzgerald's *Omar.* But the harder he presses into detail the less entirely

Yeats Eliot Review, vol. 8, nos 1 & 2, 1986.

ANSWERING TO THE LANGUAGE

almost completed. I declined. It seemed to me McQueen must have been chosen because he becomes. This is not, I think, because what he proposes is far-fetched (though occasionally it is) but rather because the echoes are often very faint and/or distant. Yes, the reader feels some connexion is very probable; but this or that example of it seems nonetheless weak and unconvincing. It will not be worth offering an anthology of Childrée and the less persuasive among the examples Unger offers. Each reader of this book will arrive at his own.

In a late chapter Unger considers Eliot's objection to the very kind of book he has written. In 'The Frontiers of Criticism' (which still seems to me a very important statement about the nature and limits of literary criticism) Eliot considers and points to the inadequacies of two kinds of criticism: the lemon-squeezer school which crushes every drop of meaning out of a poem without revealing a personal response to it; and the school which deals in explanation by origins, of which John Livingstone Lowes's *The Road to Xanadu* is the classic. Eliot's essay is interesting because it both confirms the validity of Lowes-style source hunting (Lowes showed, once and for all, that poetic originality is largely an original way of assembling the most disparate and unlikely material to make a new whole) and admits its fascination, yet dismisses it as a means of getting any closer to 'the *poem* . . . as poetry': 'When the poem has been made, something new has happened, something that cannot be wholly explained by *anything that went before*. That, I believe, is what we mean by 'creation.'

Unger confronts this objection to his own book but does not, I think, answer it, because there is no answer. What comes to the literate reader as echo because it is, part of a common stock ('those are pearls that were his eyes'), is part of the experience of the poem. Echoes which are there, not from a common stock, but from remote sources peculiar to the poet, are not part of the poem until scholarship makes them so, and in doing that, scholarship can have a dismembering effect. The poem loses unity, loses its surface, its primary rhetorical force, and becomes a series of sign-posts pointing off in all directions into the undergrowth of literature. There is no one so blind to a poem as a scholar who has spent a decade, or an uninterrupted summer, working at it. Now there was no need to look (in Crumow's phrase) the regional thing the real thing, either in landscape or in history.

What then is the use of the kind of book Unger has written? Not, I think, to help us read Eliot better. To recover the poems you will need to let a good many of Unger's remoter discoveries and suggestions sink like sediment to the bottom of the pool of memory. But from this book we learn something about Eliot, and something about the nature of poetic composition. We are forced to stop and consider the process by which poets absorb literary influences; the distinction (if it can be made) between an influence and a source, and the nature of poetic originality. The subject of this book, in other words, is broader than appears to be the case; and when reviewers of contemporary poetry are prone to slip lazily into unconsidered talk about 'influences', it is salutary to have a book which enforces a careful consideration of just what the word means.

This is a scholar's book, though it tries, and with some success, to break out of the more arid aspects of the decorum of scholarship. 'In the course of writing,' Unger tells us on p.12, 'I became aware that I was experiencing *recognitions*, ideas and understandings that were new to me, and I decided to let the book develop in that way — to produce a book that would be the record of an ongoing experience.' This makes it all seem a little more exciting than it really is. In the second chapter the ghost of a different, racier, less decorous piece of writing puts in a momentary appearance:

> After reflecting that one 'might as well claim *Omar*' I re-read *Omar* — for the first time in decades. But it is a poem we always remember, and on re-reading it I discovered that my light-hearted reflection was not so light-headed after all. I am not about to say *Ecco!* and offer the earliest and utterly persuasive demonstration that *Omar* is the source, or a source, of *Four Quartets*. The fact is that on first re-reading the poem I discovered that one might indeed 'claim' *Omar* or at least 'offer the suggestion' that with a thing here and a thing there seeming to correspond with things in the *Quartets*, why shouldn't it be possible to entertain the proposition, etc., etc.?
>
> This is exactly (sort of) what I decided to do: to compose a *tour de force* but not a farce — making the strongest possible case. But some of the purpose is already undermined and weakened, some of the force has gone (pp. 17-18)

After that little outburst of personality the book returns to a more sober and traditional tone and language. Probably it is as well that it does. Perhaps Unger has it in him to write a different kind of book. This one, in the meantime, is civilized, useful, and interesting.

II

A 'Penguin' used to have a certain clout. It signified a status, it meant a large international circulation, and there was a particular look and feel to the book. All of that may still be so in some degree with a Penguin published in Britain — but even there, the imprint is rivalled by others more stylish and equally discriminating. To reclaim some of what was being lost to Abacus, Picador and Paladin, Penguin had to launch its King Penguin series.

Now, however, in addition to the international imprint, we have Penguin Canada, Penguin Australia, Penguin New Zealand, each with a degree of independence. A Penguin of a novel by Maurice Gee comes through the same distribution network, but originates in London, and is sold and

The Penguin Book of New Zealand Verse, edited by Ian Wedde and Harvey McQueen, with an Introduction by Ian Wedde (Penguin 1985).

My favourite anecdote about Maurice Duggan goes as follows: Duggan was holding forth to two literary friends in a bar. He didn't, of course, have an English accent making his speech... another group of drinkers just along the bar seemed to find Duggan's talk distracting. Finally he pushed his face threateningly towards Duggan and said 'You a Kiwi, mate?'
Yes, mate, Duggan said. Are you?

Landfall, September 1985.

AUDEN'S 'SPAIN'

I

'Spain' was first published in pamphlet form in 1938. In the 1940 collection, *Another Time*, it appeared with three of its stanzas deleted and some minor verbal alterations. The result is a tighter and better written poem, but one rather less explicit politically. It no longer insists on the identification of the 'people's army' with the principle of Love, nor upon that of Franco's 'invading battalions' with the principle of Death — but it still invites the reader to make that identification, and it could not be read as anything but a statement in support of the Republican cause. This revised form reappeared in the *Collected Shorter Poems* of 1950 and continued being reissued until the book went out of print last year. In 1963, however, granting Robin Skelton permission to reprint the original form of the poem in the *Penguin Poetry of the Thirties*, Auden did so on condition that Skelton made it clear the poet now considered 'Spain' to be 'trash which he is ashamed to have written'. And last year the poem was entirely omitted from the new *Collected Shorter Poems, 1927-57*. In the foreword to the new collection Auden refers (without naming it) to 'Spain' as a 'dishonest' poem, and justifies the description by quoting, and (it seems to me) misreading, its final lines.

Auden agrees with Valery: 'A poem is never finished; it is only abandoned.' The point of this, of course, when it comes from a poet who revises his earlier work, is to require of us that we consider the latest version of any poem as the proper text. But what of a poem which the poet withdraws and declares to be 'trash' and 'dishonest'? The writing of the poetry and the revisions are his business, certainly; but the reading is ours. He cannot require either that we suppress our interest or that

London Magazine, March 1968

we accept his judgement; nor can he *effectively* withdraw a poem — particularly one like 'Spain' which has circulated widely and excited a good deal of admiration. On the other hand, it is entirely his right — even if a mistake — to omit from a collection any poem which (for whatever reason) he no longer likes.

Of the possible texts my ideal would be one which admitted all the minor revisions of the second version, but at the same time preserved the deleted stanzas. But this is not an important point. What I have to say applies with equal force (if it can be said to have force) to both versions. I will refer throughout to the first.

II

'Spain' was a poem with a purpose — the same purpose Auden expressed in 1935 when he wrote:

Poetry is not concerned with telling people what to do, but with extending our knowledge of good and evil, perhaps making the necessity of action more urgent and its nature more clear, but only leading us to make a rational and moral choice.[1]

The poem dramatizes the moment of moral choice; it expresses the alternatives metaphorically as 'death' or 'the Just City' and it finds them represented in the opposed forces in Spain. It is in all this consistent with everything Auden had written during the first decade of his career, and the logical and imaginative climax of that decade. Retrospectively one may say it was predictable (though no one could have *made* the prediction) that the poem should be as it is. That is part of its strength. The Spanish war seemed to enact an ideological battle that had been until then *merely* ideological. It must have been in some degree comforting to have it out of the realm of abstraction, confirmed as a matter of life and death. 'On that tableland scored by rivers/Our thoughts have bodies; the menacing shapes of our fever/Are precise and alive.'

'Our thoughts have bodies.' That no doubt was how it felt. The poem is nourished by everything Auden had written before it; but something else is added: the sense that the *moment has arrived*. 'The struggle' (as it was called) had become explicit. A decade spent anticipating it is expanded and becomes, in the rhetoric of the poem, the whole of human history:

> Yesterday all the past . . .
> Tomorrow perhaps . . .
> . . . But today the struggle.

That is the poem's rhetorical structure; and like all successful structures — engineering or literary — it has an obviousness, a simplicity that

ANSWERING TO THE LANGUAGE

commands assent. It *is* obvious, but someone had to think of it first.
Its success is not merely that it elevates its subject, but that the subject becomes more general by being so particularized. Yesterday all the past. 'I understand.' 'Tomorrow perhaps.' two. But today the struggle. This is the eternal present, the whole of life, the persistent pressure of alternatives and of the need to choose. These Murray achieves density without those accretions that The opening stanzas are not, as has been argued, arbitrarily in their particulars in length poetry and nothing else can offer, an art that arrests one's otherwise forever frustrated sense of the richness of the life that lives only in the moment.

> Yesterday all the past. The language of size
> Spreading to China along the trade routes; the diffusion
> Of the counting-frame and the cromlech;
> Yesterday the shadow-reckoning in the sunny climates.
>
> Yesterday the assessment of insurance by cards,
> The divination of water; yesterday the invention
> Of cartwheels and clocks, the taming of Horses.
> Yesterday the bustling world of the navigators.

That past is a long way off, a distant rumble which is brought rapidly nearer. The first six stanzas lead us through a primitive past, a medieval past, a modern past, without quite bringing into focus, or losing, a scene which is recognizably Spanish. At the end of stanza 4 the counter-statement is introduced: 'But today the struggle.' Statement and counter-statement — as much musical as conceptual in their effect — are repeated in stanzas 5 and 6. They are firmly established, but not prolonged to a point where their sharpness would be lost. Stanza 7 introduces a different tempo.

It is pointless to argue that this past is in some degree 'unreal' — just as it is pointless to complain that the future promised later in the poem is whimsical and unappealing. The strategy — and it is a measure of Auden's poetic tact, or knowhow, that he sticks to it — is to enlarge a present moment of choice caught between a past and a future both of which in this light are mere abstractions.

Stanzas 7 to 14 (the poem's second 'movement') show us in turn the romantic poet, the scientist, and the poor, each avoiding the choice — the 'change of heart' — which the present requires; and beyond these the nations '[combining] each cry', invoking the evolutionary process that once founded 'the city state of the sponge', raised 'the vast military empires of the shark/And the tiger' and established 'the robin's plucky canton' — calling on this Life Force to 'intervene' and resolve the hour of crisis. But the Life Force answers only by thrusting responsibility back on the petitioners:

> 'What's your proposal? To build the just city? I will.
> I agree. Or is it the suicide pact, the romantic
> Death? Very well, I accept, for
> I am your choice, your decision. Yes, I am Spain.'

Here, just past the poem's mid-point, Spain is for the first time named. This is where History — and the poem — have brought us; where we go from here depends on us.

The poem's third movement (Stanzas 15-19) opens with the beautiful description of those who have heard this reply ('I am your choice, your decision') and responded. It concludes with the two stanzas identifying Franco's battalions as the political projection of private neurosis, and the 'people's army' as the political projection of friendship and love.

Stanzas 20 to 23 introduce tomorrow — a future left tactfully imprecise, pleasantly ironic, and yet delicately evocative too.

The final movement returns us to 'today', rising to a strong climax which reiterates that choice is what the moment requires of us —[3]

> The stars are dead. The animals will not look.
> We are left alone with our day, and time is short, and
> History to the defeated
> May say alas but cannot help or pardon.

III

It is not surprising that 'Spain' should seem to be more widely known than any other Auden poem, and that even those unsympathetic to him and to it, nevertheless, concede (as Peter Lowbridge puts it) that, 'For better or for worse (it) remains the great poetic memorial to the Civil War.'[4] Only a part of the reason for the poem's success was its subject. Other English poets more passionately committed to the Republic — some of them killed in the war — wrote poems about it. None of their poems had the extra-literary success of Auden's. The important differences are, first, of course, that his talent was greater than theirs; but second that he had equipped himself over a period of years to deal precisely with *this* subject. He had a terminology, a myth of his own making, with which to meet it.

It has been argued by at least two critics that 'Spain' misses the 'grandeur' of its occasion.[5] On the contrary it seems to me the 'grandeur' can have existed only in the *conception* of the war, not in its brute reality — and it is the conception Auden catches so perfectly. If we want something of the reality we will read Orwell perhaps, or Professor Hugh Thomas's history. But here in Auden's poem is unmistakably the faith motivating those of the European Left who went to defend the Republic. This is what motivated Orwell, and what he returned to. Orwell saw the Left break up under pressure in Spain. His own sympathies were with the P.O.U.M. and the Anarchists, not with the Communists, and he wrote ([illegible]) [illegible] complain, [illegible] about British left-wing [illegible] the war. Yet in the end he validates this simplification himself when he admits that

> Walking on that early shore, in our bodies,
> [illegible] wasp-waisted:
> [illegible]
> ropework is crabbing on the tide's flood,
> swarming, sway, and shouting,
> entering the rivermouth over the speedy bar.

His talent is first for observation, then for making the best use of it without explanatory clutter. I suppose you have to have looked hard at cows, for example, to receive the full shock of recognizing how hard Murray has looked.

> A sherry-eyed Jersey looks at me. Fragments of thoughts
> [illegible]
> It is sophistication trying to happen.

Or this of a horse and rider:

> We talk with him about rivers and lakes; his polished horse
> is stepping nervously,
> printing neat omegas in the gravel, flexing its [illegible]
> off flies;
> his big sidestepping horse that has kept its stones.

Or this, less economical, but marvellous in its way, of fast-flowing mountain water:

> a harelip round a pebble, mouthless cheeks globed over a boulder,
> a finger's far-stretched holograph, skinned flow athwart a snag
> — these flexures are all reflections, motion-glyphs, pitches of
> impediment
> say a log commemorated in a log-long hump of wave,
> a buried rock continually noted, a squeeze-play
> through a cracked basalt bar, maintaining a foam-roofed, two-sided
> [illegible]

Or this, where the birds' unusual swooping flight, both exactly observed and mimicked by the run of the lines, is used as an image of something quite other and abstract:

> There'll always be religion around while there is poetry
> or a lack of it. Both are given, and intermittent,
> as the action of those birds — crested pigeon, rosella parrot —
> who fly with wings shut, then beating, and again shut.

[illegible]
action of a flock of ibis landing:

the dissension among the supporters of the Republic was mere 'froth on the surface'.[6] What mattered was that Franco's army had to be opposed.

IV

Now let me switch for a moment to the level of gossip and consider Auden's experience of the Spanish war. Out of a number of casual remarks made over a period of years by a variety of writers one can put together a sketchy narrative of his visit to Spain early in 1937.

He volunteered as a stretcher bearer on the Republican side.[7] No one has ever suggested he carried a stretcher. Roy Campbell says he played ping-pong in a hotel in Malaga.[8] Robert Graves says he played ping-pong in a hotel in Sitges.[9] Claud Cockburn, on the other hand, says Auden took his visit to Spain too *seriously*.[10] Cockburn wanted him to write about the war. Auden 'wanted to *do* something'. 'When Auden came . . .' Cockburn says, 'we got a car laid on for him. . . . We thought we'd whisk him to Madrid and the whole thing would be a matter of a week . . . But not at all: the bloody man went off and got . . . a mule . . . and announced that he was going to travel through Spain with this creature. From Valencia to the Front. He got six miles from Valencia before the mule kicked him . . . .' A friend who was with him has said Auden was soon anxious to leave.[11] He returned to England after only a few months in Spain, and according to Spender never spoke of his experiences.[12] But it was after his return that he wrote the poem.

In 1956 in an essay outlining the stages of his return to the Anglicanism of his boyhood, Auden revealed that he had been disturbed in Spain to find churches closed and priests absent.[13] In 1962 he said, in reply to a question, that he never spoke of his visit because he had been shocked by a number of things he had seen and heard there.[14]

If we add to this gossip Julian Symons's anecdote that he once met a friend of Laura Riding's who had discovered the opening lines of 'Spain' came from a travel book,[15] we are well-placed to leap to obvious conclusions: for example, that Auden was dishonest (writing the poem when he no longer believed in the cause it supported); that he was frivolous (playing ping-pong while people were dying); that he was a dupe (being pushed around by Cockburn); that he was a coward (getting out while the going was good) — and so on. It is because I believe any such conclusions to be false that I anticipate them here.

First, then, the question of the poem's 'honesty' — whether Auden believed in what he was writing. It is sometimes objected that 'Spain' is coldly impersonal, analytical, clinical. In so far as there is truth in this, it is a measure of the degree to which the poem completes and brings to a climax a phase in Auden's writing. For ten years his stated intention had been to make poetry 'clinical'. But it is also true that this style at its best, far from appearing empty of feeling, can seem a brilliant translation of personal feeling into a public and impersonal form. The very sense of control can suggest what there is, and how much of it, to be controlled — and this, it seems to me, is the case with 'Spain'.

If one doubts the emotional authenticity of a poem one should listen to its music — and not all of those who have pronounced on Auden's poetry have been equipped with ears. What Eliot called 'the music of poetry' comes from a level at which a lie is a false note. 'Spain', like so many of Auden's early poems may have its verbal imprecisions, its areas of verbal fuzziness. But musically it seems to me faultless and, in a curious way, impassioned. I have not the least doubt of its honesty.

Some critics have objected that Auden absents himself from the poem.[16] It is a mark of our romanticism that a poem in which the poet declares (let's say), 'Here I am with my rusty Mauser defending the Republic. Any moment I may be shot and become some corner of a foreign field . . .' — declares his own courage in fact — such a poem will be hailed as honest, true to experience. But the poet who keeps himself out of the picture for the good reason that he's not *in* it is attacked for 'impersonality' and lack of feeling.

Auden has said he saw things in Spain that shocked him, and that some of these things have been described ('better that I could ever have done') in Orwell's *Homage to Catalonia*.[17] Perhaps then if one wants to know why those shocks were not sufficient to prevent him from writing his poem, one may consult Orwell. Reflecting in 1943 on the Spanish war Orwell wrote:

> The common people knew in their bones that the Republic was their friend and Franco was their enemy . . .
> One has to remember this to see the Spanish war in its true perspective. When one thinks of the cruelty, squalor, and futility of war — and in this particular case of the intrigues, the persecutions, the lies and the misunderstandings — there is always the temptation to say: 'One side is as bad as the other, I am neutral'. In practice, however, one cannot be neutral . . .[18]

One could not be neutral. That was a consequence of the view of the war shared by Orwell and Auden. If the Left was breaking up under pressure, turning against itself, telling its share of lies, committing its share of atrocities — if (to put it more simply) it was being *defeated* — that hardly altered the support these writers felt they owed to a popularly elected government against an army, helped by Hitler and Mussolini, that was attempting to overthrow it. Orwell was later to consider the question of whether it was right to encourage the Spaniards to go on fighting a war they almost certainly could not win. He concluded that it was. Auden has perhaps considered it too, or put to himself the kind of question Yeats faced shortly before his death:

89

Did that play of mine send out
wasn't certain but the English kids could 'really relate to' you had to
go to Hone Tuwhare. Around her sat a group of Pakeha women nodding
agreement. Their hands would have been clean. But, as Graham
Greene's Dr. Magiot says at the end of *The Comedians*, there are
circumstances in which it may be better to die with blood on your hands
than with water like Pilate. That I'm sure, was how it seemed to them
at the time.

There is then not the least reason for accepting Hugh D. Ford's
contention that Spain must in some way represent Auden's renunciation
of his former politics. The poem is a clear and forceful re-statement
of the politics that had informed his previous writing. And two of three
years later Auden was still making the same affirmation. In an essay
published in 1940 he wrote:

think good will and intelligence ... the Fascists been wrong for their confidence in society.

Intolerance is an evil and has evil consequences ... there but there are times when
we must be prepared to accept the responsibility of our convictions. We must
be as tolerant as we dare.
But we do have to choose, every one of us.[20]

Without effort and vigilance ... One cannot be neutral. Auden and Orwell will
also ... from this point. It is hardly surprising that Orwell, despite his
lack of sympathy with ... and the anti-intellectual ... about details in the
poem, nevertheless, grudgingly conceded that Spain was 'one of the few
decent things to be written about the Spanish war'. Of their own history
and language may be a kind of bi-cultural equality. It is not a kind we
should be hoping for, but it may be where we are heading.

Recently a brochure appeared in an Auckland University common room
... Orwell's *Homage to Catalonia* ... English ... today ... together with the 1943
... looking back on the Spanish War ... put together their two statements
... writing ... types and roles of English used ... 1700 ... Anarchist ... Communist ... Orwell's
... symbolized the ... Spanish ... may
... Orwell ... the opening page ... to reach his first impression
... most powerfully again and endless ... and reveration in New
Zealand ... the past ... through the reality as Orwell saw it, and, after
a ... of the 1950s ... Chris Christopher experience ... That, I imagine, with the
figure of ... Many a 30-year-old ... who play-ping-pong the Spanish
... New Zealand literature ... adopt ... which gives the basic premises
... black ... white is, was seldom ... commercially viable. Yet it had a
... Spain only one thing ... in
... foreigner ... sense of a place, other ... challenge. Though
prevailing repressive puritanism, deflater of pieties, above all guardian

the poem's argument does not permit descriptive pauses it nevertheless evokes strongly in almost every stanza a landscape, a climate, a culture, and a history that was in the first and the last analysis European and ideological, but in its particular manifestation was Spanish. Should Auden be needed. When has had other... for so many, how could Leigh Davis have been overlooked?

Finally it has to be said that the poems at the latter end of the book have in common with poems throughout that they would not take the... to the question of their 1940 revision, and the recent withdrawal... in his foreword to the *Collected Shorter Poems*, Auden... that in his... visions... ideologically significant... it's altogether, consciously... it hardly... a revision... former thoughts and feelings in the language in which they were first expressed.' A statement based on such a difficult distinction is vulnerable to unsympathetic scrutiny. One may object that the thoughts and feeling are *in* the language; to alter it is to alter them. Nevertheless it is perfectly clear what Auden means; and I can think of only one poem ('A Summer Night 1933') where the original version and the revised version seem to be making statements which are ideologically opposed.[22]

The 1940 revision removed two stanzas which made the poem more explicit than it is without them; but the poem is not fundamentally altered... the change... remains a very stirring and gripping of the Republican side. ... those who have heard the reply... know... in the... task... hold... that every... large-scale... those who would have... the country. Various routes... to the... Besides get right and most likely to give offence. I know the good will and honest intentions which have led the editors to include a large... in the... with... and notes. I know how warmly it has been welcomed... to be applauded. Nevertheless it is a decision with which I find myself out of sympathy, and if I don't say so, and why, my review will be less than honest. Even to someone now or in the future who sees this inclusion of Maori language poems as self-evidently right it may at least be of sociological or... interest... from... matter, and... Auden has not seriously tried to explain it. Lacking an adequate explanation most of his readers will obviously believe the omission have been ideologically self-engaging—... Or the change in Auden's political views. Perhaps... but... because... Marxist... remain. I imagine they... Maori... be extremely difficult even for Auden... but... be... connected with... present... style... also... in... *The... Review*... recently Auden wrote in... Poetry (his... McQueen... claims 'is the first Penguin anthology anywhere in the "post-colonial world" to include quantities of poetry

I kissed the... and churchill murmured 'Tena koe'
To the oldest woman and she replied 'Tena koe'
Yet the red book is shut from which I should learn Maori
And these daft English words meander on
James K. Baxter, *Jerusalem Sonnets*

They clung like birds to the long expresses that lurch
Through the unjust lands, through the night, through the
alpine tunnel;
They floated over the oceans,
They walked the passes: they came to present their lives.
(revised version)

fuss, of indifference to the naked truth, which, as I get older, increasingly revolts me.'[24] To get at that naked truth, he says, he is 'prepared to sacrifice a great many poetic pleasures and excitements'.

The point of view is perfectly intelligible. There are, however, more kinds of truth than one. Comparing 'Spain' with a recent poem like 'Whitsunday at Kirchstetten' (also in its way a political poem), one can see two kinds of truth, and the two styles that embody them. 'Spain' is the conceptual, the general, the — if you like — rhetorical truth. 'Whitsunday at Kirchstetten' is the particular, the limited, what we like to call the *exact* truth. A poet cannot give us both styles — both kinds of truth — simultaneously; but that is not necessarily to say they contradict one another. I find no problem in the fact that I admire and value both poems.

VII

'We make of the quarrel with others rhetoric,' Yeats says, 'of the quarrel with ourselves, poetry.' If politics is 'the quarrel with others' it is not, then, according to this view, fit material for poetry; and it is true that a great deal of political poetry in English seems to require some such description as 'rhetoric' (in the bad sense) or 'satire' or 'verse', rather than poetry. Yeats is constantly telling us how he and his associates worked to keep politics out of literature; and he does not mean (like those who say 'keep politics out of sport') *other people's* politics. He feared that the strength of his own partisanship would wreck the precision, the delicacy, above all the *inclusiveness* that his high conception of poetry called for. But once the 'quarrel with oneself' has been recognized as a microcosm of the larger quarrel, the perspective alters. Yeats's 'Easter 1916' is a political poem. It takes sides. It celebrates the executed rebels — but not before Yeats has told us that he has been in the habit of making jokes about them, that one was 'a drunken vainglorious lout', that the Easter Rising was perhaps unnecessary. His strategy is to put all this in the past tense. That was a time when life in Ireland was a comedy. Now it is tragedy. Each of the dead rebels

> . . . has resigned his part
> In the casual comedy . . .

> Transformed utterly:
> A terrible beauty is born.

The poem ends on a note of trumpeting partisanship, but it does not begin there.

A comparable process occurs in Marvell's 'Horatian Ode'. Marvell sets out to celebrate Cromwell, but he cannot do it without incorporating into the poem the quarrel with himself that preceded his acceptance of the Protectorate. Cromwell's energy is breathtaking, but to accept and praise it Marvell must also acknowledge that it has 'ruin'd the Great Work of time', that it has destroyed the old decorum represented by Charles.

The distinction between the quarrel with oneself and the quarrel with others is not absolute. Politics begins in private and becomes public when a choice has been made and acted upon. In his early poetry Auden's public mythology is a projection of the quarrel with himself. On the one hand there is the romantic attachment to his class and his country; on the other his feeling that both are decadent and must rediscover the will to change. This lies behind — quite a long way behind — 'Spain'; but the residue of that private quarrel remains in the poem. It is there in his delicately ironic treatment of a Socialist future ('all the fun under/ Liberty's masterful shadow'; 'the eager election of chairmen/By the sudden forest of hands'). It is there in his plain dislike for the actual *work* of politics ('the flat ephemeral pamphlet and the boring meeting').[25] It is there in the reluctance of his allegorical figures to take the step required of them. It is there in the recognition that killing in war, however we rationalize it, is nonetheless 'murder'.[26] If past and future are unreal in the poem, they are also *pleasanter* than the present — and this serves to emphasize that the choice is a moral duty, not a form of self-indulgence.

Each of these poems — Marvell's and Yeats's as well as Auden's — deals with politics and civil war against a broad national or international background. Each inevitably has that element of 'theatre', of exaggerated gesture, that Auden now finds distasteful. He is not likely, however, to want Marvell's poem, or Yeats's, removed from their collected works. I see no good reason why he should want 'Spain' removed from his.

While its events are near to us we tend to speak of a political poem in ideological terms. As the events recede into the past the qualities come to seem purely literary. When enough time has elapsed it will be scarcely more relevant to an appreciation of 'Spain' that it takes the Spanish war as its subject than it is relevant to Shakespeare's histories that they take the Wars of the Roses for theirs. In the meantime we are still conscious that what the Thirties called 'the struggle' continues to reappear in new places and new forms. For my own part I would like to think that a young left-wing poet with a hard head and a clear conception of his purpose might at this moment be playing ping-pong in a hotel in Saigon, waiting for the next plane out.

to three per year. The effect of this is to produce the sense of two different anthologies welded together and overlapping. One represents that 'core tradition' which must now be seen as extending far beyond the twenty-two names above to include many others — Eileen Duggan, ...uwhere, Flame, Apeck, O'Sullivan, Manhire, and Wedde himself, to take only the names about which there would probably be no disagreement. The other anthology is perhaps the one Wedde would most have enjoyed doing — a post-1960 collection demonstrating the progression he suggests is from the 'hieratic' to the 'demotic', the language 'growing into location'.

The very inclusiveness of Wedde's selection from the last two decades is probably what determined that he would not do anything radical with what he calls the 'core tradition'. But the result is a curiously uneven arrangement, as if you began your guest list selectively and as you went on got more and more slap-dash and what-the-hell about it until it turned into something like open house. Also the sheer number of poets precludes a close look at anyone. In an anthology of 437 pages O'Sullivan is able to give 33 pages to Baxter, 20 to Brasch, 24½ to Curnow, and 19 each ... have given 16 to Baxter, 13¾ to Curnow, 11½ to Glover and 10½ to Brasch —

... pages back, reflectively, to Eileen Duggan's ...

It has a momentum I admire. But you have to take it at a cracking

AUMLA, 53, May 1980.

A. D. HOPE

introduction and his anthology a less easy target than the others had
like Amis and Wain withered on the stalk as poets, Davie flowered and
was fruitful... to consider Davie as poet and
critic... to consider Hope is to consider a stubborn and purposeful
anachronism... Successful adaptation has occurred; and this is signalled
... I think they are. As
... (pp. 28, 60) and
... its point.

argument that the language of New Zealand poetry has at last 'grown
into location'? I am still

There might be some sort of half-truth there; but the fact that over

the black swan of trespass on alien waters

... Wedde make distinct yet
not dissimilar announcements that New Zealand poetry has 'arrived' ought

the new men are cool like spreading fern

to make us wary. Because the measure in each case is in terms of
... Curnow of 1945 (his Caxton anthology) and
the Wedde of 1985. When English poetry was shedding romantic prettiness

Remembering that saying of Lenin when the shadow was already on his
face

and dealing with truth and reality, Curnow found evidence of poetic
maturity in the harsh truths he and his contemporaries were prepared

the emotions are not skilled workers

to tell about 'real' New Zealand; Kowhai Gold was the local variant
... composition' governing the writing of Ern Malley's poems was 'there

137

must be no coherent theme, at most, only confused and inconsistent hints at a meaning held out as a bait to the reader'. They could not recognize, of course, that this principle, meant to demonstrate that the Malley poems deserved only contempt, is in fact a partial explanation of their charm and interest. The deficiency of the poetry Hope and McAuley have promoted is precisely a lack of that resonance beyond the obvious which the Malley poems, for all their awkwardness and banalities, undoubtedly have. It is a poetic principle that has its source in French Symbolism; and Hope (p. 142) quotes the relevant passage from Mallarmé: 'Les Parnassiens prennent la chose entièrement et la montrent; par là, ils manquent de mystère, ils retirent aux esprits cette joie délicieuse de croire qu'ils créent.'

Hope acknowledges that it must have 'seemed a splendid and exciting manifesto at the time' but insists it has 'turned out to be at best a narrowing road between high walls and at worst a mere blind alley'. Anything can be a blind alley if you close your eyes, but the literary history of our century cannot be undone by wishing. It is easy but of course quite misleading to point to bad examples of any poetic mode and say this proves the mode itself is worthless. The practitioners of the current mode are always legion, and most of them (whatever the mode, whatever the century) not very highly skilled. Time can be relied upon to sort out the sheep from the goats. If I feel a certain antagonism to this book, and to Hope, it is because he offers aid and comfort to academics who have preferred not to keep up with the poetry of our time.

Hope is a good poet and in The New Cratylus he is at his best when writing about the processes of writing poems. He is 'Romantic' (as I think any genuine poet who is honest is likely to be) in his attitude to poetic inspiration. There is a lot of good clear (if sometimes a little pedantic and obvious) exposition of the way metre, rhythm and rhyme work in poetry, of the relation of sound and meaning, of literary language and common speech, of the relation of 'dream work' and conscious control in writing, and of the musical sense which underwrites much that is best in poetry. There is also a timely attack on academic interpretations of poems, concluding

Too many critics of our day appear to me to use poems simply as raw material for an exquisite display of their own sensibilities. Even where they are not engaged in importing irrelevant material into the poem, they are exhausting its possibilities, they are leaving nothing for the reader's imagination, they anticipate all his possible discoveries, they forestall wonder and delight and the sense a good reader has of letting a poem reveal itself little by little. (p. 126)

— a complaint which closely matches that of T. S. Eliot in 'The Frontiers of Criticism', with its description of such critics as constituting the 'lemon-squeezer school'. One must repeat here, however, that the poem itself can be too self-explanatory for its own good, 'leaving nothing to the reader's imagination', and it is this which Hope's critical position (and sometimes his poetic practice) fails to take sufficient account of.

But along with much sense goes the parade of old prejudices and blind spots. Free verse ('tedious', 'trivial', 'effete', 'spurious', p. 58) gets a drubbing, and we are told poets like to write it because it is *easy* (p. 61, Hope's italics). It is easy, I agree, to write badly; it is also easy to write rhymed verse badly. And it may be easier to convince the unpractised and unprofessional that rhymed verse is poetry than that free verse is. To succeed, free verse must stand up without the props of rhyme and regular metre, and it would be possible to argue that in this sense it is harder to do well. But all such debates are pointless. As a poet I have written in tight forms and in free verse and don't wish to be talked out of either. I think it is one of Hope's limitations as a poet that he is not able to work outside closed forms; it is certainly his limitation as a critic that he is not able to appreciate the work of men like Eliot and Pound.

Hope's limits as a critic show in Chapter 12 when he compares a passage from Tennyson's *In Memoriam* with one from John Berryman's *Dream Songs*. They are not very notable examples of either poet's work but they are brought together because they both deal with Christmas and the death of a friend. Hope's point is simple and within its limits unarguable: Tennyson makes himself clearly understood, Berryman doesn't. If poetry and intelligibility were synonymous there would be nothing more to say. But it is the whole question of the life of the language, the energy it stores and transmits, which Hope's discussion omits. The Tennyson passage is inert. It is language serving as a vehicle. It is bland and textureless. Berryman's has some life of its own apart from its function as a conveyor of fact, idea and feeling.

'In present day America and in much of world beside', Hope writes, 'the poet feels no obligation to his reader' (p. 152). Certainly the emphasis has changed since the nineteenth century. The poet's first duty is now conceived as being to the language itself, but *that* is an obligation to the reader, and for the benefit of society as a whole. Turning English into a sweet milk custard can be left to the ad men who will always do it better.

SECOND WIND:
ALLEN CURNOW'S CONTINUUM

Continuum: New and Later Poems 1972–1988, by Allen Curnow (1988)

More than twenty years after I first published a chapter on Yeats's 'Easter 1916' defending its stirring refrain about how MacDonagh and MacBride and Connolly and Pearse were 'changed, changed utterly', I set foot in Ireland for the first time. I was on my way to lecture at the Yeats Summer School in Sligo, and at the airport information desk I asked how I should get to the Dublin railway station. The young woman replied with a question: 'Do you want Connolly or Pearse?'

Last year I visited Harvard. I was taken about Boston and Cambridge by Helen Vendler, whose brilliant running commentary mixed the expected early American history with lines and whole stanzas of Robert Lowell's — poems I know well and have always admired but which seemed to acquire by this particularity of reference new urgency and strength.

One forgets how much of the best poetry in English, at least since the Romantics, is, in a controversial phrase Allen Curnow used in the introduction to one of his two anthologies of New Zealand poetry, 'local and special at the point where we pick up the traces'. The phrase typically says what Curnow wants it to say — that the poet and therefore the poem are visibly products of a region — while protecting itself against anticipated complaints that such a view is insular. When I last wrote about Curnow, in 1963, I backed my text with references to an essay by Allen Tate defending regionalism in literature against an internationalist position which Tate cleverly described as 'the new provincialism'.

Allen Curnow (b. 1911) invented New Zealand poetry — or forced

London Review of Books, February 1989

it into being. Before his 1945 anthology, *A Book of New Zealand Verse*, there had been only poets who were New Zealanders. In a similar way Frank Sargeson (1903-82) gathered around him a group of determined associates who made a distinct New Zealand fiction. There is an unmeasurable calculus as between what the history of a region requires and the talents of the writers who are called upon to supply it. One might argue that for a population the size of New Zealand's to throw up two such men at the necessary moment is improbable — as if statistics should undermine one's literary valuation — but only if one didn't know (for example) the approximate population of Elizabethan England, or that of Classical Greece. Between them Curnow and Sargeson brought one of the 'new literatures in English' into being.

Curnow arrived at poetic maturity as the Great Depression came to an end, the Second World War began, and New Zealand celebrated its first hundred years since the 1840 signing of the Treaty of Waitangi by which the Maori tribes ceded sovereignty to the British Crown. He was a post-Eliot poet, keenly aware of the Auden generation, in tune with their politics and their poetics. Like them he inherited that view common to modern poets that there is an unbridgeable gap between the official account of public events and occasions, and a poetic response to them. Yet like Yeats in 'Easter 1916', or Auden in 'Spain 1937', he found ways of writing poems about them. He made history over into poetry without averting his eyes from the pain and destruction of colonial settlement, and the depression that was somewhere built into the psyche of generations who had travelled so far, had neither the means nor the wish to return, but hadn't entirely shaken off a sense of loss and alienation.

By the 1950s the public aspects of Curnow's poetry had been largely internalized. He was now less a national poet, but still very clearly a regional one. Collective pain, blood sacrifice, simply the anguish of being conscious of place and history — it was all there; but so were the corresponding affirmations, rooted in particularities as 'New Zealand' as Lowell's were 'Boston' or Yeats's 'Ireland'.

And then, about 1957, Curnow fell silent. There was an Audenesque piece from New York in 1961; there was a retrospective selection from OUP in London in 1963; there were some plays. But for fifteen years there was nothing else — no new poems. New Zealand poetry in the 1960s was dominated by James K. Baxter (born 1926) — a Byronic figure, at once careless, prolific and brilliant, who had (in the phrase I think Russians use of writers after Gogol) climbed out from Curnow's overcoat, and who for a few years seemed destined to eclipse his master.

In 1972 Baxter died, aged 46, and Curnow published *Trees, Effigies, Moving Objects*, a sequence of seventeen poems. Baxter's writing life was over and Curnow's second had begun. *Continuum* represents Curnow's second wind — his complete poems since that date, the six collections

99

presented in reverse chronological order. In praising this book I don't want to seem to do it at the expense of, or in unfavourable comparison with, what he wrote up to 1957. His has been a major voice at every phase of his career. But poets who survive as poets seem to grow in cunning, and learn to use their talents without the wastage of false starts and mistaken directions. There are few pages of *Continuum* in which I don't feel instantly in the presence of a rock-solid artisan-artist, knowing what he is about, moving at his own pace, inventive, unpredictable, writing poetry which strikes me, as it has done serially over the years, as unsurpassed by the work of any other poet at present writing in English.

There are two ways of talking about later Curnow, neither satisfactory. To describe his themes and structural devices misses the incidental felicities without which they might be just interesting, or profound, abstractions. To concentrate on the felicities is to lose the sense of larger patterns. The first is the academic vice, the second the journalist's. But the measure of Curnow, as of any poet, is his language, line by line and phrase by phrase. He can pack it tight, so your head spins; or produce momentary explosions. But his best effects are a transparency that very simply gives you a 'meaning' and at the same time forces you to doubt or extend it. 'An Upper Room' begins with a typically open and ambiguous syntax:

> Where is the world? Upstairs.
> At the end of the corridor. The last room.
> I have drawn the curtains back, under the window
> I am waiting for my students, my sixty-first
> year is high cloud that alters as it filters
> the sun, good light while it lasts, for reading.
> I can hear them growing up the stairs.

Why that opening phrase? One is forced to recall how much in the sequence in which this occurs (*Trees, Effigies, Moving Objects*) touches upon subjectivity and objectivity, the puzzle that the world 'out there' exists without us, yet is 'ours', each of us possessing a different one. So that which exists without us also dies with us. Here the world is 'upstairs' because that is where the poet is, waiting while the light lasts for his students who are 'growing up the stairs'. They, like the light that will fail, promise the end of the world.

Five poems later, where 'the turn' is of the tide, the word 'waiting' is called in again for inspection:

> Olive, olive-budded, mangroves wait for the turn,
> little as it means, to call that waiting.
>
> A green car follows a blue car passing a brown car
> on the Shore Road beyond the mangroves which wait

no more than the tide does because nothing waits.
Everything happens at once. It is enough.

That is not to say there is nothing to cry about,
only that the poetry of tears is a dead cuckoo.

Curnow's 1979 collection, *An Incorrigible Music*, concerns, I suppose one
can say, murderers and victims, and each of us is both. The victims are
various — a caught fish, a stabbed fifteenth-century Medici, poisoned
snails, a murdered woman in a literary novel — and Curnow's way to
his subject is often oblique. Here is the opening of the poem about the
poisoned snails:

Fluent in all the languages dead or living
the sun comes up with a word of worlds all spinning
in a world of words, the way the mountain answers
to its name and that's the east and the sea *das meer,*
la mer, il mare Pacfico, and I am on my way to school

barefoot in frost beside the metalled road
which is beside the railway beside the water-race,
all spinning into the sun and all exorbitantly
expecting the one and identical, the concentric,
as the road, the rail, the water, and the bare feet run

eccentric to each other.

In every line the hand is sure; but that sudden bringing down, which
is a marvellous lift, of 'and I am on my way to school/barefoot in frost'
is the touch of a master.

The book was to revolve around a poem in five parts, 'In the Duomo',
about the murder of Giulano de' Medici in the Cathedral at Florence
in 1478 — a poem which begins and ends with images of fishing at Karekare
on Auckland's west coast where a favoured rock is called 'the cathedral'
and is seen as an inversion of the interior forms of the Florentine 'duomo'.
The caught fish bleeding in a rock pool is both Christ and Leviathan.
The blood at the altar flows from the veins of a sinner. Once again,
to talk of the scaffolding may be to miss the poem; but Curnow, son
of an Anglican priest, who himself trained for the ministry before yielding
to doubts and the world, seldom moves far, or for long, from the traditional
symbolism that partly determined his habits of mind. He may stretch
it, subvert it, secularize it, master it, but it has remained a vehicle, almost
a second language which he commands as easily and inventively as he
does his first:

. . . Here the linens, the sacred
silverware are arranged and the blood is poured
by experienced hands which do not shake

> serving up to Messer Domeneddio god and lord
> the recycled eternity of his butchered son,
> this mouthful of himself alive and warm.
>
> This is homoousianus, this is the cup
> to catch and keep him in, this is where he floats
> in a red cloud of himself, this is morning sun
>
> blotting the columns, the ogives, the hollowed throne,
> smoking the kite-high concavity of the cliff.
> This is the question, *Caught any fish?*
>
> > Say, *No.*
>
> *I am teaching Leviathan to swim.*

Defenders of Eliot's *Four Quartets* are invited to make the comparison and measure the relative linguistic inventiveness and force.

What was intended to be the whole book (*An Incorrigible Music*) was complete and in the hands of his publisher when Curnow, having retired from the English Department of the University of Auckland, took off for a sojourn in Italy. He was there throughout the fifty-four days of the Aldo Moro kidnapping, April to June 1978, which with extraordinary convenience (life obliging art) coincided with 500th anniversary of the Medici murder, subject of 'In the Duomo', and ended with the body of the murdered prime minister in the boot of a car parked near Jesus Square in Rome. Curnow found himself 'guest in a stricken house' — but what a guest! There can have been no one in Italy so perfectly prepared to offer the cruel and squalid events generous accommodation. It must now have looked as if his book, called back from the printer, had a large space waiting for this death.

> All the seas are one sea,
> the blood one blood
> and the hands one hand.
>
> Ever is always today.

'Moro Assassinato' is one of the most powerful of his longer poems, a brutal aggregation of detail (Curnow working with the eye of a one-time journalist) given its place in history, in myth, in Christian iconography, but always with the imagination coming back to the fact that these, killers and victim, were 'ordinary' human beings, sharing the same lavatory in the 'Prison of the People', ironing a man's shirt before sending him to his death, noticing too late that a pair of socks were being worn wrong side out.

The effect on the book as a whole is to humanize it, to remind us how much more urgent blood as reality is than blood as symbol. By that recognition the symbol is strengthened, and we are back where we began.

> Christ set it going and ascended
> leaving the engine running.

That is the engine of the R4 in which the victim is to die. His last word is imagined as 'yes' — repeated eleven times, once for each bullet entering his body.

The title poem, coming last in the book, brings us back to the local scene — Curnow trying to count herons on the mud flats at low tide:

> The small wind instruments in the herons' throats
> play an incorrigible music on a scale
> incommensurate with hautboys and baroque wigs.
>
> There's only one book in the world, and that's the one
> everyone accurately misquotes.

Coming and going, their numbers changing like the birds on Ezra Pound's wire, the herons won't be counted. Their 'scale' (size and music) is the natural one, and incorrigible. The world's 'one book' is surely itself, and the only possible accuracy is a misquotation because it exists in time. Herons only stay still on Graecian urns.

The themes and preoccupations carry forward into Curnow's 1982 collection, *You Will Know When You Get There*, but in two long poems, 'A Fellow Being', and 'Organo ad Libitum', there is a new tone. One might describe these as comedies to the tragedy of 'Moro Assassinato'; or as poems of wit — so long as neither description suggested a lesser scale or any sense of loss.

'Organo ad Libitum' begins with a funeral — your own. You're 'got up to kill', carried shoulder-high in your box to the sound of organ music and to an accompaniment of verbal play hardly in keeping with the occasion. From this funeral scene we move, by the accident or non sequitur of attending a Walerian Borowczyk movie on a wet day in Paris, to a nunnery where the nuns have poisoned the Mother Superior.

> and they danced
> their hot pants down on the stony
> gallery for joy of their nubility
> crying 'La Mère est morte!' they
> swung on the bellrope naked making the
> bell-mouth boom at the sun

After this bizarre and joyful eruption we return soberly (though the syntax continues to enjoy itself) to the

> cards the flowers the municipal
>
> oil-fired furnace the hole
> in the ground one after after
>
> another thereafter before you
> know where you are you were.

Now eternity presents itself in the form of 'sleeping off life' in a motel room with only a Gideon's Bible and a paperback to pass the absence of time. Our organist at his console becomes (*'dissolves to'* as they say in movie scripts) the pilot of the Air New Zealand DC10 that crashed in Antarctica. The funeral car doors close with a discreet *'chlomp'*, and a decision on 'belief in a hereafter' is still pending. Why should there not be palingenesis? This thought too is given its head, but its possibilities prove to be, like everything else in the poem, largely verbal — an exercise of the mind. 'What cannot be spoken about must be passed over in silence,' Wittgenstein says; to which poetry might be heard adding, 'and the silence spoken about at length'.

> the organist
> locks up the console
> Handel
> booms at the sun
> Tiziano's
> rapt airborne virgin in the Frari
> was an assumption
>
> . . .
>
> *chlomp*
> and they made the bell-mouth swing
> swinging on the bell-rope
> naked.

So the end of the poem brings us back to that Borowczyk movie, the presence of which seems after all to have a perfect logic. Think hard enough about death and if it doesn't knock you flat, your sense of life will be the richer for it.

'A Fellow Being' makes its twenty-page way around the figure of an American, Dr Rayner, who came to New Zealand in the late nineteenth century and made a fortune as self-proclaimed 'Originator of Painless Dentistry' and as a ruthless exploiter of Auckland's west-coast kauri forests. The year of Rayner's death, 1931, was the year when Curnow first came (from the South Island where he grew up) to that coast, and the poem ends with an imagined crossing of paths:

> your soul could have dragged itself
> as far as the dawn clifftop
> over Anawhata or been torn
>
> from death duties or been sucked
> up and scaled off with the sea fog
> or spilled into the creeks which drain
> the steepnesses worming
>
> its way the dragonflies and
> the mosquitoes rise in their day

on wings of success humming
the way money hums and the saw-teeth

your life-cycle and mine
humming the hymn of it's finished
to the tune of it's just begun

Even exploiters and despoilers of nature are one with it if the vision
is generous.

You Will Know When You Get There is all about death. It opens with
a short poem about a ferry crossing in the Bay of Islands in which the
phrase 'at the end of the world' takes on a double meaning, and ends
with the title poem where the world's end is once again simply one's
own. The poet walking down to Karekare beach at sundown to pick
mussels off the rocks hears each wave breaking as the slamming of a
door — less discreet, more final than that *chlomp* of the funeral cars:

one hour's light to be left and there's the excrescent
moon sponging off the last of it. A door

slams, a heavy wave, a door, the sea-floor shudders.
Down you go alone, so late, into the surge-black fissure.

Since 1982 Curnow has published three or four poems each year. It
seems they arrive singly, take their own time to reach a point where
words go down on paper, and then are worked on, and over, at length.
The concentration is steady and intense; and though they may sometimes
spring from events and occasions abroad they are always written at home
in an isolation that is not just geographical, but a state of mind:

As they pass down hill
away from you their backs, and uphill towards you
their faces, the ages, the sexes, the ways

they are dressed, even one 'smile of recognition',
beg an assurance the malice of your mind
withholds. Look down, confess it's you or they:

so empty your eye and fill it again, with
the light, the shadow, the cloud, the other city.

That is one image of the poet, protecting the otherness out of which
poems are made. Another is a long-ago memory of 'Mr Prisk' ('The
Pug-Mill') in his dug-out under the hill, making bricks one at a time.
At the sound of a bell his horse 'Up above in the sun . . . plods a muddy
zodiac' and another lump of clay drops down on to the work bench.
Mr Prisk is like one of those underground dwarf artisans in German
mythology. He has become his function. He knows how to make bricks,

and he will go on making them: 'so long / as there's a next there's no last'.

'I am that child', Curnow says of the boy watching; but he is also Mr Prisk.

WHAT BECAME OF MODERNISM?

Five American Poets, with an introduction by Michael Schmidt (1980)
The New Australian Poetry, edited by John Tranter (1980)
Carpenters of Light, a Critical Study of Contemporary British Poetry, by Neil Powell (1980)
Mirabell: Books of Number, by James Merrill (1980)
The Book of the Body, by Frank Bidart (1980)
Skull of Adam, by Stanley Moss (1980)
The Poems of Stanley Kunitz 1928-1978, by Stanley Kunitz (1980)

What became of the Modernist movement? It was initiated by Pound and Eliot about the time of the First World War and in America it set off a further wave of innovation (often referred to as 'post-Modernism') after the Second. Beats, Black Mountain Poets, the New York school of the fifties — all these and others, though clearly different, are unimaginable without Pound, early Eliot, William Carlos Williams, and perhaps Wallace Stevens as forerunners. This is the main stream of modern American poetry. In England the picture is very different. Pound is grudgingly acknowledged, distrusted, kept at a distance. Eliot holds his place, but not the revolutionary Eliot. Eliot didn't convert England — England converted him; and *Four Quartets* is Modernism neutralized by good form. Who then won the poetic war in England? It was, I think, the Georgians, because there were two strands in Georgianism, one sentimental and rural, the other urban and honest. Wilfred Owen passes the baton to the political poets of the thirties. 'Georgian' becomes a term of abuse but the baton passes nevertheless and it says 'the true poets must be truthful' and 'the poetry is in the pity', Owen's dicta.

London Review of Books, May 1980.

Truth, realism, 'values', common sense, worthy purpose — these are the glories and the limits of modern English writing (fiction too). They pass into the universities and are the predominant criteria of judgement in schools of English and in journals. The English poem is as useful and unstylish as the English car. It is a vehicle, and judged as such; and this is because there is in the British literary climate something of that 'philistinism' Donald Davie says was characteristic of the Movement: 'We would not entertain for a moment the idea that poetry could be, in some degree, or from some points of view, a self-justifying activity.'

Why should it be that, insofar as it's possible to abstract 'the modern English poem' and 'the modern American poem', the former seems to someone with no axe to grind (I mean myself) less spacious, less athletic, less inventive, less stylish, less magical than the latter?* One reason might be that a tighter, more unified society determines more readily what are the important subjects *outside* poetry, which in turn (to put it very simply) puts too much emphasis on what is being said and not enough on the way of saying. A second might be that a European (and particularly French) sense of the mystique of language itself entered poetry in English through Modernism, and insofar as Modernism has thrived in America and been rejected in England, so correspondingly the language of the modern American poem tends to come to life of itself rather than live as poor relation off its 'subject'. A third might be that all modern poetry lives by extracting and refining the energies and the music of spoken language, and modern educated spoken English in England tends to be a stilted class-ridden affair by means of which speakers strive to assert or to conceal their origins. (Perhaps the hope for British poetry ought to lie in regional speech, and of course in Ireland, Scotland and Wales.) One might even hazard as a fourth reason that the university scene into which the practice and promotion of British poetry has been largely absorbed is a haven of reason and moderation, and that these are inimical to the best in poetry.

In all the arts there are broad movements which are inexorable. You may choose to swim against the tide, and perhaps do it very well, but you can't turn it back; and English poets for half a century have mostly chosen to swim against what my hunch as literary historian tells me will prove to have been the major tide of poetry in this century. That broad tide is represented by the Modernist movement.

Open form, the aggregation of numinous fragments without logical or narrative structure, the movement of spoken rather than written language, incompleteness of statement so that the reader is invited into the poem and required to participate in the imaginative act — these are some of the features of the Modernist poem. They are common to

*What seemed so clear to me in 1980 no longer seems so in 1989.

the work of widely divergent inheritors of Modernism, and they are seldom found in the modern British poem which is most often the short, well-made article, completing the statement, closing the account, shutting the gate on the reader who must stand outside the linguistic action, looking in.

The five American poets of Michael Schmidt's anthology are not introduced as representing an avant garde school. They are if anything somewhat conservative; but they are characteristically American in inheriting Modernism's sense of openness, of possibility, and of an obligation to push forward the development of poetry in English. It is, if you want to see it negatively, an over-technical, almost technological view, which carries with it the danger that the poet will strive beyond his means. (I feel this in some poems by all five, and particularly in those of Robert Hass.) But it produces also a sense of spaciousness and energy in and beyond the language of the poem. James McMichael has a fine delicate touch in brief evocative lyrics and can open out into longer forms. John Matthias at his best achieves a steady tone, a dense texture, a clear focus on complex material. And in some of Robert Pinsky's poems ('Sadness and Happiness', for example) there is a momentum, a sense of invention and language rushing forward, keeping it up, which I find exhilarating.

John Tranter's *The New Australian Poetry* is committed to Modernism. Its editor's theoretical position is familiar to me and on the whole congenial. I find much to admire in the book, plenty of talent and good reading and only one poet whose inclusion seems incomprehensible. But I felt more and more troubled as I read on, and even slightly bored, by something that bothers me equally in the work of the younger New Zealand poets. It is not that one necessarily demands 'Australianness', explicit regionalism, of Australian poets. It is, rather, that one demands of poetry — any poetry — the real, the concrete, the particular, not on any theoretical grounds but simply because without it the language will always seem under-employed, lacking in texture. The aspect of Modernism that seems to predominate in Australia and New Zealand at the moment (probably in America too) is the one drawing ultimately from French Symbolism, specifically from Mallarmé. 'Poetry is not made with ideas, my dear Dégas, it's made with words.' Mallarmé's put-down is perfect and right when directed against the notion of the poem as vehicle for an 'idea'. It is something the English poets need to take to heart. It is the source of that magical quality Modernist poetry at its best possesses. But like all critical ideas it needs to stand against the background of its counterstatement to make safe sense. Removed, it becomes a doctrine of verbal abstraction.

What are some examples of the best Modernist texts? Let's propose Pound's Cantos 2, 18, 47 and 49 and Eliot's *The Waste Land*. And if we

109

add to those some of the best poems by W. C. Williams (an altogether slighter but historically important poet), we have something to go on. In each case the poem is open, the language mostly informal, unliterary, there is a lack of finality about the writing, energy is more important than finish, logic and narrative need not apply, the reader feels himself to be in the atelier (and perhaps handed a brush), whereas reading Yeats, for example, one has entered the stillness and finality of the Musée. But what the poems of Pound, early Eliot and Williams at their Modernist best force upon us remorselessly is things, scenes, sounds, voices, particulars — a real, teeming world. Mallarmé's 'Poetry is made with words' is complemented by Williams's 'No ideas but in things'. When modern poetry loses the sense of what John Crowe Ransom calls 'things in their thinginess', it slides away into verbal gesture, a mime of meaningful speech, and the result is always something narrowly personal and ultimately boring. This is quite different from the 'personal' as one finds it in late Lowell or late Berryman or in the Pisan Cantos, where the personality of the poet registers an intransigent world and confronts it, neither giving way. In *The New Australian Poetry* I was impressed, sometimes dazzled, by the way so many of these poets could sustain fantasy, invention, surrealism, a sort of meta-discourse without meaning or reference, like the game children play of going around the room without touching the floor. But how long can you watch even the cleverest juggler before you begin to say 'So what?'

In that confrontation of Mallarmé and Dégas there are in fact two abstractions proposed. There is the abstraction of Dégas' 'ideas' ('I have some wonderful ideas for poems'). But there is also the abstraction of Mallarmé's 'words'. A mystique of language for its own sake is the power source and the danger of Modernism. Michael Schmidt's five American poets avoid (the best of their work avoids) both abstractions. The language has a life of its own and a life in relation to a recognizable real world, as in James McMichael's 'Compline':

> Gudique is the chastening.
> She is not a fish.
>
> She is not the rocks where she browses
> nor the pools.
>
> The river when it opens
> is not Gudique.
>
> When its forgetfulness
> falls from it,
>
> when a cold wind leaks
> upward through the drifts and folds and

110

pours over the banks
and over the ferns

this is not Gudique.
Gudique is the chastening,

the river forgetting
Gudique is the river.

The best of the Australians achieve something like this conjunction; but there is too much in Tranter's anthology that is no more than verbal gesture.

Neil Powell's *Carpenters of Light* is probably a better book than I am prepared to admit. Its limits (academic prissiness apart) are the limits of his understanding of Modernism. He uses the term frequently but never in such a way as to make me feel he has fully entered into the experience of any Modernist poem. Consequently his attempts at tight-rope walking between American and British elements in recent English poetry seem to me of limited value. He is judicious in attempting to answer the question 'What is traditional poetry?' I'm left unsure what his answer is, if one is given. I find his chapter on Donald Davie useful, but a better understanding of the American side of the debate is needed before that crucial case (Davie both as poet and as critic) gets the discussion it calls for. He treats Larkin, if not with more respect than he deserves, at least with more than is good for the future of British poetry. He discusses Roy Fuller's poetry but then doesn't give it anything like the space it requires and consequently seems to slight it. And where does Ted Hughes fit into his picture? Telling us that in a larger book he would give his judgement on this poet is another way of saying the book is incomplete. Finally his argument that we must all be nice to one another, and tolerant, and not resort to 'rhetoric', is Jack Hornerish and a good death-recipe for the future discussion of English poetry.

Of the books by individual poets James Merrill's *Mirabell: Books of Number* is a maddening expenditure of manifest talent on a silly fiction. Two characters, David Jackson and the poet, conduct interminable seances at which spirits of the dead gradually unfold the Truth about the universe. It is at once a whimsical and grandiose scheme, combining myth, religion and science (God is Biology). There is some camp fun now and then when the spirit of Auden intrudes speaking from the other side, and we learn that Chester Kalman is being prepared for reincarnation as a future black leader in South Africa.

Frank Bidart's *The Book of the Body* elicits the voyeur in us. Such fascination as it has is that of the case study in abnormality, and no one confident of his poetic style would find room for Jerome Kern words like 'suddenly' and 'somehow', nor sprinkle his text with words italicized for emphasis. Yet Bidart's book makes a point and compels an acknowledgement when put alongside Stanley Moss's *Skull of Adam*. Bidart's, one has to concede, is interesting for the human material it contains. Moss's book by comparison is bland, vacuous, sleek and slack — and the attempt to give it some gravel (poems called 'Snot', 'Shit' and 'Vomit') are embarrassingly trumped up.

Stanley Kunitz is now in his middle seventies and his *Poems 1928-1978* contains 150 short poems, an average of three per year over a period of half a century. Reading his work in reverse order, as one does here (the latest poems come first, then his collections of 1971, 1958, 1944 and 1930), one can see that although he has remained indifferent to the main thrust of Modernism, and in particular to the Modernist ambition to resurrect (by the aggregation of numinous fragments) the long poem, nonetheless his poetry has loosened up, becoming freer, more open in recent years. Reading back through the book takes one just perceptibly through styles of past decades, while at every point Kunitz is pre-eminently himself and a master of his art. Often his style has a slight stiffness about it, an awkwardness that is as individual as a way of walking, and not at all a disability. It is there even when he rises to his most packed and forcefully eloquent:

> In the zero of the night, in the lipping hour,
> Skin-time, knocking-time, when the heart is pearled
> And the moon squanders its uranian gold,
> She taunted me . . .

There is a strange rich charm about this poet, whose work I am glad to have read thoroughly for the first time. The book is beautifully designed, a rare pleasure to hold and to look at, matching the poems and suitably honouring Kunitz's half century of patient practice.

THE SWARM OF HUMAN SPEECH? ROBERT DUNCAN AND DENISE LEVERTOV

In May 1981 I took part in the International Poetry Festival in Toronto as a guest of the League of Canadian Poets. The following notes were prompted by reading and listening to the poetry of Robert Duncan mainly, but also of Denise Levertov. They don't pretend to be a 'criticism' of either poet's work but represent my wary reflections on practical poetics prompted by the presence of those two notable figures.

Breakfast at the Bond Place Hotel where most of the visiting poets are housed: Robert Duncan comes down early, breakfasts with the first poets to arrive, talks non-stop, moves to another table as his first companions leave, and so on. This way he gets in at least two hours' mainly monologue to start the day. His voice is loud, harsh, yet musical and continuous, punctuated by a braying laugh. The first morning, not knowing he is to be among the poets, I think idly that the incessant talker with Henry Beissel (Chairman of the League of Canadian Poets) looks like Robert Duncan who visited Auckland some years ago. Meanwhile a stranger, a woman at my table, says, 'I'm a grump in the mornings, I know it, but that *man* over there. Who is he? I can't stand his voice and I can't stop listening.' I make soothing noises. I'm following his monologue too and I begin to be sure it's Robert Duncan.

Duncan's conversation is in some ways like his poetry. Both marvellous and flawed — marvellous for fluency, copiousness, invention, and music; flawed in their lack of concern for the individuality of the word. It's a totalitarian voice that treats language as a crowd. I deplore the *mot juste* approach which picks out words so singly there's no flow. But if poetry is too predominantly a matter of movement, the language becomes

PN Review, 35, 1983.

abstract. It lacks reference, it lacks texture — an essential aspect of its multiple function goes unused. Listening, even reading, one enjoys the music while at the same time the language doesn't engage the whole mind. Last year in San Francisco I was told by someone who claimed to be a friend of Duncan's, and who certainly at least knew him well, that he had heard Robert assert he is now first among America's living poets. It may be a dangerous way for a poet to think but it's not unusual. Told Swinburne had died, Yeats is said to have murmured, 'And now I am king of the cats.'

At his reading and in his conversation Duncan seems defensive. (One who talks so much can hardly fail to give away his anxieties.) He mentions a reviewer who hated his poetry but then revealed that he also hated Whitman and Blake. It seems a way Duncan has of both acknowledging and defending his rhetorical position; but it fails to recognize the form any critical objection to his poetry would be likely to take — that the terms of such an objection would not necessarily apply to Whitman nor to Blake. At his reading he says 'rhetoric went out with Brooks and Warren' and that he is a 'bad boy' because he's still writing it. But did rhetoric go out with Brooks and Warren? If it did, it came straight in again with Ginsberg and the Beats.

> In the great figure of many figures the four
> directions and empires
> change into four times, and opposites of
> opposites meet and mate,
> separating and joining, ascending a ladder of litanies
> until they are 'sent' —
> losing themselves in each other's being
> found again
>
> Now, because I am Fire and you are Water,
> Water and Fire kiss and embrace.
> Water and Fire dance together. This,
> the grand mimesis,
> imitates the wholeness we feel true to What Is.
>
> *
>
> We must go back to sets of simple things,
> hill and stream, woods and the sea beyond,
> the time of day — dawn, noon, bright or clouded,
> five o'clock in November five o'clock of the year —
> changing definitions of the light.

(from 'An Interlude')

When Duncan reads lines like these he conducts himself with one hand so his audience is given the run of his line and its pauses both by the voice and by the movement of the hand. I choose this example at random from *Bending the Bow*, the poems he read at Toronto not being, so far as I know, available in print. But here is the characteristic Duncan music. I am myself distinctly an ear rather than an eye person; I listen for music in poetry, and my sense of structure is musical. But language is more than sound, and in the lines quoted the elements of concretion are thin, faint, and constantly fading off. Fire and Water are images of states of feeling — they are rhetorical assertions and the rhetoric is conventional (just as the line in which they first appear is close to conventional pentameter). It's not less rhetoric one wants, perhaps, but stronger rhetoric. Even the apparent movement into concretion, 'hill and stream, woods and the sea beyond', is hardly more than the notion (or notation) of a landscape.

Here are again some lines taken more or less at random, but from a famous early piece, 'The Venice Poem':

> Where shall my heart feed, drink deep
> the carnal waters until the dry heart
> flowers? Those images then
> like great tears swim
> in lust's malicious eye;
> transform its glare
> where the heart feeds;
> render a rare music.

Duncan's peculiar quality is there, a kind of baroque, tending to euphuism. It feels as if it belongs more in the seventeenth century than in the twentieth. Whatever virtues it has they are not those of economy, nor of concretion, nor, I think, of precision — though it might be wrong to accuse him of imprecision. But 'carnal waters', 'dry heart', 'great tears', 'lust's malicious eye' — could this really be where Modernism and its various sequels have been leading? And in later sections of this poem, where he becomes expository, even didactic (on the subject of homosexuality), there is not an improvement — if anything it's worse, because the exposition destroys his music, the trajectory of his native eloquence.

Henry Beissel, introducing Duncan's reading, says Duncan made a resolve not to publish a book for fifteen years, and he has stuck to it, but soon the fifteen years will be up. Duncan hotly denies any such resolution, and Beissel apologizes. I have a feeling there's some foundation for what Beissel has said, but in any case it's easy to see how it might have got about. The poems for which Duncan is known seem mostly to have appeared between 1940 and 1965.

When I puzzle over what is lacking in Duncan, I think first that everything is conceptualized, composed into a formal picture, before it has become real. Cooked without ever having been raw. And then I see that what is lacking is observation — and I think 'of course', remembering the poet at the breakfast table. The energy is self-generating and takes little account of the world outside. Only the ego is alert, fearful, defensive — it looks out as from a fortress for reactions to itself. It doesn't look out to lose itself in a discovered world.

> The whale-shark dark with the universe
> pushes up a black nose of loneliness
>   against the thin strands, shakes
> the all-night glare of the street-lamps
>   so that for a moment terror
> touches my heart, our hearts, all hearts
>   that have come in along these sexual avenues
> seeking to release Eros from our mistrust
>
> Our nerves respond to the police cars cruising
> a part of the old divine threat. How in each
>   time the design is still moving. The city roars
> and is a lion. But it is a deep element,
>   a treacherous leviathan.

('Night Scenes' from *Roots and Branches*)

He is unconcerned about a word like 'heart' which still seems to him servicable in its old conventional signification — and that alone, that apparently thoughtless repetition of what has seemed worn out, shop-soiled, in the language, sets him somewhat apart from the Modernist tradition he is reputed to be heir to. (Ginsberg, who is sometimes said to be shoddy in such matters, has I think, a harder, more precise diction.) It is not one police car, or one experience of police cars; it's already generalized — 'police cars', the idea of them — to which 'our nerves respond'. The city's roar makes it 'a lion'. The step is so automatic one may glide over it unimpressed, failing to notice that it's not even appropriate — that a city's 'roar' is continuous, a lion's occasional. The two halves of the image don't illuminate one another because they're not based in observation. But the city is not merely a lion — 'it is a deep element / a treacherous leviathan' — both ocean and whale? It is words Duncan is drunk with — words dissociated from exact reference, merely quivering with the memory of what it was once their first function to signify.

In his article on the Black Mountain poets Donald Davie says he will not 'dissect' any samples because that is what 'the Beatniks and Black Mountaineers alike want to avoid: the graduate seminar class which spends happy hours winkling out the symbols and the ambiguities in a dozen lines . . .'. I agree. Nor do I favour a Brooks-and-Warrenish irony over poetry of full feeling. What I'm analysing (insofar as these notes are analytical) is perhaps not precisely Duncan's poetry but my own response to it. I don't claim that my own is the one right response — only that it's a legitimate one, and not based on misunderstanding. Comparison is always a help, and a reading of Gary Snyder's poems (a poet with the same inheritance) makes the point immediately. One is never for a moment in doubt with Snyder that there is a world *out there* with which the world *in here* is in direct communication. And to say this is as it should be, is only a way of saying that poetry, of all the verbal modes, must use the full resources of the language. There ought to be a maximum agitation of the responding mind and nerve ends. The signal ought not to be faint. The word cluster which constitutes the poem must be registered vividly, and that won't occur if a significant part of the action of language (I mean quite simply *reference*) goes unexercised.

Try putting it in the other way about. What does Snyder's poetry lack which Duncan's has? Eloquence? Of a kind, yes — but that is the sort of plush Snyder makes one feel poetry can (should?) do without.

I think this over in relation to the great movements in painting since Cezanne. Haven't the movements forward been always steps towards greater immediacy — either of a world, or of the action of painting itself? It's not description that's required but a sense of the object, of a 'reality'. As soon as a technique for projecting this sense becomes shared, used, begins to turn into convention, it's discarded for another (the principle of 'Make it New'). Description leaves out the describer; and with no viewer there's no life in the object. In Duncan there is a viewer but no object. Or put it another way, there's a voice in an echo chamber. Duncan is the great Narcissus of the ear.

Let me take another tack on the subject. The Festival includes a session on Poetry and Politics in which I and John Montague lead off a panel discussion. I argue, not for the purity of poetry — because I don't like the word, or the ideal, or the feel of 'purity' — but for its integrity. I know the pull of the strong subject — to make the poem a vehicle for a conviction. But the 'subject', whatever it may be, goes cold and dies and sooner or later your poem is the vehicle for a corpse. (Who were those 'slaughtered saints' about whom Milton wrote a protest sonnet?) I argue that poetry deals with the existential, not the political. Its subject can never be politics (which is a matter of analysis), though it may well be the feelings engendered by politics. Only when the political experience has been taken right inside the self, below the armchair opinion, can it come out again into poetry. This is what makes the difference between Pound's half-baked 'political' Cantos of the 1930s, and the Pisan Cantos where the politics have been lived through and become part of the man.

This discussion occurs before Duncan reaches Toronto but I feel sure he is the last poet who would need to be told these things. He is in one sense the living embodiment of the integrity of poetry; and it's on this that he and Denise Levertov fell out after many years of friendship and association. Levertov has traced the curve of their relationship in

117

her essay on Duncan. It's clear that early on she placed herself in something of a pupil-to-master relation and that she feels she gained from this. But as her determination increased to oppose the Vietnam War, not merely in her day-to-day life (something which Duncan did too) but in her poetry as well, it appears the work which resulted alarmed the master more and more. She has written about the severance lucidly and generously, without concealing that it has been serious. (The extent to which Levertov has committed herself to this role of political poet is illustrated by the fact that she doesn't join the Poetry & Politics panel of which she was to be a member. She arrives late at the Festival because she has been in Washington taking part in a rally protesting at America's actions in El Salvador.)

I'm in complete agreement with the wholeheartedness, the intransigence of Levertov's stand at the time of the Vietnam War, and since. I sympathize with the feeling that in the late sixties/early seventies something in the nature of a revolution occurred in American society, and that any serious writer (any serious citizen) had a duty to be involved. But when I read the Levertov poems that came out of that commitment I feel on the whole (sadly) that Duncan was right — right, and possibly also partly to blame. It seems to me Levertov, beginning her career with a beautiful talent for precision and delicacies of feeling, has tried, under the influence of her master, to project herself on a scale she simply hasn't the architectonic (Arnold's word) power to sustain. There's a sense one has that the poet is floundering, that she lacks focus, as though she's feeling for a governing principle and not finding it, lacking in fact Duncan's confidence in a flow of rhetoric pouring forth from one centre. Her Vietnam poems are written from within the charmed circle, preaching to the converted (preaching anyway) — writing which makes no great demands on itself, or maybe the wrong demands. There is always this temptation to confuse the poetry and its subject. It's a mistake history doesn't make.

Nor does Robert Duncan make it. And there's an irony here in that Duncan has written a few Vietnam poems which I think are better than any of Levertov's, and I suspect he gets away with it by being very literary, echoing Blake and Whitman and Ginsberg-echoing-Whitman, so that the piece feels like a very practised and purposeful exercise in pastiche, precisely circumscribed by that intention. It doesn't hector you to go along with its worthy opinion. Rather it says 'Given that I hold this opinion, how about this as a means of finding for it a literary form'. 'Up Rising' begins

> Now Johnson would go up to join the great simulacra of men
>   Hitler and Stalin, to work his fame
>   with planes roaring out from Guam over Asia,

all America become a sea of toiling men
        stirred at his will, which would be a bloated thing
        drawing from the underbelly of the nation
        such blood and dreams as swell the idiot psyche
        out of its courses into an elemental thing
        until his name stinks with burning meat and heapt honors

And 'Earth's Winter Song' opens with a directness and simplicity that Duncan seldom achieves (but again complicated, I think, and protected, by its literariness):

The beautiful young men and women!
Standing against the war their courage
has made a green place in my heart.

Duncan doesn't make the mistake I think Levertov has made, of fearing that the poem he is moved to write may be trivial — that it will fail its examination when asked the question 'What is your point? For what purpose do you exist?' Poems don't exist for any purpose except to arrest the instant — or the instance. If they do that, the question 'What for?' won't arise. Only imperfect poems need worthy purposes.

But Duncan has claimed as a poet to 'live in the swarm of human speech'. That's easily said but difficult to see in the writing. For all the 'post-modern' panoply, and the quasi-mystical associations with Black Mountain and with all that's 'en avant', Duncan's syntax and diction (but it's the syntax I think that matters most) is extraordinarily conventional — almost a killing weight. Isn't that what one means by 'eloquence'? He stands in for the old masters again.

In Goya's canvas Cupid and Psyche
have a hurt voluptuous grace
bruised by redemption. The copper light
falling upon the brown boy's slight body
is carnal fate that sends the soul wailing
up from blind innocence, ensnared
        by dimness
into the deprivations of desiring sight.

But the eyes of Goya's painting are soft,
diffuse with rapture absorb the flame.
Their bodies yield out of strength
        Waves of visual pleasure
wrap them in a sorrow previous to their impatience.

Those lines are from the much anthologized 'A Poem Beginning with a Line by Pindar'. They are eloquent; but in syntax and diction do they differ much from a purplish passage in the Art section of a Sunday newspaper?

JAMES K. BAXTER: THE POET AS PATRICIAN PARIAH

James K. Baxter: A Portrait, by W. H. Oliver (1983)

In the nineteenth century biography and literary criticism were confused. Matthew Arnold demonstrated that Keats 'had flint and iron in him' in order to make a point about the worth of the poetry. In this century the reaction away from biographical criticism has led to an equally unsatisfactory isolation of the text from the poet who produced it.

There is of course a relation between the poet and the text. Responding to a poet's work is in many ways like responding to a human personality. The work has the stamp of a character — not quite the character of the poet, but close to it.

All poets of stature have weaknesses which are as characteristic as their strengths. During their lifetime we may indentify the work as readily by the weaknesses as by the strengths, and this sometimes leads to feelings of irritation. It did in the case of Baxter.

Once the poet dies, irritation tends to pass and attention focuses on the strengths. Jim the hairy nuisance has become Hemi the secular saint. On the whole W. H. Oliver avoids hagiography in this book, but the pull towards it is not entirely absent.

The mystery about Baxter, the sense of contradictions unresolved, is no larger than that which surrounds many important writers, but for me it is certainly there. How could the commander of such poetic power be guilty of so much that was half-baked or even absurd? How could the rebel be capable of such servility? How could the great trader in pieties be so turbulent?

Denis Glover used to say that Baxter carried about a portable hell-

New Zealand Listener, November 1983.

pit into which he cast himself whenever the mood took him and the audience was suitable, dragging himself up to peer over the rim with haggard and suffering eyes. His mother, the redoubtable Millicent, declared that Jim invented an unhappy childhood because he thought a poet should have one. Yet his self-torment was real enough and neurotic enough to amount to a form of self-destruction. When he could stop inventing sins and laying extravagant penalities on himself, he was capable of enjoying the world, investing it with wonder, and seeing himself with a sense of proportion. Those moments of relaxation, humour and acceptance constitute grace in his poetry. His sense of guilt was his devil, and it probably destroyed him.

That Baxter should have been a poet was almost laid down in his parentage. His mother was the daughter of two remarkable literary scholars — J. Macmillan Brown and Helen Connon — and a scholar herself. His father, Archibald, was a rebellious pacifist whose refusal to fight in the First World War involved him in a kind of bravery hardly surpassed by an average V. C. winner. Archibald Baxter was also a man who inherited the whole tradition of English poetry and could quote from it at length. With these parents it isn't surprising that Baxter was impatient of formal education. He had little to gain from it, and was consequently not very successful at coming to terms with it.

There is something Byronic about Baxter, and not just in the Scottish inheritance and the egotism of his sense of sin. Baxter's family credentials lead Oliver to describe him as a patrician. He was that, in New Zealand terms; but he was also (and again this is like Byron) a patrician pariah. The Baxter family's pacifism during the Second World War rendered them suspect and alien in their small community. This sense of alienation was something Baxter preserved throughout his life.

Patricians often use the language as they use everything else — profligately. Sir Walter Scott said that Byron used his pen with the careless ease of a man of quality — and Matthew Arnold showed what that meant in terms of slovenly diction and bad grammar. The sensibility of a barbarian, Arnold concluded, and the language of a schoolboy — yet he allowed Byron greatness too, for catching the spirit of the age, and for finding a medium in which to reach out beyond provincial England and address Europe at large.

Baxter's use of the language was characterized by a secure voice, a wonderful economy, an eye for detail and a trust in letting it speak, a too casual resort to shop-soiled symbol and metaphor, a tendency to pronounce ex cathedra when he had nothing to say, and a fluency the equal of Byron's. Like Byron he could speak out to the world at large, beyond the usual confines of poetry. His best lines, put alongside the best of Allen Curnow's, can seem like the work of a simpleton, but a simpleton with certain distinct advantages, most notably, complete confidence.

W. H. Oliver's book observes, at least until its final page, the decorum of the historian. It gives us a set of facts, in chronological order. These are accompanied by another set of facts — the photographic record. Side by side the two sets of facts don't pretend to solve the mystery of Baxter — rather, they put it before us, leaving us to attempt our own explanation if we want to. That is one of many reasons for admiring the job Oliver has done.

There is little that is new, almost no gossip (Oliver is not writing the kind of inquisitive, probing biography that must sooner or later come), and for me there is only one of those really odd or unexpected facts that can cast new light on a biographical subject. The one (and it may not, to other readers, offer anything at all in the way of shock or illumination) is that when Jim was ready to offer his first book of poems for publication, it was his mother who took him along to the Caxton Press with it. I had never thought of Baxter as cosseted — or rather, as *willing* to be.

Having stuck to the decorum of the objective historian, Oliver on his final page steps forward as himself, claiming friendship and expressing nostalgic regard. I like the personal, where it is relevant, to be made plain; but if that is the kind of book your subject permits you it should be apparent from the beginning . To change roles on the final page is like signing yourself into the register without having paid your dues.

For a time, Oliver says in his final paragraph, Baxter 'was my fellow-Catholic'. True — but it seems to me the statement leaves too much unsaid. Like Baxter, Oliver was a convert. So was Robert Lowell, one of the great influences on Baxter, and also Allen Tate, Lowell's mentor: all poets — and all very much literary men in their conversions. Tate later renounced his Catholicism; so did Lowell — and so has Oliver.

In Baxter's last poems a Zen attitude to experience is in clear conflict with the Catholic one. Neither stylistically nor philosophically had he reached anything like the end of the road. He was 46 when he died, and he needed another couple of decades in which to come to terms with the elements at war in himself. Had he had them, the final statement and the resolved style might have been very different.

LES MURRAY: AUTHENTIC OZ

Selected Poems, by Les Murray (1986)
The Daylight Moon, by Les Murray (1988)

One of my most uncomfortable memories is of arriving at a *Poetry Australia* conference, called a 'Write-In', in Sydney in 1975, and being told by Grace Perry (a mentor of Les Murray's) that I was on in ten minutes, solo, to give a talk. When I pointed out that I had agreed only to appear on panels and readings and that I had no talk prepared, Dr Perry said that was OK — unprepared would be quite acceptable. And for those ten minutes she chatted non-stop so I couldn't begin to think what I was going to say.

Faced with an expectant audience I began to talk about a literary argument that had raged in New Zealand in the 1950s between Allen Curnow, who had held that a truly indigenous literature would be regional and nationalist, and some of his younger challengers, who argued that mature New Zealand writing ought now to be international, taking its local roots for granted. What I had to say was embarrassingly haphazard and halting, but I felt that it struck a chord. The reason, I afterwards discovered, was that Les Murray and Peter Porter were present (that 'Write-In' may have been the occasion of their first meeting); and although the terms of the debate are not quite interchangeable between Australia and New Zealand, they are close enough to seem familiar.

Murray was, of course, and is, the regionalist and nationalist, Porter the internationalist. What added interest and spice to their disagreement was that the two greatly admired one another's poetry. In fact if Murray is well known outside Australia, some of the credit must go to Porter's promotion of his work.

London Review of Books, February 1988.

Les Murray (b. 1938) grew up on a dairy farm in northern New South Wales, an only child whose mother died of what seems to have been a medical misadventure when he was twelve. The farmhouse was hardly more than a timber shell with an iron roof — there was no lining or ceiling, and conditions were primitive. He was a fat boy, and still quakes inwardly when he finds himself in a schoolyard, remembering taunts of long ago. (One of his cleverest poems, 'Quintets for Robert Morley', is a tribute to the skills, social, psychological and physical, developed by the world's heavyweights.)

At school, works by Australian writers disappeared from the curriculum once senior classes were reached and the study became 'serious'. For a long time poetry left Murray unmoved, though he does remember reading all of Milton in a single long weekend. But somewhere late in his schooling a door opened. He mentions in one place help he received from a skilful teacher of English. In another he describes something like a moment of revelation 'one evening in the mid-fifties' beside the Coolongolook, one of the rivers of his home territory, in which the certainty that he was to become a poet arrived.

In 1957 Murray arrived at Sydney University, whose motto *Sidere Mens Eadem Mutato* he likes to translate 'We're gonna make this place as much like Oxford as we can'. He dabbled, dressed in a Parisian beret and navy polo-neck sweater, played the poet, and left without completing his degree. He hitch-hiked around Australia, returned to Sydney with no money and no prospects, and for a brief time lived in a cave on the Bondi golf links. At some time in the 1960s (I'm uncertain of the chronology) he made his first visit to Europe, completed his Sydney B.A., and found work in Canberra as a translator. But his profession was poet. He consistently argued that society owes its artists a living, and since the Whitlam Government of the early 1970s behaved as if it thought so too, Murray has been able to sustain himself and a family on grants, writer-in-residences, and royalties. As he ingratiatingly puts it, 'I finally Came Out as a flagrant full-time poet in 1971, and have not held a paying job since then.'

Central to a great deal of the literature of Australia and New Zealand is the question of identity. The Romantic inheritance is strong, but perhaps also confusing, because while it fortifies, through a mystique of landscape, notions of local difference, it is, nonetheless, a derivation from the European source. Physically and psychologically we are products of a particular soil and climate. Intellectually and socially the lineage is more complex. Along with custom, law, language, and history, more of ourselves is delivered from the parent culture than the post-colonial mind, impatient for definition, is commonly willing to admit. On the other hand, in one and a half or two centuries of settlement a great deal has been said, thought, written and enacted in the new place. And then there is the fact of growing up together in a society and physical setting remote from all others, so that in many ways (but not in every way) an Australian of British stock will have more in common with a Chinese Australian than with his London cousin. These problems of definition demand precision and subtlety at the same time that they promote extravagance and assertion.

Murray tends, I suppose, to extravagance and assertion. Where questions of identity arise he writes always confidently and consistently and his work is never without its Oz framework. His view is essentially that of the Jindyworobak movement of the 1930s and 1940s, but perhaps with more force and confidence, and with more poetic talent, than any of the Jindyworobaks could muster. Like them he holds that the truest Australian consciousness is rural and agrarian; but because 'culture has followed commerce', rural Australia has been neglected and relegated to Third World status. The cities, mimicking the larger world, tend to distort and conceal the real Australian identity.

Murray claims always to speak for rural Australia against the cities; for Pacific-centred rather than Eurocentric Australia; for the people against literary and academic élites; for the Celtic against the Anglo-Saxon tradition; and for Republican against Royalist Australia. It is a peculiar and peppery mix. In public argument Murray continually presents himself as the poor boy from the back-blocks standing up to the city slickers. He is frequently on the attack, often simplifying, and usually surprised and hurt when his opponent strikes back. He is also extremely effective at delivering insults, as when he wrote of one of his literary adversaries that he was 'the only man I know who can be simultaneously at your feet and at your throat'.

Authentic Australia, he insists again and again, is a 'vernacular republic'. The appropriate literature for the New World must be written 'against the grain of Literature'. It requires what Murray calls the Golden Disobedience — disobedience of the dominant literary sensibility:

I grew up near and often in the great forests of the New South Wales lower north coast . . . my father had been a bullock driver and timbergetter in those forests before he married and started dairyfarming — and yet even I was almost seduced by the myth of the alien bush, as I began learning to write poetry. A received sensibility almost had me subscribing to its agenda, in spite of my awareness that the bush wasn't alien to me at all, but a deeply loved vastness containing danger and heavy work, but also possessing a blessedly interminable quality which was and is almost my mind's model of contemplation.[1]

Contradictions abound. The writer who insists on an Australian consciousness and the severing of ties with the Mother Country is obsessed with his Scots ancestry and the Celtic literary inheritance. The country conservative, deeply distrustful of leftist causes and fashionable radicalism, addresses anti-monarchist meetings and designs an Australian flag which leaves out the Union Jack. The spokesman for 'the people' against intellectuals and high culture writes poems whose verbal density and range of reference are about as populist as champagne and caviar. The believer in the innate virtue of productive labour and the sweat of rural brows is unabashed demanding, and receiving, a living from government hand-outs.

Perhaps the oddest element in it all is Murray's Catholicism. He is a convert, received into the church in 1964 (possibly through the influence of his wife), and what Catholicism means to him inwardly, spiritually, is never clearly revealed. In his prose it figures mostly as a large club with which to strike down modern urban intellectuals, conceived of always as rationalist and radical foetus-killers. The absolute authority of the church is never questioned. No apparent — or anyway public — attempt is made to explain how it is, for example, that while Marxist radicalism is foreign to the mystique of the great Australian continent and therefore an aspect of colonialism, Catholicism is not. Nor is it easy to see how he can write of a Scottish group who were praying over their crops to make them grow, and claiming to have encountered the spirits thus conjured,

That is pagan stuff, belonging to an old tradition whose gods and powers have long been superseded by a higher revelation. I am a Christian, and thus not obliged to be indiscriminate in religious matters.

while at the same time according, as he does consistently, a sort of Jindyworobak priority and authority on Australian soil to ancient rituals and mysticisms of the Aborigines. But any challenge offered to his intellectual superstructure which includes references to his Catholicism will be dismissed simply as 'anti church'. Murray's faith is not available for questioning.

The terms of Murray's dialectic received their clearest definition in his essay 'On Sitting Back and Thinking about Porter's Boeotia',[2] an essay which takes off from Peter Porter's poem 'On First Looking into Chapman's Hesiod', and which seems to have followed on from their interchange at that 1975 *Poetry Australia* 'Write-In'. Athens and Boeotia are seen as 'two models of civilization between which Western man has vacillated; he has now drawn the rest of mankind into the quarrel, and resolving this tension may be the most urgent task facing the world in modern times'. Athens is the 'urbanizing, fashion-conscious principle, removed from and usually insensitive to natural, cyclic views of the world'. It is 'always scornful of rural, traditional-minded, predominantly small-holding Boeotia'. 'The Boeotians, living to the north-west of Attica, were held to be rude, boorish and stupid, their country swampy and cheerless, their arts old-fashioned and tedious.' Boeotia is 'mistrustful of Athens' vaunted democracy' which is based on 'the labour of a large slave population'. Poetry, having its roots in the soil, is the Boeotian art, drama the Athenian. The English repression of Gaelic languages and literature was an Athenian repression. As for Australia, its home-grown would-be Athenians (*Sidere Mens Eadem Mutato*) are going against the grain of the place: 'our culture *is* still in its Boeotian phase, and any distinctness we possess *is* still firmly anchored in the bush'. The only good Australian Athenian, then, is not a dead one but Peter Porter, who has had the good sense to live as an expatriate and to admire Boeotian Murray from afar.

To some of this Porter has replied in passing in an article in the Melbourne journal, *Scripsi*: 'I rest my case on the conviction which will probably be unpopular with more Australians than just Les Murray — that we are unflinchingly European people, and still owe more to those far-off shores than we do either to the landscape or the original inhabitants of the continent.'

Murray's mind, always powerful and inventive, gains some of its strength from being untroubled by fine shades and subtleties. Pondering on what it is that makes the difference between him and Allen Curnow, two poets remarkable for the multiple pressures they impose on the language of their poems, it occurred to me that Murray's skill is that of a natural linguist; Curnow's is that of a genuinely philosophical mind. If Curnow forces language to bear burdens, it is because he is trying to make it measure up to a sense of how elusive and difficult 'reality' can be. Murray, on the other hand, demands a great deal of language because he wants it to be worthy of, and to celebrate, a vision of reality which is fundamentally bold and simple.

In more narrowly literary terms Murray's position has been anti-Modernist. His 1974 review of *The Pisan Cantos* no doubt owes a lot to Noel Stock, but I think it is better than Noel Stock could have written, and it is one of the most succinct and comprehensive anti-Pound statements I have read. I don't think I would want to disagree with a word of it. Everything it says against Pound is true. It only leaves out, and suggests a blindness to, the things which Pound did not only well, but better than anyone else had ever done before.

He was crushed by the weight of what he embraced. His verse, increasingly with the years, has a sort of interminable cunning obliquity common to the socially insecure and the mad, in so far as both desperately want to be heard but are terrified of giving themselves away. Everything is allusion and significant winking, every impending lucidity in the Cantos is hurriedly deflected by magpie philology, in case any of the sophisticated readership which the writer courts and fears should ever impute a barbarian simple-mindedness to the clever boy from Philadelphia.

For Murray the great fault of what he calls Franco-American Modernism is that it was the creation of two men, Eliot and Pound, who were in flight from New World egalitarianism, which they believed could not be reconciled with their ideal of high culture. Because they were involved in burying their own origins and inventing for themselves a tradition which was not in fact the one they had inherited, they turned modern poetry into something secretive, occult, specialist — alien to people outside the literary-academic circle. It soon became the preserve of the universities, which were entrusted with, or anyway claimed possession of, the keys that would unlock its mysteries. This in turn meant that young people were not exposed directly to the shock of new poetry, but received it through the normalizing and selective filter of the teaching process.

There are a dozen things, and perhaps a dozen more, to be said against all this; but like most things Murray argues, it contains a hard core of truth, and one which is usually overlooked or ignored.

In his anti-Modernism he shares some ground with compatriots James McAuley and A. D. Hope; but his advantage over them (apart from sheer talent) is in his practice as a poet. He was never disposed, as they were, to re-enact old laws about rhyme and regular metrics, nor to insist that twentieth-century experimentation with form had been charlatanism and non-poetry. Like any serious poet writing today, Murray inherits and profits by what has been done in a variety of schools and by a number of very different masters. He describes his own procedure as 'Trying to make not so much "high" as rich and flexible art out of traditional and vernacular materials.' He is also, no doubt, describing his own style when he writes that 'the central and best tendency of Australian poetry' has been 'an enlightened, inclusive, civil mode of writing which belongs ultimately to the middle style, but allows itself to dip up and down at need'.

Murray has a marvellous gift of phrase which is sometimes purely descriptive and celebratory, but often pushing also towards an abstract idea. More than any other poetry I can think of, except perhaps the early work of Judith Wright, his has caught the distinctive feel of the Australian experience without rendering it in a way which makes it seem underdog, outback, offbeat, downcast, outlaw — proper stuff only for ballads and popular yarns. He has managed this because his roots are in his own country experience; and there is no doubt of the genuineness of his sense that his gift is dependent on loyalty to that experience. But his loyalty, however little he may emphasize it, is also to the language and to the best traditions of poetry in English. He says the poet must 'speak to the tribe', but speaking *for* it might be more accurate. What Auden said of his and Louis MacNeice's readers must be true also of Murray's: 'our handful/of clients at least can rune'. If you can't 'rune', a lot of Murray will pass you by. But if you can, there is something reassuring about even his denser, more opaque passages. As with Lowell, there is an authority in the writing that is felt immediately and is more important than simple intelligibility.

Walking on that early shore, in our bodies,
the autumn ocean has become wasp-waisted:
a scraped timber mansion hung in showering
ropework is crabbing on the tide's flood,
swarming, sway, and shouting,
entering the rivermouth over the speedy bar.

His talent is first for observation, then for making the best use of
it without explanatory clutter. I suppose you have to have looked hard
at cows, for example, to receive the full shock of recognizing how hard
Murray has looked:

A sherry-eyed Jersey looks at me. Fragments of thoughts
That will not ripple together worry her head

It is sophistication trying to happen.

Or this of a horse and rider:

We talk with him about rivers and lakes; his polished horse
    is stepping nervously,
printing neat omegas in the the gravel, flexing its skin to shake
    off flies;
his big sidestepping horse that has kept its stones.

Or this, less economical, but marvellous in its way, of fast-flowing
mountain water:

a harelip round a pebble, mouthless cheeks globed over a boulder,
a finger's far-stretched holograph, skinned flow athwart a snag
— these flexures are all reflections, motion-glyphs, pitches of
    impediment
say a log commemorated in a log-long hump of wave,
a buried rock continually noted, a squeeze-play
through a cracked basalt bar, maintaining a foam-roofed, two-sided
overhang of breakneck riesling.

Or this, where the birds' unusual swooping flight, both exactly observed
and mimicked by the run of the lines, is used as an image of something
quite other and abstract:

There'll always be religion around while there is poetry

or a lack of it. Both are given, and intermittent,
as the action of those birds — crested pigeon, rosella parrot —
who fly with wings shut, then beating, and again shut.

(The same peculiar opening-and-closing flight is caught, in another poem,
in 'the daily / parrot gang with green pocket-knife wings'.)
    Then there is this, catching as perfectly as a slow-motion camera the
action of a flock of ibis landing:

> Leaning out of their wings, they step down.

Or an image of winter in the country, when

> The white faced heron hides in the drain with her spear.

In these examples the gift of phrase is tied down to particulars; but it can also expand to embrace something so large the particulars must be random and yet exactly right, as in the poem 'Jozef', about Murray's wife's grandfather who came in old age as an immigrant from Hungary:

> but this field's outlandish: Australia!
> To end in this burnt-smelling, blue hearted
> metropolis of sore feet and trains.

Murray has also (like Wordsworth of the *Lyrical Ballads*) a real gift for narrative. In the midst of his richly ambiguous sequence of seven poems about the police (one only, 'The Breach', included in the Carcanet *Selected*) 'Sergeant Forby Lectures the Cadets' is a murder mystery brilliantly adumbrated and laconically solved in 37 lines. And he has written a verse novel, *The Boys Who Stole the Funeral*, in 140 Lowellian, or open, sonnets.

Murray's poems are full of sly humour, concentrating at times into sharp wit:

> In the midst of life we are in employment.

Or this of his time at Sydney University:

> a major in English made one a minor Englishman.

He is clever too at distancing himself wryly from modern technology, as in his line about computers failing to take over the work of translators because they insisted on reading 'out of sight, out of mind' as 'invisible lunatic'; or his description of 'a new car streaming cricket scores' as 'a sit-in radio'.

On the other hand I would say that Murray's ear is not always dependable, and that he is not gifted in the use of fixed regular forms. It might be more exact to say that he has a brilliant linguist's ear, not a musician's. For that reason, when invention flags he is inclined to let aggregation do the work of form. There is a good example of this in a recent poem, 'The Dream of Wearing Shorts Forever'. The title and the opening lines, seem to catch exactly a mixture of faint comedy and romantic release that the idea of shorts signals in Australasia:

> To go home and wear shorts forever
> in the enormous paddocks, in the warm climate,
> adding a sweater when winter soaks the grass,

to camp out along the river bends
for good, wearing shorts, with a pocketknife,
a fishing line and matches,

or there where the hills are all down, below the plain,
to sit around in shorts at evening
on the plank verandah —

At that point what seems to me the 'poetry' runs out. The remaining 70-odd lines are a catalogue of varieties of human dress for the lower part of the body, or for coolness — entertaining, I suppose, clever, but disappointing because lacking that peculiar lift with which the poem opens.

Murray's other weakness is that he sometimes gets caught up in detail which, however good in itself, can clog the movement of the poem. That's why his free-running sequence, 'The Buladelah-Taree Holiday Song Cycle' seems to me in many ways his finest achievement, and one of the great poems of Australia. It is less packed verbally than many of his poems — but that is partly illusion. It is a poem which is full of its subject — the great holiday migration which Murray treats as Australia rediscovering its identity, refilling its spiritual tanks. But that sense of a poem crammed with what lies outside poetry, rather than with the action of language, is only achieved through language. What the language of this poem has in fact is a maximum of unambiguous reference, or signification, combined with an exhilarating grammatical momentum. The way the long lines are sustained throughout is the measure of a kind of psychic energy. It is like Whitman without the ego. And its pace, together with its range of reference, is what distinguishes it from Ronald M. Berndt's translation of the Moon Bone Song Cycle of the Wonguri-Mandjigai people which superficially it imitates, but which, wonderful in its own way, is static by comparison, and dependent on repetitions.

Murray's new book, *The Daylight Moon*, selected as the Poetry Book Society's spring choice, is a collection partly celebrating his return from many years living in Sydney to live again in the region where he grew up. (Approximately the first third of this collection forms the last thirty-two pages of the *Selected*.) The whole range of Murray's qualities is richly on display, even to the book's brave dedication, 'To the glory of God'. I once thought of dedicating one of my books to my favourite Hollywood star, without her permission. I never thought of God — but I'm sure He will be pleased with most of what He's offered here.

Three of the shorter poems (and probably some of the longer ones as well) would go into my anthology of Murray at his very best. 'Louvres' is a marvellous, witty, tropical-Oz poem, as if the mind of John Donne had been reborn and entirely reprocessed by the experience of growing up in some place like Brisbane. 'The Edgeless' is something of a puzzle poem, to which the solution may be — I'm not sure — a word that occurs nowhere in the text. 'Tropical Window' is one of those pieces of writing where literal seeing becomes metaphorical — 'I see' meaning 'I understand' — and the two are inseparable. The same is true of 'Leaf Spring'.

In poems like these Murray achieves density without those accretions that can clog the movement of his lines. It is wonderfully disciplined writing, offering what poetry and nothing else can offer, an art that arrests one's otherwise forever frustrated sense of the richness of the life that lives only in the moment.

AT HOME WITH THE POETS

The Penguin Book of New Zealand Verse, edited by Ian Wedde and Harvey McQueen, with an Introduction by Ian Wedde (Penguin, 1985)

I

My favourite anecdote about Maurice Duggan goes as follows: Duggan was holding forth to literary friends in a bar. He didn't, of course, have an English accent, but his speech was what we call 'educated'. It was also voluble, colourful, rich in vocabulary and confident. A large Maori among another group of drinkers just along the bar seemed to find Duggan's talk distracting. Finally he pushed his face threateningly towards Duggan and said, 'You a Kiwi, mate?'

'Yes, mate,' Duggan said. 'Are you?'

II

A 'Penguin' used to have a certain clout. It signified a status, it meant a large international circulation, and there was a particular look and feel to the book. All of that may still be so in some degree with a Penguin published in Britain — but even there, the imprint is rivalled by others more stylish and equally discriminating. To reclaim some of what was being lost to Abacus, Picador and Paladin, Penguin had to launch its King Penguin series.

Now, however, in addition to the international imprint, we have Penguin Canada, Penguin Australia, Penguin New Zealand, each with a degree of independence. A Penguin of a novel by Maurice Gee comes through the same distribution network, but originates in London, and is sold and read there and at large. A Penguin by Sam Hunt, on the other hand, is edited on the North Shore and printed in Hong Kong. A few copies may go abroad; but local Penguins are mostly books for which there is no significant market outside New Zealand.

All of which is to make a point that may be overlooked. In 1960, when Allen Curnow's *Penguin Book of New Zealand Verse* was published, the poets Curnow had chosen were being given some kind of international airing. And even if, in the longer term, Curnow's selection and introduction would be statements for New Zealand to consider, a certain decorum was required which recognized that in the first instance they were addressed to a wider world.

I'm sure a lot of people strong on national independence will not lament the change. In the end we have to arrange our own priorities; and there's a danger of posturing when you think you have a larger stage. Colonial writing, as distinct from genuine regional writing, takes its cues from whatever is conceived to be the 'centre', and looks there anxiously for applause. Nevertheless, there is always the opposite danger that a small literary community can go quietly mad together and not even notice. If Matthew Arnold was right (as I'm sure he was) to fear British insularity and to look to Europe for some confirmation of local estimates of the worth of British poets, how much more does a literary community in a population of three million need to maintain communication with a wider world! Not to be overborne by it, or to let it be the determinant of what we value, but to act as a point of reference, a way of getting outside ourselves and our collective solipsism.

The cover of my review copy of the Penguin is already curling up towards the ceiling. Something has happened to the glue at the back of the spine, so it looks as if a mason bee has got in there. To my eye the print looks too black on paper that is too white and too thick. And why that ragged right margin to the introduction, as if to suggest anything Wedde writes even in prose will approach the condition of poetry?

These personal and perhaps idiosyncratic grumbles are only to signify that there is to me an insular feel about the new Penguin, both in its physical appearance and in its selection and introduction. Not that great international and current themes (feminism, decolonization, the rights of ethnic minorities, the linguistic base of poetry) are ignored. They are played over insistently. But when you have heard them all non-stop for a decade from the full boring metropolitan orchestra, don't their late local echoes seem more than ever provincial? 'Communication with a wider world' should mean something more than eavesdropping and copying.

So (to take just one example) when Wedde writes of 'the full context of a "New Zealand poetry" where male hegemony has achieved the dubious status of orthodoxy', I feel a huge yawn rise in me. This is not thinking. It is a contemporary semaphore, signalling Virtue. It doesn't derive from the facts of men and women writing in New Zeland now, or twenty-five years ago when Curnow edited the first Penguin, or forty-five years ago when the Weetbix Card series 'Great New Zealanders' included Katherine Mansfield as our greatest writer. It invokes a fashionable untruth about the wickedness/blindness/prejudice of past male editors, and assures readers that Wedde and McQueen are not wicked/blind/prejudiced in the same way. But in fact Wedde and McQueen are no more generous than Curnow was to women poets of the period Curnow anthologized, and presumably for the same good reason — that in those decades there were more men than women writing tolerable poems. Curnow anthologized Blanche Baughan, Ursula Bethell, Robin Hyde, Ruth France, Gloria Rawlinson, and Ruth Dallas; and if he missed out on Eileen Duggan that was because he and she couldn't agree on what poems of hers to include. I doubt of course that Curnow would be as generous to contemporary women's poetry as Wedde/McQueen have been; but neither would he be as generous to the men. Unlike our present editors, Curnow was never embarrassed by the notion of excellence, or by the fact that talent is undemocratically distributed.

Since it's as well sometimes to spell things out laboriously, let me say that I don't believe that during my lifetime any male editor in New Zealand, either of a literary periodical or an anthology, has ever discriminated against a woman writer on the basis of gender. When a woman, Fleur Adcock, recently edited the Oxford *Contemporary New Zealand Poetry* she selected seventeen male poets and four female. That is not at all the selection I would have made; but it was hers, and at least the women chosen must be confident they are there because an editor thought they deserved to be. What a male editor does when he solemnly signals that he is being virtuous in his treatment and selection of women is to deprive the women of that confidence. The same is true of the Maori poets selected for this anthology. It's an odd irony that an ostentatiously 'liberal' editor leaves only the Pakeha males sure of having been selected on their merit and not in order to demonstrate the editor's.

III

All of Ian Wedde's public statements about the Penguin suggest an entirely equal partnership from the beginning by the two editors, with a great deal of easy agreement, and where there was disagreement, amicable give and take. There is no evidence to suggest otherwise; but it must be an incomplete picture of how the partnership came about. Some years ago Penguin approached me to write an introduction to a new *Penguin Book of New Zealand Verse*, which, as I recall it, Harvey McQueen had almost completed. I declined. It seemed to me McQueen must have been chosen because he was a schools inspector who had edited a Longman Paul anthology, *Ten Modern New Zealand Poets*, which had sold well. It was a formula anthology, designed to give a balance of sexes, ages, races, and I didn't think it likely I and its editor would agree. And in any case, why should I write an introduction to his anthology? Couldn't he write his own? Or did the publishers think Harvey McQueen's name needed some ballast?

When I declined I was offered a say in the contents; and when I still said no, I was offered equal partnership as editor. I think I refused for the same reason I had in the late 1960s declined to do the Oxford anthology which was later done by Vincent O'Sullivan. I wanted to be sure that if poems of mine were represented they were there because someone else thought they should be.

The proposition was then passed on to Ian Wedde and he accepted it. Now it's impossible to know whether or not the public front conceals real divergences of taste and intention. Wedde acts as spokesman, both publicly and in the introduction — so much so that it's difficult not to think of it as the Wedde Penguin. If Wedde has made any serious compromises he seems content to live with them.

IV

Recent anthologists of New Zealand poetry have tended to invoke some kind of historical sanction for what has been relinquished from or added to the canon. In 1945 Curnow pointed to unease in the environment as proof of honesty, or clear-sightedness, a recognition of 'reality'. Earlier poets, his argument implied, had not been able to face up to the truth of alienation, dislocation, in the new land. They had sentimentalized their lives and New Zealand and had failed to begin the painful process of adaptation.

Chapman and Bennett (1956) in their Oxford anthology didn't so much argue with this as imply a new generation, only ten years younger and living mainly in the north, had made the adjustment earlier poets had failed to make. They were 'at home' in New Zealand. Now there was no need to look for (in Curnow's phrase) 'the regional thing, the real thing', either in landscape or in history. The subject of these younger poets was 'the concerns of poetry everywhere' — urban (or suburban) rather than rural; domestic rather than historical or mythic.

In his Oxford anthology of 1970 Vincent O'Sullivan doubted that it was possible to abstract what was 'peculiarly New Zealand's' (another of Curnow's phrases) from the great variety of poets and poetry. He preferred to make his choice according to some (undisclosed) measure of excellence, and let the poems speak for themselves. This made his introduction and his anthology a less easy target than the others had been, but also less interesting.

Wedde has elected (properly I think) to risk an historical overview. Although uncomfortable with any notion of progress, he hasn't been able to avoid it. His claim is that the language of recent poets has 'grown into' its location. Successful adaptation has occurred; and this is signalled by a relaxed, less 'willed', more 'demotic' language, as distinct from the 'hieratic' language of poetry before (say) 1960.

Each of these arguments (including O'Sullivan's refusal to argue at all) is in some degree valid and useful — and this is so even where they appear to contradict one another. It is surely true, as Curnow implied, that when New Zealand poetry stopped romanticizing the place, it became more truthful, and better; and these poems were not the reports of homesick poms, but of the native-born who could say 'I have no other home than this'. It is equally true that although there has been, and remains, an anxiety at the heart of the colonial and post-colonial experience (and I'm talking here of the colonizers, not of the colonized) there was something untypical, overstated, even (in Wedde's term) *willed* in the degree of unease present in some of the early poems of Brasch and Curnow, where the plains were 'nameless' and the cities 'cried for meaning', and where there was 'never a soul at home'. So the reaction against it represented by the Chapman anthology had its point.

Similarly one can see what Wedde means on the subject of poetic language. It is not merely that Wedde's own poetry, or that of almost any one of his near contemporaries, is written in a manner more relaxed, less anxious, less contrived, than that of the poets in Curnow's two anthologies. The older poets too have climbed down off their stilts. Curnow himself has become more idiomatic, Smithyman more frankly anecdotal; everyone has grown more casual (or is it more subtle?) about form and more colloquial in language. Do these developments justify Wedde's argument that the language of New Zealand poetry has at last 'grown into location'?

There might be some sort of half-truth there; but the fact that over the past forty years Curnow, Chapman and Wedde make distinct yet not dissimilar announcements that New Zealand poetry has 'arrived' ought to make us wary. Because the measure in each case is in terms of a literary fashion unrecognized by the other cases. This can be seen most clearly by comparing the Curnow of 1945 (his Caxton anthology) and the Wedde of 1985. When English poetry was shedding romantic prettiness and dealing with 'truth' and 'reality', Curnow found evidence of poetic maturity in the harsh truths he and his contemporaries were prepared to tell about 'real' New Zealand; 'Kowhai Gold' was the local variant of the Georgian enemy common to the modernism of that time. Now, at the end of two decades during which the language of poetry everywhere in the English-speaking world, but especially in America, has become progressively more informal, Wedde finds in that informality evidence of post-colonial adaptation.

But what a sensibility conditioned by all that has happened up to 1985 finds commendably relaxed, the sensibility of 1945 would probably have found merely sloppy. And conversely what looked admirably watertight and shipshape in 1945 may look anxious and over-managed in 1985. We need not be slaves of fashion; but nor can any of us be entirely free of it. It plays some unavoidable part in our judgements; and the anthologist who recognizes this will be protected against naive historicist pronouncements.

Of the four anthologists Curnow was the one who (in 1945) began in something like a vacuum. The others have had him as a point of reference, a place to take off from, a statement to argue with. Yet it is still Curnow who reads most authoritatively overall and most tellingly sentence by sentence. Wedde's prose by comparison is oblique, mannered, sometimes unfrank, and often cluttered with confusing metaphors and analogies. If someone clever and uncharitable should go at it in detail I think it might be shown to be a very frail structure indeed.

V

Who's in and who's out? For the moment I set aside the poetry in Maori. So I'm writing about poetry in English, by Pakeha and Maori.

The short answer, looking anyway at living poets, might be that just about everyone is 'in'. Wedde apologizes for leaving out the recent immigrant poets who came and went again — Hart Smith, Bland, Doyle. In a more selective anthology the apology wouldn't be necessary. To go so close to all-inclusiveness when dealing with recent decades means you have to explain and justify what's omitted rather than what is chosen. (Why is Riemke Ensing absent? And Michael Morrissey?)

In his *Listener* review Terry Sturm emphasized how much this Penguin favours work written post-1960, and how much is gone that was in previous anthologies. The favouring of post-1960 work is true, and not altogether surprising. All our anthologists have tended to favour their contemporaries and the decades in which they came to intellectual maturity. And what Wedde has chopped from the past consists mainly of the work of poets who, though present in earlier anthologies, were minor figures. Some readers won't like the decision to drop J. R. Hervey, for example, or Mansfield; but I don't think anyone will be shocked. It is simply a matter for mild disagreement. Similarly with the thin representation of nineteenth-century poets. It may well be that there is some rediscovering to do; but in the meantime none of the anthologists who have tracked back there has returned enthusiastic about what he found. If there is a blindness, it is so far shared.

What strikes me is not how much has been put into the basement but rather how much that is familiar remains in place and in a reasonably stable order over the past twenty-five years. This can be simply demonstrated by taking the twenty-two poets (more than half of them now dead) who are represented in Curnow's Penguin (1960), O'Sullivan's Oxford anthology of 1970 and his revised anthology of 1976, and the new Penguin, putting them in order according to the space allotted to them. The result looks like this:

Curnow (1960)	O'Sullivan (1970)	O'Sullivan (1976)	Wedde (1985)
Fairburn	Baxter	Baxter	Baxter
Glover	Curnow	Brasch	Curnow
Mason	Brasch	Curnow	Glover
Curnow	Fairburn	⎧ Fairburn	Brasch
Bethell	Glover	⎩ Smithyman	⎧ Hydc
Brasch	Smithyman	Campbell	⎩ Stead
⎧ Smithyman	Mason	Johnson	Fairburn
⎩ Sinclair	Campbell	Glover	⎧ Bethell
Baxter	Bethell	Mason	⎩ Smithyman
Baughan	Johnson	Joseph	Baughan
⎧ Stead	Spear	Stead	Campbell
⎩ Rawlinson	Hyde	Bethell	⎧ Joseph
Spear	Joseph	Spear	⎩ Mason
Hyde	Rawlinson	Hyde	Johnson
Dallas	Dallas	Rawlinson	Rawlinson
Johnson	Witheford	Dallas	Sinclair
France	Sinclair	Witheford	Dallas
Joseph	Stead	Sinclair	⎧ Witheford
Witheford	Baughan	⎧ Baughan	⎩ Spear
Campbell	France	⎩ France	France
Oliver	Oliver	Oliver	Oliver
Tregear	Tregear	Tregear	Tregear

Although reputations rise and fall, there is a measure of agreement which surprises me. I can imagine a very interesting anthology which redrew this map in quite radical ways, and that is something I might have expected from Ian Wedde. Instead, we have the statement that 'a core tradition needed to be respected'[1] and an anthology which does just that.

O'Sullivan omits only a few poets who are in Curnow's Penguin and adds in 1970 eleven new names and a further five in 1976 — about one new poet for each year. Omitting a very few names that O'Sullivan has added, Wedde adds twenty-seven, stepping up the rate of increase to three per year. The effect of this is to produce the sense of two different anthologies welded together and overlapping. One represents that 'core tradition' which must now be seen as extending far beyond the twenty-two names above to include many others — Eileen Duggan, Tuwhare, Frame, Adcock, O'Sullivan, Manhire, and Wedde himself, to take only the names about which there would probably be no disagreement. The 'other' anthology is perhaps the one Wedde would most have enjoyed doing — a post-1960 collection demonstrating the progression he suggests is from the 'hieratic' to the 'demotic', the language 'growing into location'.

The very inclusiveness of Wedde's selection from the last two decades is probably what determined that he would not do anything radical with what he calls the 'core tradition'. But the result is a curiously uneven arrangement, as if you began your guest list selectively and as you went on got more and more slap-dash and what-the-hell about it until it turned into something like open house. Also the sheer number of poets precludes a close look at anyone. In an anthology of 437 pages O'Sullivan is able to give 33 pages to Baxter, 20 to Brasch, 24½ to Curnow, and 19 each to Smithyman and Fairburn. In 570 pages Wedde/McQueen have given 16 to Baxter, 13¾ to Curnow, 11½ to Glover and 10½ to Brasch — yet these are still the poets who receive most space. It seems to me an anthology which can find something less than 10 pages for Smithyman while allowing 4¾ for Michael Harlow, or 3½ for Barry Mitcalf, is not getting its proportions right. Discriminations are being made (why, otherwise, not equal space for all?) but only half-heartedly. The book bounces us along with a taste of this and a whiff of that. It all happens too fast and too randomly.

There are, of course, pleasures and surprises — the surprises mainly in the latter part of the book. I was glad to be reminded of the promise lost when Hilaire Kirkland died; of the surprising energy Heather McPherson can generate out of current feminist clichés; of the durable freshness and oddness of Christina Beer's poems; or to come on surprising images in Alan Brunton ('War is a cow/ with an udder of thorns', for example, which sent me 300 pages back, reflectively, to Eileen Duggan's 'War shows what each man's country means to him'); or to discover a poem as charming and funny as Peter Olds's 'Thoughts of Jack Kerouac and Other Things'. Some of these no doubt belong where they are, in the *Penguin Book of New Zealand Verse*. Others would be more appropriately found in a more open and less definitive selection. In other words I don't think the two shadowy anthologies hidden inside these covers have been satisfactorily accommodated, one to the other.

As for David Eggleton's 'Painting Mount Taranaki' — I'm sure I would have enjoyed it more if Wedde hadn't tried to make so much of it so insistently. It's a poem that shows lively invention, energy and stamina. It has a momentum I admire. But you have to take it at a cracking pace not to notice that, for all its dash and occasional brilliance, it rides on a syntax that is often ill-sprung and commonplace.

Wedde, Manhire and Murray Edmond are the real strengths at this end of the book and there should have been more of them and less of others. But if there was room for so many, how could Leigh Davis have been overlooked?

Finally it has to be said that the poems at the latter end of the book have in common with poems throughout that they would not take the forms they do, or use English in quite the ways they do, if some poets who have never given a moment's thought to the 'location' New Zealand had not been read here. But this is something Wedde omits altogether to mention. Being influenced is hardly a condition specific to provincialism; but refusing to acknowledge it may be.

VI

at the church I murmured, 'Tena koe'
To the oldest woman and she replied, 'Tena koe' -
Yet the red book is shut from which I should learn Maori
And these daft English words meander on
                    James K. Baxter, *Jerusalem Sonnets*

All of which may seem a very grudging and griping response to the hard work these editors have done. I'm sure they know it's in the nature of the task they have undertaken that every knowledgeable reader will feel he or she could have done it better. I come now, however, to the gripe most difficult to get right and most likely to give offence. I know the good will and honest intentions which have led the editors to include a large amount of poetry in Maori with translations and notes. I know how warmly it has been welcomed and will continue to be applauded. Nevertheless it is a decision with which I find myself out of sympathy, and if I don't say so, and why, my review will be less than honest. Even to someone now or in the future who sees this inclusion of Maori language poems as self-evidently right it may at least be of sociological or historical interest if I can succeed in digging out of myself why my reaction is as it is.

In one or two ways the editors are obviously vulnerable. They have been criticized for engaging Margaret Orbell as their adviser — not because she lacks competence but because she is not Maori. More obvious, I suppose, is the fact that they themselves are not Maori speakers or readers. This wouldn't be so bad if Wedde hadn't taken it upon himself to reprove Curnow for his 'textcentric' appropriation of Maori poems into a Pakeha context by representing them only in English translation. Theirs (his and McQueen's), Wedde claims, is 'the first Penguin anthology anywhere in the "post-colonial world" to include quantities of poetry

141

in an indigenous language'. I predict it will be the *only* one in which the editors offer poetry in a language they don't know!

What makes this anthology truly distinct from all those that have preceded it in New Zealand is the poetry in Maori, and this is precisely the part of their work which the editors, through ignorance of the language, have been unable to control. All Wedde's comments on his principles of selection shift uneasily between the criterion of excellence and that of representation; but I suspect what it came down to in practice was that the poems in English were chosen because they were good of their kind while the poems in Maori were chosen because they were poems in Maori. How can I or Wedde or anyone not competent in the language put any sort of value on what is offered in Maori? Our ignorance may be lamentable but it is a fact — and this is a fact which underlines the very large white lie on which this anthology is founded.

An anthology is an historical document. It should tell us what has happened, not what ought to have happened, or what we think may happen in the future. Between the English language poems in this anthology a continual dialogue has gone on involving influence, reaction, interaction, imitation, rejection. No such dialogue has occurred between the poems in Maori and those in English. To represent Maori poetry as part of a lively New Zealand literary scene is simply dishonest. It has not been; and whether it will be in the future no one can say. This is the latest decoration our poetry has taken for itself — its latest claim to 'difference'. It is 'Kowhai Gold' 1985 style — New Zealand poetry with Maori in its hair.

I wonder whether writers in the Maori language will be pleased by this; or if they are, whether they are right to be. Some, surely, will feel it to be at least as much an 'appropriation' as Curnow's (which, I should add, also made me uneasy) — and one which does their language no useful service.

> Call and assemble together Aotearoa
> All the tribes throughout the land
> Come and give your support
> To my cultural activities
> Let the nets be cast
> Cast them far and wide
> Then drag them back
> Filled with our cultural pursuits

> Kōhine Whakarua Pōnika (p.260)

> We greet you rarest White Heron of One Flight,
> Rising as the rays of dawn from the far horizon.
> Welcome Queen Elizabeth, and your consort, Philip.
> Bringing with you your son and daughter. Welcome.

> Wiremu Kīngi Kerekere (p. 296)

May the waters of Waikato continue to flow and grieve,
For the misfortunes and disasters of the land
Which are commemorated at Turangawaewae marae
And are deplored; and for which tributes are paid by the tribes
Whilst tears flow to alleviate our sorrows.
Long may you hold the secret sovereign power of your ancestors
Te Atairangikaahu!

Kīngi M. Īhaka (p.266)

In the days gone by
Whatever happened was Maori.
O people, bring up, raise up
This generation.
Aue! Aue! Aue!

Hera Kātene-Horvath (p.224)

I float
On the wind
From my twirling pois
Soaring high
In the drifting clouds
I travel far away

Hirini Melbourne (p. 499)

There's some famous butter,
Nati is its name,
The place where they make it
Is Ruatoria!
Welcome, Prime Minister!
You have come to perform
The opening ceremony
For this food-producing work!

Apirana Ngata (p.121)

It may be that the Maori behind these verses, and many like them, is fine, noble, striking, inventive or beautiful. If it is the translations haven't done justice to the originals. On the other hand if the translations match the quality of the originals then they might be better left unexposed to comparison. Either way the loss is to the mana of Maori.

'Maori is the language of the land' Peter Tapsell told an audience of writers in Auckland recently; English is 'good for science and practical matters', but 'for human subjects Maori is incomparable'. And a few weeks later Arapera Blank, one of the Maori poets represented, was telling a meeting celebrating the launching of the Penguin that New Zealand poetry by Pakehas was 'too difficult'. She had tried Jim Baxter and found there were 'too many things you had to look up'. Sam Hunt

143

wasn't so bad. But for poems kids could 'really relate to' you had to go to Hone Tuwhare. Around her sat a group of Pakeha women nodding agreement.

Because we all know the political, and practical, and even moral importance of these claims for Maoritanga and the Maori language we are likely to be silent rather than dissent. After all, if English has also become (in the writing of Ihimaera and Tuwhare no less than in Curnow and Frame) 'the language of the land', we don't need to assert the fact; and if it brings with it an inheritance which includes Shakespeare, the English Bible, the Romantic poets, Dickens, Melville, Henry James, and so on up to the great moderns, Peter Tapsell's remark about 'a language suitable for human subjects' can be allowed to pass in silence. Where the Maori language is helping to build a new Maori consciousness and confidence, let it have all the space it needs, and the blessings of all persons of goodwill. Whether much will have been done for confidence by this Penguin is something for others to answer.

But somewhere at the back of my mind there is a thought for that British and European culture which is my particular inheritance and which has become also a part of the inheritance of most who are of Maori blood. The idea that our hold on it is secure, or that we go on possessing it without effort and vigilance, seems to me false and dangerous. It is also falsely romantic to think that geography takes absolute precedence over history in determining where the allegiances lie. So much of what we are collectively is laid down in the language, like a genetic code. To have two races both lacking secure possession of their own history and language may be a kind of bi-cultural equality. It is not a kind we should be hoping for, but it may be where we are heading.

Recently a brochure appeared in an Auckland University common room announcing a new periodical called *English Today*. It was colourful (it used the slogan 'the language that went to the moon'), enthusiastic, modern, emphasizing the exciting variety of modes of English used now by 700 million people. Across its front someone had scrawled MORE MONO-CULTURAL OPPRESSION. That graffito, crude and absurd though it may be, is at one with the spirit of a whole cluster of liberal orthodoxies which have been powerfully influencing literature and education in New Zealand during the past decade.

Back in the 1950s R. McD. Chapman and James K. Baxter[2] saw the figure of the Man Alone as a projection of the position of the artist in relation to a philistine society. New Zealand literature had no real status. It was ignored in schools and universities, and read by so few New Zealanders that it was seldom commercially viable. Yet it had a curious vigour and confidence, because the writer saw himself as having a function as outsider, bearer of unpalatable truths, challenger of the prevailing repressive puritanism, deflater of pieties, above all guardian of the grail of language in which (as Maurice Duggan insisted) our humanity and our civilization were kept alive.

All that has changed. New Zealand writing has gradually acquired a kind of official status and is being absorbed into the liberal orthodoxies of the education system as moas once sank into bogs.

Is it wrong to complain of this change, from which it might be argued that writers have gained so much? Maybe; but not, I think, wrong to point out the new dangers that arise as the old are overcome. The Wedde/ McQueen Penguin is in many ways a good and interesting anthology; but somewhere behind every word of Wedde's introduction quivers his fear of the charge of elitism, racism, sexism. It is a fear that clouds the vision, makes discriminations shifty, and blurs the edges of the prose. I can imagine a chorus made up of the Departments of Education, Internal Affairs, Foreign Affairs, Social Welfare, Maori Affairs, Women's Affairs, joined by University English Departments, schools high and primary, the PSA, the FOL, welfare groups, the churches (and so on) singing a sort of murmured karanga to this bi-cultural — *landmark*, it would probably be called. Few of the welcomers would be readers of poetry; all would be sure that they knew what was right.

This Penguin is in fact a perfect expression of New Zealand intellectual life as it strikes me at the moment. There is so much that is fresh and free and lively and well-intentioned — so much to celebrate and to welcome. But along with that freshness there goes an uncertainty, a lack of clarity, a lack of toughness or intellectual daring, a sort of good-boyism as crippling in its way as the old-boyism it has replaced. It causes me to recall almost nostalgically the bad times when the word culture made the bosses reach for their revolvers. Living under the constraints of those times was unpleasant. But a loud laugh was then an acceptable form of rebellion; and there was a general sense that the battle lines were clearly and cleanly drawn.

TWO

FICTION

KATHERINE MANSFIELD AND T. S. ELIOT: A DOUBLE CENTENARY

Two writers born within three weeks of one another exactly one hundred years ago: T. S. Eliot in St Louis, Missouri, on 26 September, Katherine Mansfield in Wellington, New Zealand, on 14 October, 1888. I have studied and written about them both over a period of several decades; but it wasn't until I was invited to lecture on one and then the other, in different places, on the occasion of their centenaries, that it occurred to me not only how exactly contemporary they are, but also that although there are plenty of people expert on one or the other, I am the only person who might without too much exaggeration be described as 'expert' on both.

So I have prepared a paper which brings them together — not to present close critical analyses or significant new biographical facts, but chiefly as a way of celebrating and reflecting on a double occasion.

One key to the temperament of each and to the strategy by which each proceeded in the literary world, is expatriation. Having had three years' schooling in London, Mansfield returned there in August 1908 with the ambition of becoming a writer. Eliot went first to Paris in 1910 and to England in 1914. Both were leaving behind cities and societies they felt to be limiting to their intellectual and literary development. Both had to argue family into permitting their travels. Each was subsidized — in fact the adventure was made possible — by a wealthy, uncomprehending, but generously disposed father; and in each case the allowance was continued after a marriage which the family had good reason to feel apprehensive about.

This lecture, published here for the first time, was delivered, in slightly different forms, first at the University of Victoria, B.C., Canada, then at a Mansfield Symposium at the University of Liège, Belgium, and finally at a Katherine Mansfield day at New Zealand House, London, during October 1988.

Eliot and Mansfield were alike, I think, in being a curious combination of theatricality and secretiveness. Both were good at mimicking accents and mannerisms — especially (for comic effect) those of Cockneys and people of 'inferior' class. They were both middle-class young persons of their times — which means, by the standards of 1988, that they were both snobs. Both had keen critical intelligence. Both were good at taking on the protective colouration of the immediate environment. Perhaps because the society from which each came had not imprinted itself as deeply on their personalities as might have been the case if they had grown up in Europe, they were able to adopt roles, to play at being English, for example, without feeling English. And the same was true of their literary development. As a young poet Eliot simply *became* Jules Laforgue — took over Laforgue's manner, his voice, his persona, and made himself into a modern poet. Mansfield, one could say in a few stories *became* Chekhov even to the point of plagiarism,[1] and made herself into a modern fiction writer. Both, it's to be noted, took a foreign language writer as the instrument by which their modernity was to be achieved. In that way the oppressive dominance of *English* literature was evaded; and in that way something new was brought into literature in English.

Both learned to speak in an accent which was neither quite that of the country they had grown up in nor that of their adopted country. Both were the children of businessmen fathers and sensitive artistic mothers. Eliot's mother has been described as 'not particularly interested in babies',[2] though she produced seven; and Mansfield's fiction represents her mother, in the character of Linda Burnell, as a woman whom child-bearing had left drained and emotionally disengaged. For Mansfield, security in earliest childhood came from her grandmother; for Eliot it came from his nurse.

But for both of them, the family they removed themselves from remained, not the centre of their emotional lives, but the foundation on which everything else was constructed. And for both, the landscapes of childhood remained more vivid and significant than those of their adopted country.

I'm speaking thus far of likenesses. The differences when we set them side by side are also illuminating. Eliot, it seems to me, was of an essentially timid and fearful disposition. Mansfield, though she had her times of fear and even panic, was by nature bold and adventurous. Eliot has a line about 'the awful daring of a moment's surrender'. One has the impression that the young Mansfield surrendered to the moment fearlessly — though she had cause sometimes to regret it.

Eliot grew up in a strongly religious household — one where duty and good works counted for more than faith, and where Christ was more example than divinity. This conditioning no doubt explains his seriousness of purpose. But in religious matters he was to rebel against his family by becoming more traditional, more orthodox — Catholic, as he liked to describe it, though not Roman Catholic.

Mansfield had no such conditioning in her early years. She appears remarkably free and untormented — a high-spirited pagan for whom the notion of art had replaced traditional religion as the source and receptacle of the highest truths and the finest achievements of humankind.

Both were ambitious and hard-working. Both, in the spirit of the times, wanted to 'make it new'. But Mansfield knew that her job was to work at her art. She never lost her faith in it. Eliot, on the other hand, as he grew older became so obsessed with questions of religion, society, and by extension politics, the importance of poetry as poetry receded in his life. It became an instrument, a vehicle, indirectly even a weapon. Since his faith was not in art, art had to serve his faith.

I've mentioned Mansfield's boldness and Eliot's timidity. These contrasting qualities are particularly apparent in their sexual behaviour while they were young. Eliot yearned, but held back. Mansfield seems to have pressed forward even when she wasn't yearning. She acquired early on the notion that the artist must go in pursuit of 'experience', and that governed her sexual behaviour.

Eliot's early poetry is full of the melancholy of desire unfulfilled; her stories are full of the pain of consequences. One of the most interesting of recent biographical theories is Claire Tomalin's that the tuberculosis which killed Mansfield was indirectly a consequence of gonorrhoea, the one lowering her resistance to the other.[3] There can be no doubt that Mansfield's attempt in her early years in Europe to live the kind of life which the pill and antibiotics made possible for a later generation of women inflicted damage, both physical and psychological. If that had not been the case, I might now be comparing two major figures in the history of literature, rather than one major and one minor; because I don't feel that simply in terms of talent there is any great disparity.

In fact Mansfield's genius seemed to become more and more available to her as she matured, while the reverse was the case with Eliot. The years in which the poet in him became progressively frozen under layers of Catholic-puritan angst were the years she needed to make the most of her potential as a fiction writer. Had she lived I find it impossible to imagine that she would have had cause to reflect on 'the years of l'entre deux guerres' as 'years largely wasted' as Eliot does in *Four Quartets*.

While I'm making these comparisons and contrasts I'm sure it would be regarded as some kind of dereliction in the year 1988 not to mention gender. As the gifted male child of affluent parents Eliot was given the best of educational opportunities. He studied at Harvard, the Sorbonne and Oxford. No such opportunities were offered Mansfield. But I have to add that this weight of formal learning, though it helped Eliot make his way in a wordly sense, appears from a purely literary point of view

151

to have given him no particular advantage. In fact Mansfield was freer intellectually and imaginatively. As a writer she ranged widely and settled on what was useful to her. Her comments on Shakespeare, on Dickens, on D. H. Lawrence or Dostoyevsky or Chekhov, were almost always acute and confident. It is hard to see what she would have gained by more rigorous formal training; and it is possible to argue that for Eliot there was at least as much loss as gain in it. Certainly his studies in philosophy seem only to have promoted the worst quality of his prose — its tendency to a kind of lumbering circularity.

So much for generalization. Now let's close focus a little on these two — the American and 'the little colonial' — making their way in literary London at the time of the First World War. Inevitably they were aware of one another, and inevitably their paths crossed.

They met, probably for the first time, at Garsington in 1916. The following year Eliot's first collection of poems was published — *Prufrock and Other Observations* — and Clive Bell recalls taking 'ten or a dozen copies' of the book and distributing it among Lady Ottoline Morrell's guests.[4] And he adds 'Katherine Mansfield read ["The Love Song of J. Alfred Prufrock"] aloud. As you may suppose, it caused a stir, much discussion, some perplexity.' So it seems that Ottoline and Philip Morrell, John Middleton Murry, Aldous Huxley, Lytton Strachey, Mark Gertler, as well as Bell and others, may have first encountered that landmark of poetic Modernism in her reading of it.

A short time later she was at a dinner party where the guests included Eliot and Robert Graves (in her letter about it she mis-spells both names). She took a great dislike to Graves who talked incessantly about the War in a way she felt to be 'stupidly callous' — no doubt (although she doesn't say so) because she had her dead brother in mind while she listened. Meanwhile Eliot, she tells her correspondent, 'grew paler and paler and more and more silent' as their host 'cut up, trimmed and smacked into shape, the whole of America and the Americans'.

It was an occasion to make the two outlanders feel a certain kinship. She and Eliot left the party together; and in her account the streets they walked through take on something of the flavour of Eliot's early poetry with 'little ugly houses', 'amorous black cats', and 'high up in the sky [. . .] a battered old moon'.[5]

In 1919 Mansfield's second husband, John Middleton Murry, began his editorship of the *Athenaeum*; and on the strength of his reading of the *Prufrock* collection, he asked Eliot to join him as assistant editor. Eliot was grateful, hesitated, and decided it was safer to stay in his job with Lloyds Bank; but he agreed to contribute, and according to his own recollection (in 1959) was soon 'reviewing some book at length as often as three weeks out of four for a considerable time'.[6]

Mansfield was deeply involved in the establishment of the paper under its new editor, and she worked hard at her regular reviews which were widely read, highly regarded, and to some extent prepared the ground for her reappearance in 1920 as a fiction writer.

She was primarily working out what it was proper to expect of the *new* fiction — fiction that would match and express the post-War sensibility. But there are signs that she was also arguing out with herself questions about modern poetry which Eliot's presence on the scene seemed to provoke. His poetry was something she could neither dismiss nor quite accept.

In May Virginia Woolf sent her two of the Hogarth Press's earliest publications, one of which was Eliot's *Poems*. She wrote back

Eliot — Virginia? The poems *look* delightful but I confess I think them unspeakably dreary. How one could write so absolutely without emotion — perhaps thats an achievement. The potamus really makes me *groan*. I don't think he is a poet — Prufrock is, after all a short story. *I* don't know — These dark young men — so proud of their plumes and their black and silver cloaks and ever so expensive pompes funebres — I've no patience./

A month later she is writing to Ottoline Morrell, apparently about poetry in general, but really, I think, with Eliot in mind:

The Brontes — Last night in bed I was reading Emily's poems. There is one:

> I know not how it falls on mc
> This summer evening, hushed and lone,
> Yet the faint wind comes soothingly
> With something of an olden tone.

> Forgive me if I've shunned so long
> Your gentle greeting, earth and air!
> Yet sorrow withers e'en the strong
> And who can fight against despair?

The first line — why is it so moving? And then the exquisite simplicity of 'Forgive me' . . . I think the Beauty of it is contained in one's certainty that it is not Emily disguised — who writes — it is Emily. Nowadays one of the chief reasons for ones dissatisfaction with modern poetry is one can't be sure that it really does belong to the man who writes it. It *is* so tiring isn't it — never to leave the Masked Ball — never — never — [8]

The question here is about impersonality, which Eliot's critical theory was just then making so much of. That image of the Masked Ball is like the one about the dark young men 'so proud of their plumes and their black and silver cloaks': she is reluctant to see lost from poetry a directness and naturalness which Eliot's theory and practice seemed to reject. And although 'Gerontion' was only written in May/June 1919 it seems to me possible Mansfield had seen one of the drafts which Eliot customarily put about among friends when he was working on something new; because her next paragraph has what looks like a faint but distinct echo of the poem: 'The house is full of women today. The peevish old lying cook in the kitchen . . . says it is *I* who make all the work.'

But if she tried to reject Eliot's poetry — or anyway its theoretical implications — she couldn't get it out of her head. In August of the same year she is writing in her journal about plans for stories:

Tchehov makes me feel that this longing to write stories of uneven length is quite justified. *Geneva* is a long story, and *Hamilton* is very short, and this ought to be written to my brother really, and another about life in New Zealand. Then there is Bavaria. 'Ich liebe Dich, Ich liebe Dich,' floating out on the air . . . and then there is Paris. God! When shall I write all these things and how?[9]

And she adds, 'Is that all? Can that be all? That is not what I meant at all.' Prufrock's reiterated line has come to represent her own state of mind — hovering on the brink of stories, but unable to press forward and write them.

But now, just as she is becoming thoroughly immersed in the literary life of London, ill health forces her to leave it. Early in September, having written an informal will in the form of a letter left with her bank telling Murry 'don't let anyone *mourn* me. It can't be helped',[10] she departs for Northern Italy to sit out the winter.

But she kept writing her reviews for the *Athenaeum*; and even tried to maintain an influence over it by sending Murry detailed comments on issues as they reached her. In November she responds to Eliot on Ben Jonson:[11]

I have a suspicion Eliot is finding himself as a poet in his analysis (not quite the word) of caricature. I feel he is seeing why he fails, and how he can separate himself from Sweeney through Sweeney. But this may be sadly far-fetched.[12]

The comment is 'off-the-cuff'; but it is not 'far-fetched'. In fact it goes straight to the heart of the matter. She sees at once, something insufficiently recognized by the scholars and critics who wrote about Eliot in the succeeding three or four decades, that an essay by Eliot on Jonson is also, and perhaps more importantly, an essay by Eliot about Eliot.

In the same issue, along with Eliot on Jonson, Mansfield is found reviewing yet another pair of novels about the War. 'We suppose it will be long and long', she reflects, 'before the novelist, looking about for a little wood wherewith to light his fire, does not turn instinctively to that immense beach strewn with wreckage.'[13]

'The peculiar tragedy of the consumptive' she writes in another review, 'is that although he is so seriously ill, he is — in most cases — not ill enough to give up the precious habits of health.'[14] Mansfield's energy during this period, or anyway her persistent hard work in turning out a review of at least one book every week and often more, seems to me something that hasn't been sufficiently commented on. Being fiction reviewer for a weekly paper meant that much of what she had to read was of minor interest. She was living now away from England, suffering bouts of illness, growing weaker, and her life was consequently more circumscribed. There were crises with the mail as well as emotional crises. And all the time she kept up her prodigious correspondence with Murry, and wrote fiction as ideas for stories came to her. Yet the standard of her reviews is consistently high. When the subject is indifferent she makes up for it in the quality of her writing.

So between April 1919 and August 1920 Mansfield and Eliot appeared frequently together in the pages of the same journal. She is there every week; he is there two and sometimes three weeks out of four. It's hard to think of an example of two reviewers on a paper keeping up such a regular stream of wit, intelligence and originality. It was in these pages that Eliot wrote his essays on *Hamlet*, on Swinburne as critic and as poet, on 'Rhetoric and Poetic Drama', on Massinger, on Charles Whibly and on George Wyndham, as well as the piece on Jonson, and two essays under the title of 'The Perfect Critic', all of which were to reappear in *The Sacred Wood*, making up I should think almost two thirds of the book that was to establish his reputation as *the* new critic of the age. There were also pieces by him on Kipling, Yeats, Pound, Henry Adams, and a number of others, not reprinted.

Mansfield did more of the bread-and-butter reviewing; and the interest in many of her pieces died with the book under review. But among her reviews we find pieces on Jane Austen, Conrad, Dostoyevsky, E. M. Forster, Galsworthy, Rider Haggard, Knut Hamsen, Jack London, Rose Macaulay, Compton Mackenzie, Somerset Maugham, George Moore, V. Sackville West, Gertrude Stein, Frank Swinnerton, Hugh Walpole, and Virginia Woolf — names which, though not equally distinguished, are all still remembered at this date. And we find her writing about a name still well-known in New Zealand — Jane Mander.

Evidently Murry and Eliot at this stage in their working relationship got on well. When Murry included in a letter of April 1920 a list of the 'nice people' in his life, Eliot came third. Mansfield responded with some surprise. But two days later she wrote asking Murry to invite Eliot to supper. She was now just returning to London after a miserable and lonely winter in the Mediterranean. No doubt there was a hope that she could once again take her place on that London literary scene; and if Eliot had become Murry's friend, he must be invited to visit.

Two letters that will appear in Volume Three of Mansfield's *Collected Letters* refer to the visit. [15] In one she is, in characteristic Mansfield fashion, anticipating it: 'I have asked them both [i.e. Tom and Vivien Eliot] here for Thursday or Friday. What will they be like, I wonder? The grey door of my room keeps opening and opening in my mind and Mrs Elliot [*sic*] and Elliot enter. I cant see her at all — only something conscious and over-confident.'

I suppose gossip, of which there was plenty, must have been the source of this negative expectation. And one has to suppose that Mansfield didn't know enough about Vivien Eliot's nervous problems to make any kind of allowance for her peculiar behaviour. Her sketch of the event is cruel, but also vivid and convincing. It comes instantly, without reflection (they are still on the stairs as she takes up her pen); and there is in it something nightmarish, as if she had perceived Vivien Eliot's mental disturbance and, in her own hypersensitive state, over-reacted to it:

The Elliots have dined with us tonight. They are just gone — and the whole room is *quivering*. John has gone downstairs to see them off. Mrs E's voice rises 'Oh don't commiserate with Tom; he's *quite* happy.' I know its extravagant; I know [. . .] I ought to have seen more — but I dislike her so *immensely*. She really repels me. She makes me shiver with apprehension . . . I don't dare to think what she is 'seeing' From the moment that John dropped a spoon & she cried: 'I say you are noisy tonight — what's wrong' — to the moment when she came into my room & lay on the sofa offering idly: 'This room's changed since the last time I was here.' To think she had been here *before*. [. . .] And Elliot, leaning towards her, admiring, listening, making the most of her — really minding whether she disliked the country or not —

I am so fond of Elliot [. . .] But this teashop creature.

And the letter goes on to describe how when Murry returns from seeing the Eliots off he defends Vivien and (Mansfield says) 'I feel as tho' Ive been stabbed.' Clearly it was not going to be the Murrys and the T. S. Eliots as it had been the Murrys and the D. H. Lawrences.

There are, of course, different ways of grouping those four people at the disastrous supper party. On the one hand there is the focus which history — and this paper — gives: Eliot and Mansfield are the writers of consequence, Murry and Vivien are their respective spouses. But in 1919 Mansfield hadn't yet made her spectacular re-appearance as a fiction writer. It was Murry and Eliot who were (or were becoming) public figures: two young men who both aspired to write poetry and criticism, each clearly aware of the other as a competitor, both ambitious and working extremely hard, both, probably, neglecting wives who in different ways might be considered invalid; and the wives themselves both sensitive — hypersensitive — and endowed with literary talent. What is perhaps especially odd is to consider that when Eliot began to publish Vivien's stories in the early issues of his magazine the *Criterion* (this was after Mansfield's death), they had a distinctly 'Mansfield' look and feel and flavour. 'This teashop creature' whom Mansfield 'disliked so *immensely*' was to become one of her many posthumous imitators.

At the end of the summer Mansfield is away again to safer climates in an attempt to preserve her lungs. She lives out the winter in the South of France, then moves north to Swiss mountain resorts. There she reads Eliot's contribution to the American periodical, the *Dial*, and writes to a friend.

Poor Eliot sounds tired to death. His London letter is all a maze of words. One feels the awful effort behind it — as though he were being tortured.[. . .] I don't think people ought to be as tired as that.[. . .] It is wrong.[16]

Could Eliot have had a more attentive reader? The date of the letter is October 1921, the month when Eliot, exhausted and worried, was diagnosed as suffering from a nervous condition which required him to take three months' leave from his job at the bank.

So their paths crossed again, but this time at a distance. In Switzerland that summer and autumn of 1921 Mansfield had been producing probably her finest work — and at a prodigious rate. As her burst of creative energy ran down, Eliot's began. He took up the manuscript of *The Waste Land*, first at Margate, then at Lausanne where he went to be treated by a nerve specialist, and where the poem was completed.[17] So the two outlanders were both in Switzerland that autumn, both seeking cures, and both writing their very best work. She picked up from a letter he wrote to the *Times Literary Supplement* that he was there, and commented to a friend in a letter, 'It seemed to me very fitting that his address should be Lausanne'.

The following year saw the publication of the work each had completed in Switzerland — *The Waste Land* and *The Garden Party* — each in its way a landmark in the development of modern literature in English. Eliot's poem established certain revolutionary principles so powerfully that they became ineradicably part of the history that every poet writing in English would henceforth inherit. Mansfield's book established in English what Elizabeth Bowen calls 'the "free" story'. Both, as it had turned out, were liberators. Eliot had opened possibilities for poetry, both in form and in subject, that had not seemed to exist before. Elizabeth Bowen says of Mansfield 'How much ground she broke for her successors may not be realized . . . she was to alter for good and all our idea of what goes to make a story.'[18] And Virginia Woolf, who wrote when Mansfield died, 'I was jealous of her writing — the only writing I have ever been jealous of',[19] saw in those stories some of the new possibilities that existed for the craft of fiction in the twentieth century. Woolf was surely a major beneficiary of Mansfield's 'breakthrough'.

It's fairly certain that Mansfield never saw *The Waste Land*; but 'Prufrock' stayed with her, and the poem she had described as 'after all a short story', she came to see as 'far and away the most interesting and best modern poem'.[20] This was in August 1922 and she added, 'It stays in one's memory as a work of art.'

Eliot stayed in her memory too — 'French polish Elliot' she had called him — but a letter to Dorothy Brett of February 1922 shows how closely she had observed him:

Yes he is an attractive creature; [. . .] He suffers from his feeling of powerlessness. He knows it. He feels weak. He's all disguise. That slow manner, that hesitation, sidelong glance and so on are *painful*. And the pity is he is too serious about himself, even a little bit absurd. [. . .] He wants kindly laughing at and setting free.[21]

Those comments are probably Mansfield's last on Eliot.

So far I've been looking at these two through a window provided largely by Mansfield's writing. What Eliot thought of her has remained undisclosed. Now, however, with the publication of the first volume of his letters to coincide with the centenary, we get our first glimpse from the other side, and it adds something typically dark and Eliotic to the picture.

Late in 1922 Mansfield entered the Gurdjieff Institute at Fontainebleau where she was to die only a few months later; and it seems Eliot became anxious — extremely anxious — when his patroness, Lady Rothermere, went there too and pronounced Mansfield to be the most intelligent woman she had ever met. In the same letters Lady Rothermere referred to Eliot's periodical, the *Criterion*, which she was funding, in ways Eliot found unsettling. He must have put the two things together and concluded that Mansfield was influencing Lady Rothermere, possibly in favour of his rival editor, Middleton Murry. (He had already described Mansfield as 'a dangerous WOMAN' who controlled Murry.)[22]

Now Vivien Eliot wrote a wild letter to Ezra Pound saying that Mansfield 'hate[d] T. more than anyone' and was 'pouring poison in [Lady Rothermere's] ear'.[23] Pound wrote back soothingly and said after all Mansfield probably *was* the most intelligent woman Lady Rothermere had ever met. Eliot replied angrily that she was not — she was 'simply one of the most persistent and thickskinned toadies and one of the vulgarest women' Lady Rothermere had met. For good measure he added that she was 'a sentimental crank'.[24]

So we may conclude he wasn't disposed to admire her writing. After her death he is said to have asked Richard Aldington to 'deal with' her 'inflated reputation' in the *Criterion*, but if the article was written it never appeared.[25]

Eleven years after her death, however, Eliot addressed himself briefly to the subject of her fiction in the course of three lectures given in America and published as *After Strange Gods*. There he brought together three stories — 'Bliss' by Katherine Mansfield, 'The Shadow in the Rose Garden' by D. H. Lawrence, and 'The Dead' by James Joyce. It is a clever conjuction in that all three stories deal with a painful revelation in marriage that a loved spouse has had, or is having, an association with another person. But the use Eliot puts this to is theological, not literary.[26] Mansfield's story is described as 'brief, poignant and in the best sense, slight'; it's said to show the great skill with which Mansfield could handle 'perfectly the *minimum* material'; and this in turn defines it as 'feminine'. But its 'moral implication is negligible'. Lawrence's story, we are told, has 'an alarming strain of cruelty' and 'an absence of any moral or social sense'. Only Joyce passes Eliot's new critical test. Joyce may have lost the Catholicism of his boyhood, but his sensibility, Eliot insists, remains 'orthodox' — and this is somehow proved by the fact that the suffering husband, at the end of the story, feels that 'His soul had approached that region where dwell the vast hosts of the dead.'

After Strange Gods was not a book Eliot remained pleased with. Among other things, it contains his most overt and disturbing anti-Semitic statement; and a reprint has never been permitted. The circumstances in which it was written are relevant. In 1932 Eliot had at last decided that he could no longer live with Vivien. The nervous creature Mansfield took such a dislike to had to be abandoned — but how was it to be achieved? Eliot set off to give his lectures at the University of Virginia intending not to return to her; and from America he arranged, through lawyers, for her to be notified of his decision.

In what must have been a state of more-terrible-than-usual anxiety he clung to the only certainty in his life — not poetry or literature, but religious orthodoxy. Privately he was tidying up his life. Publicly the world had to be called to order and literature brought to judgement. So Lawrence was consigned to Hell, Mansfield to a 'feminine' Limbo, and Joyce admitted into Heaven. There is not a worse or more revealing example of the decline of Eliot's critical talents as they yielded to other, more pressing interests.

I don't intend to discuss 'Bliss'. It seems to me one of the least successful of Mansfield's later stories. In fact it very nearly deserves the fury Virginia Woolf unloaded on it when she first read it.[27] Almost every *other* story in that 1920 collection, or any in the 1922 collection, is more deserving of attention; and one can't help feeling that Eliot chose it only because it made such a neat parallel in subject matter with the stories by Lawrence and Joyce.

Of course Eliot was to go on. His work — especially that done before 1930 — was to gather in the power and range of its effects, so that by the 1940s and '50s he was the towering figure in English letters, his eminence unchallenged. I don't think that was unwarranted. *The Waste Land* still seems to me the great modern poem — the great poem of the twentieth century; and Eliot was the dominating critical presence. There was nothing to parallel that in the effect of Mansfield's work, although the best of her stories, and her letters and journals, simply bristle with talent and with promise. She survives partly for having brought into English the seriousness and respect for the short story that belonged previously to the French. But even more, perhaps, she survives in those letters and journals as a great example of the writer as writer. She was, Ottoline Morrell said, 'as aware of herself as a writer as Queen Victoria was of being a Queen'.[28] She lays before us as few writers have done, the psychic state, the inner condition, of the artist whose material is language.

This is not the place to argue out at length how well Eliot sustained his talent as poet and critic. I've argued it elsewhere; and it's enough to say that while academics have tended to treat everything he published as of more or less equal interest, practising writers, who make up the tribunal he most valued, have been more inclined to see a dramatic falling away in his poetry, matched by a drop in intensity in his criticism. And it's not irrelevant to recall that Eliot himself, especially in the 1930s, likened himself to Coleridge, 'condemned to know that the little poetry he had written was worth more than he could do with the rest of his life'.[29]

So if you can share my view for a moment, we are looking not at a single tragedy but a double one. Our writers were born in 1888. By 1923 one was dead; but I think it's true to say that by that year the other — as *writer* — was dying. Why this should have been so is hard to say; and all talk of cause, if pressed too far, will seem intellectually naive. But I come back to the common fact of expatriation. In Mansfield's case certainly, but perhaps in Eliot's too, it seemed in the early years of the century unavoidable. Her talent, which was fostered in the richer European soil, might have withered in colonial Wellington. But the cost of that transplantation was enormous, and it is reflected partly in the way her writing, once she knows her illness will probably be fatal, turns back towards the home country and family for some of its richest material and its best effects. Similarly in the case of Eliot — by 1930 he is writing to his friend W. F. Stead that after so many years in London he has to get back to Massachusetts and Missouri for natural imagery.[30] And long after that wonderful vision and lyric intensity of his early poetry is gone, there are brief moments which light up, and they usually draw upon his American locations.

How well the lesson has been learned (or needs to be learned) might be argued over; but Mansfield and Eliot belonged to a generation that demonstrated very clearly that the best of literature in English wasn't necessarily going to be written by Englishmen. It was simply no longer predictable where the best new poets and fiction writers might spring up.

They felt it necessary to bring their talents with the language back to its centre — London — and in different ways they paid a high price for that. It's a price which a century later doesn't have still to be paid — or not in the same way. The world is a smaller place, with many viable centres. We all move about in it more rapidly and easily. And there's surely a general recognition that literature in English, like gold, is where you find it.

Everyone who writes it, or tries to write it, and everyone who reads it, has cause to reflect on this double centenary.

KATHERINE MANSFIELD'S LIFE

Katherine Mansfield: A Secret Life, by Claire Tomalin (1987)

Katherine Mansfield, unlucky in life, has been lucky in death. Where some figures sink under successive waves of literary fashion, she remains buoyant. One Mansfield vanishes but another takes its place. If you measure simply by the fictional product you might conclude she has had more than her fair share of attention. If you take, not the work but the writer, then the attention seems entirely justified. Three major books on her to appear in the past decade have all been biographies — one by an American, one by a New Zealander, and now one by an Englishwoman. In all of them she appears not only as a writer of some importance in the development of modern fiction, but also as a presence in and influence upon the lives and work of a number of major figures, most notably D. H. Lawrence and Virginia Woolf.

In her foreword, Tomalin (who refers to Mansfield throughout as Katherine) points out that she is

of the same sex as my subject. It may be nonsense to believe that this gives me any advantage over a male biographer. Yet I can't help feeling that any woman who fights her way through life on two fronts — taking a traditional female role, but also seeking male privileges — may have a special sympathy for such a pioneer as Katherine, and find some of her actions and attitudes less baffling than even the most understanding of men.

I'm not disposed to quarrel with this; but I'm interested in an element of conflict, or contradiction, I think I detect between Tomalin, 'the woman who fights her way through life on two fronts' dealing with Mansfield,

London Review of Books, November 1987.

and Tomalin the feminist. She would say they are the same. But whereas the subject of this book, if she could read it, would respond warmly, and be grateful for the parts which spring from Tomalin's sympathy with the woman who wanted to work, *and* marry, *and* have children, I feel quite sure she would be distressed and angered to discover herself casually described as 'sexually ambiguous, with a husband and a wife, and lovers of both sexes'. Inevitably Tomalin's publishers seize on this flamboyant description for their press release, only improving it by changing 'a husband' to 'two husbands'.

What I'm saying is that Tomalin, so sensible, careful, accurate and intelligent in most of what she has to say, is inclined, in the area of sexuality, to slip into the clichés and trigger-words of the feminist movement. She's not alone in this. Rather, she's letting the times do her thinking for her. Just as it was once fashionable to present Mansfield as some kind of otherworldly, pure, mystical person, it's now fashionable to present her as 'bi-sexual'; and though the new view might be marginally nearer the truth than the old one, both are wrong.

The principal, and almost the sole, ground for the 'bi-sexual' Mansfield is a journal written when she was eighteen in which she described a beach holiday spent with Edith Bendall, a Wellington artist then aged twenty-seven.

Last night I spent in her arms — and tonight I hate her — which, being interpreted, means that I adore her: that I cannot lie in my bed and not feel the magic of her body: which means that sex seems as nothing to me. I feel more powerfully all those so-called sexual impulses with her than I have with any man. . . Gone are all the recollections of Caesar and Adonis [two young men she had recently been in love with]; gone the terrible banality of my life. Nothing remains but the shelter of her arms.

A page or so later she writes:

O Oscar! am I peculiarly susceptible to sexual impulse? I must be, I suppose — but I rejoice. Now, each time I see her [I want her] to put her arms round me and hold me against her. I think she wanted to too; but she is afraid and custom hedges her in, I feel.

In the next journal entry she is once again in love with Caesar and bored with Edith.

Mansfield had come back to New Zealand after three years' London schooling at Queen's College, Harley Street, full of advanced ideas about art and society. She had read Wilde and was imitating him in her journal — hence the invocation 'O Oscar!' Bi-sexuality, or anyway the idea of it, was a part of the pose. But when Edith Bendall, who married, bore a child, and lived to 107, remembered her relations with Mansfield she simply denied anything passionate or out of the ordinary, and said that Mansfield, whom she found charming and delightful, but who, she said, used people for her own purposes, must have chosen to misunderstand her maternal and protective embraces.

Tomalin is sceptical of these denials, as she is of those of Mansfield's 'wife', the ever-devoted Ida Baker, whom Mansfield referred to variously as 'Jones', 'the Mountain', and 'the slave', whom she said often she hated and once said she thought of shooting with her revolver, and whom she would not allow to touch her. This modern 'we know better' tone in dealing with the elderly survivors seems to me the part of Tomalin's book that is less than satisfactory. Either we are all bi-sexual, in which case the designation means nothing; or elderly women know as well as young ones do whether their relationships with other women were or were not sexual. And when Tomalin writes that 'none of Mansfield's sexual relations with men appears to have given her happiness or satisfaction' (p.37), I wonder what this means exactly. If 'satisfaction' means pleasure in sex, how could it possibly be known? Mansfield never made any such declaration; and if she didn't enjoy sex with men she was surprisingly consistent, until ill health restrained her, in going after it. Even Tomalin's description of John Middleton Murry's role in Mansfield's life as 'crucial and largely unfortunate' (p.95) seems to me glib. Is it right to ignore, as Tomalin does, that farewell letter in which Mansfield wrote 'I think no two lovers ever walked the earth more joyfully — in spite of all'?

The 'affair' with Edie Bendall seems to have been much more in the mind than of the body. And, more important, it almost certainly preceded Mansfield's first full heterosexual experience. Once her sexual orientation is established there is, as far as I know, not a single deviation from it.

It is true that she gave her first husband, George Bowden, the impression that she was lesbian. But she did this in order to escape from him, since she had married him only because she was pregnant to someone who could neither marry nor support her. Once she had achieved Mrs Bowdenhood it was not to a woman's arms she escaped but to the lover who had made her pregnant. Yet this incident too is allowed to hover as evidence of 'bi-sexuality'.

Meanwhile, Mansfield's mother, having heard of her daughter's marriage, was steaming from New Zealand to London — a voyage of six weeks. She met Bowden and was probably told of the 'lesbianism'. Ida Baker was named. But Baker could hardly be blamed for a pregnancy — something Bowden knew nothing of. Mansfield was packed off to Worishofen in Bavaria to have the embarrassment discreetly. There the pregnancy miscarried, Mansfield began writing the German Pension stories which became her first book, and had an affair with a Polish writer, Floryan Sobieniowski, from whom she contracted gonorrhoea and who, much later, blackmailed £40 from her for the return of letters which, she told her second husband, she would pay 'any money' to have back. Tomalin's claim to be writing a biography which is new and distinct from those that have gone before rests largely on what she makes of this relationship — or rather of its consequences.

She makes two points — one medical, one literary. The medical point I accept entirely. For the twelve or so years that were left to her Mansfield's life becomes increasingly one that can't be described separately from her medical condition; and all the proliferating horrors of that condition, including susceptibility to the tuberculosis which killed her, sprang, Tomalin demonstrates, from the venereal infection made worse by an operation for the removal of an infected fallopian tube, an operation which would have had the effect of spreading the infection further through the body.

Recently I had for review Volume II of the projected five-volume Mansfield *Collected Letters.** What struck me on this reading of those letters, was that Mansfield seems an invalid long before tuberculosis gets a hold. Her body is wracked with aches which strike different bones and joints at different times. Walking becomes difficult. She suffers what she calls 'heart attacks'. Menstruation (referred to as 'Aunt Martha') is irregular, sometimes absent, sometimes profuse. Add to that the increasing burning sensation in her left lung, and long exhausting fits of coughing, which heralded the onset of tuberculosis, and the picture is grim indeed. Only Tomalin's account makes sense of it.

I'm less persuaded by Tomalin's other argument, which is that Mansfield feared Sobieniowski because he had been the first to introduce her to the work of Chekhov and knew that her story 'The Child Who Was Tired', published in *In a German Pension*, was virtually plagiarized from the Russian writer. Tomalin sees this as the reason why Mansfield would not have her first book republished, even when lucrative offers were made; and why she would pay £40 to get her letters back from Sobieniowski. She also supposes that this plagiarism must have been kept secret from Mansfield's second husband, John Middleton Murry.

I accept that the story must have become an embarrassment; but it could have been deleted from any reprint. Letters from that period of Mansfield's life were bound to be embarrassing. And if they contained secrets from Murry, why did she write to him, after he had got them back from the Pole, 'As to the letters, they are yours. I'd like them destroyed as they are, but that's for you to say, darling'? Tomalin doesn't quote this passage. What doesn't seem to have occurred to her is that the letters, which don't survive, might have contained references to the medical consequences of the affair with Sobieniowski.

The Collected Letters of Katherine Mansfield, Vol. II, 1918-1919, edited by Vincent O'Sullivan with Margaret Scott, Clarendon Press, Oxford, 1987.

Mansfield spent half her life in New Zealand. Tomalin gives one tenth of her book to those years, and there is nothing to suggest she has ever visited New Zealand. She makes mistakes that might easily have been avoided. For example, when the young Mansfield, touring remote parts of the North Island, buys 'a Maori kit', Tomalin explains that this is 'a version of traditional Maori costume'. But a Maori kit is a basket of woven flax (the Maori word is *kete*). Later we have Mansfield wearing her 'kit' in London.

It is easy to defend Tomalin's emphasis. Mansfield's adult and literary life is her subject and that was lived mostly in London and Europe. On the other hand, she always saw herself as an outsider — 'the little colonial'; and a large proportion of her most highly regarded stories are set in New Zealand.

I have sometimes confronted this problem by asking myself, is she a New Zealand writer at all? If the answer is yes, it may seem more than anything because she is not any other kind of writer. She had no regional or metropolitan attachment, nor class allegiance, nor dialect, to place her among British writers. Yet the New Zealandness is hard to pin down. It has been laid over, concealed — deliberately. This is an essential aspect of Mansfield which I think Tomalin doesn't appreciate; but it has been neglected by other biographers as well.

Mansfield first met Murry after he had accepted her story 'The Woman at the Store' for his literary magazine, *Rhythm*. Tomalin describes the story, rightly, as 'striking . . . her first deliberate portrayal of her native country, a vivid and almost sinister evocation of the atmosphere of the sparsely inhabited wilderness, the poverty and ignorance of the people settled there, the "savage spirit" of the place'. This story combines a harsh regional realism with Mansfield's principal theme, the woman as victim, whether of men, biology, or fate. It is an extraordinary story because it reveals at its end that the woman is a murderer without in the least diminishing one's pity for her or one's sense that she is the victim. Two other stories written at the same time (about 1911) also deal with New Zealand in a harsh realist manner that foreshadows a whole line of New Zealand fiction in the 1930s and '40s.

But that was a manner Mansfield herself abandoned. When, after some years of experimentation, she returned to her New Zealand subject, the relations of men and women remained. The study of Stanley and Linda Burnell in 'Prelude' and 'At the Bay' is more precise, sensitive, subtle, and comprehensive than most fiction writers could manage in ten times the space. But where is New Zealand? It is there as background, a faint wash. The 'savage spirit' of the place which in the earlier story 'walked abroad' after sundown and 'sneered at what it saw', has been put down — and I'm sure this was deliberate. When the contents of a collection of stories was being discussed in 1920, Mansfield wrote to Murry, 'I couldn't have "The Woman at the Store" reprinted' — she didn't say why. A few months later, reviewing Jane Mander's *The Story of a New Zealand River* for the *Athenaeum*, she quotes a passage in which Mander refers to several trees by their Maori names (the only common name they possess) and asks, 'What picture can that possibly convey to an English reader? What emotion can it produce?'

'Prelude' and 'At the Bay' avoid what she had evidently come to see as a problem by neutralizing the background. Not only that, they civilize the colony. They are rather genteel, middle-class stories. Their lesser characters — Alice the servant girl, and Mrs Stubbs, for example — belong more to the comic underplots of nineteenth-century English fiction than to a New Zealand reality. Elizabeth Bowen, commenting on the New Zealand stories of the kind Mansfield suppressed, says 'their flavour and vigour raise a question — could she have made a regional writer? Did she, by leaving her own country, deprive herself of a range of associations, of inborn knowledge, of vocabulary?' Tomalin's book offers nothing that would help to answer those important questions.

There are 600 million users of the English language, and every writer in English is a regional writer. No one expects an English novelist to write in an explanatory way so that a reader on the continent of Africa who has never seen an oak, or a rose, will understand what it looks like; and the reverse expectation, that the African writer should somehow explain himself to a Londoner, is equally asking for artificiality, a kind of falsity that will get into the tone of the prose. 'Prelude' and 'At the Bay' are wonderful portrayals of their small cast of central characters; but there are passages of literary archness (like the opening description of the dog, the shepherd and the cat in 'At the Bay') which seem designed to put an English middle-class reader at ease. They seem to say 'Relax. You're not on foreign soil. This is fictionland.' There is a parallel, I think, in Mansfield's letters to Ottoline Morrell, which are often so brilliant, but in which so much of the real Mansfield is either concealed or disguised. Virginia Woolf complained of Mansfield's perfume. Her writing is often perfumed too. Tomalin's sub-title is 'A Secret Life'. There's a sense in which New Zealand became part of the secret.

Another element of falsity springs from her extreme physical and emotional suffering. It causes her to revolt against her own skill at dead-pan comic-satiric representation. She wants to teach herself to be what is called today 'a caring person'. Again one sees the true Mansfield most clearly in early stories — which is not to say they are her best. *In a German Pension*, published before she was twenty, is immature work. But the pure talent is there; and there is something clean and surgical about its wit. She sees so clearly and represents so exactly — human folly can be relied on to do the rest.

Every way she turned she was baulked. She chose freedom from the narrowness of a colonial society, but lost a large part of her real subject matter. She chose sexual and emotional freedom and as a consequence, Tomalin shows, was locked into a progression of illnesses which killed her at the age of thirty-four. Denied a full life, she tried to replace it with a kind of mysticism which was really alien to her brave, bold, questing and worldly temperament. Although the finished products are few and slight, they are important; and the records of her effort to be a major writer are copious. She remains one of the most brilliant and extraordinary of modern women.

KATHERINE MANSFIELD'S LETTERS

The Collected Letters of Katherine Mansfield, Volume II, 1918-1919, edited by Vincent O'Sullivan with Margaret Scott (1987)

This is the second volume of what is now projected as a five-volume *Collected Letters of Katherine Mansfield*. It covers the period from January 1918 to September 1919. The two largest blocks of letters are those Mansfield wrote daily to her de facto, and after 3 May 1918, de jure husband, John Middleton Murry from Bandol in the South of France and then from Looe in Cornwall. Because her letters to Murry were published almost complete in 1951, 250 of the 350 pages of this volume are to be found in that 1951 edition. There is much less that appears here for the first time than was the case with Volume One; but in the final section of the book there are a number of very interesting letters that haven't previously been available.

The overwhelming impression is of Mansfield's heroic and losing battle against the onset of tuberculosis. Her natural high spirits, brilliance, and flair are pitted against her fear, loneliness, and boredom. She can be seen trying to manage her world against terrible odds — sometimes succeeding, often failing.

The letters of this period to Murry, which I haven't read through in full for many years, strike me on this reading slightly differently. Previously I was aware chiefly of her positive qualities — cleverness, inventiveness, humour, and high courage. I'm more aware this time of the dark side, and even of an element of falseness which I don't feel in the least inclined to condemn. She is trying always from a distance to manage Murry's emotions — to keep her hold on him. She's very

Dominion, October 1987.

demanding. She needs constant responses, and gets them, despite evidence that this day-by-day correspondence, together with his war work, and with his attempts to keep himself in the race as a young critic, editor and writer, was a destructive burden, almost too much for him to carry. His letters to her, which can now be read in Cherry Hankin's edition, often look like sad imitations of hers, or attempts to give her what she wants. He is the lesser personality and the lesser writer, doing his best to meet her requirements. She half-perceives that living without her is for him almost less difficult than living with her. But she keeps him acting up to the fiction that they are an Eloise and Abelard, perfect lovers kept apart by unavoidable circumstance, exchanging letters that may one day be published. By 'fiction' I don't mean that this is entirely untrue. Her love is real, if only because her need is absolute; and the letters have been published and republished. But there is something remorseless, deliberate, frantic, and will-driven about the whole exchange. Mansfield's consciousness of her talent, and her determination to make use of it, is almost as naked in these letters as the talent itself.

In human relations Mansfield is not always honest or admirable. She encourages in Murry a dislike and distrust of their friends and literary acquaintances; yet at the same time she may write warmly to these people. In this, I suppose, she reveals her fear, stronger when she was away from him, that she might lose him to someone else. Meanwhile he was compulsively flirting with most of their female friends — a habit which doesn't seem to have altered his emotional dependence on her.

Away from him and from London, Mansfield sustains herself with dreams of the future, and with poetry — especially Shakespeare and the Romantics. If there is one lesson especially that modern prose writers might learn from her it is what a resource poetry can be. Her reading of it continually enriches her sense of language and her skills in using it. It becomes as important as observation. Observation provides her with subjects and occasions; but language is the vehicle. In this period one sees Mansfield growing as a writer while physically her condition declines.

The elements of falseness, self-dramatization, over-writing are almost inseparable from the evidence of enormous literary talent. Extravagances which in a lesser writer would be absurd, Mansfield can get away with. Even her most fluting letters to Lady Ottoline Morrell contain phrases, sentences, whole paragraphs one would not be without. But perhaps the most honest letters are the gritty, economical notes, full of instructions, and sometimes of insults, to Ida Baker, the devoted and cloying friend whom Mansfield often insisted she hated, but on whom she often depended. Writing to Baker she doesn't conceal and she doesn't dress up. Her suffering and her blackness are there. She is tart, bossy, frank, and just occasionally conciliatory, as when she writes,

I don't *want* to quarrel, though I believe you think I do. The truth is that for the time being my nature is quite changed by illness. You see I am never for one single hour free of pain . . . This, plus very bad nights exasperates me and I turn into a fiend, I suppose. And when you turn to me and say 'you *did* have a bag of herbs IF you remember' as though those words of yours came out of an absolute cavern of HATE I realize 'the change'. All the same, and knowing and realizing this as I do I *still* ask you to come to Hampstead — until I am better.

This volume concludes with Mansfield setting off for Italy with Baker, happy to have escaped the sentence to a sanitorium which might have saved her. To a reader who knows the extreme miseries that were to follow, her pleasure in setting forth is a sad irony.

Like Volume One, this book is beautifully produced, impeccably edited and annotated, a credit to its editors and publisher, and entirely worthy of its subject. But it does arouse one's curiosity. Margaret Scott was at work on these letters back in 1971 when she was awarded the first Katherine Mansfield Menton Fellowship. By the mid seventies one had the impression most of the work had been done, but Mrs Scott seemed stuck, unable to complete an introduction or bring the text to final readiness for the publisher. It was then announced that Vincent O'Sullivan would help her complete the task.

When Volume One appeared of what had been projected as a three-volume edition the editors were listed as Vincent O'Sullivan and Margaret Scott, in that order (alphabetical? or priority?), and the edition was to be four volumes. Now, in Volume Two, the editors appear as Vincent O'Sullivan *with* Margaret Scott, and the edition is to be five volumes. Further, whereas Volume One gave no indication of how the work had been divided up, this one declares, 'In this volume, as in Volume I, the transcriptions of the letters were made by Margaret Scott. Vincent O'Sullivan is responsible for the annotations, dating, and other editorial aspects of the edition.' Is taking responsibility for all annotations the same as having done the work on which they are based? My impression many years ago was that Mrs Scott had done much more than transcribe letters. She had, I thought, worked on and solved a great many problems about people, places and events they referred to. I find it hard to believe that O'Sullivan hasn't made use of this work, though of course he must have done a great deal himself.

If one considers simply the product — this beautiful and scholarly edition — and the long process of editing it has entailed, it adds up to a sad story with a happy ending. On the other hand, thinking about the gradual displacement of the original editor, I can't help wondering whether it doesn't also conceal a happy story with a sad ending.

KATHERINE MANSFIELD'S FRIEND

Brett: From Bloomsbury to New Mexico: A Biography, by Sean Hignett (1984)

Anyone who studies the lives of D. H. Lawrence or Katherine Mansfield, Ottoline Morrell or Bertrand Russell, will at some point encounter the figure of 'Brett', the deaf painter of aristocratic family who emerged from the Slade School around the time of the First World War along with Carrington (another young woman who went by her surname only), Mark Gertler, C. W. R. Nevinson, Isaac Rosenberg, and Stanley Spencer. Brett's connexions thereafter were more literary than artistic. She knew the 'Bloomsberries' and attended Lady Ottoline Morrell's house parties at Garsington. For a time Ottoline was her patroness and close friend, as well as fellow-aristocrat.

Part of the interest Brett (the Hon. Lady Dorothy) aroused derived from her family. Her father, Lord Esher, was a close adviser to three British monarchs. Brett had recollections of childhood dancing lessons watched by Queen Victoria. When Edward VII's coronation had to be postponed while the King recovered from an operation for appendicitis, Dorothy was under a cloud in the family because she had had the same operation and it was thought Esher must have carried the 'germ' from his daughter to the king. At the dinner to celebrate her coming-out ball she was seated beside Winston Churchill. (She failed dismally to impress him.) Her sister Sylvia married the White Raja of Sarawak.

Whenever the problems of Brett's private life were discussed, either by herself or her friends, her father was blamed in whole or in part. The rest of the blame went to Esher's friend 'Loulou' Harcourt (a male), who had made a very explicit advance to her when she was a child.

Times Literary Supplement, January 1985.

But in what way Esher was to blame is not clear. She was extraordinarily sheltered when young; but she made her own way out of that, through the route of the Slade, and went on to live a life much more independent than that led by most women of her time. She was certainly somewhat shy of sexual advances — but she didn't receive many. All she needed, it seems, was a little encouragement and tuition; but the only males to offer it (and I will return to them) were in different ways unsatisfactory. She was isolated, probably, much more by her deafness than by the lingering subterranean damage at which she and her friends, full of fashionable Freudianism, liked to hint. It is difficult not to suspect that the 'Loulou' Harcourt episode became something of a ready-made face-saver for the lack of a sexual life. And Esher, at least judging by his letters, seems to have been one of the very few people who took his daughter and her artistic ambitions seriously and tried to share her view of the world. He never provided for her as lavishly as she wanted; but while she lived in England he saw to it that she had a studio and an income. He complained, but he always cleared her debts.

There were difficulties getting her into the Slade. Professor Frederick Brown seems to have doubted her artistic abilities. More important, he doubted her seriousness. In due course she proved herself, even winning some prizes. She also attached herself to Brown, or he to her. Although he was a much older man, it seemed for a time they might marry. Then Brown explained to her 'the facts of life' and 'what it would be almost impossible for him to do at his age', after which they regretfully drifted apart.

But Brett's period at the Slade, and immediately after, under its influence, may have produced her best painting. Of the reproductions this biography offers, 'Umbrellas at Garsington' (1917), her 1918 portrait of Ottoline and one of Aldous Huxley done in 1919, together with 'War Widows' (1916), impress me more than those of paintings done later in New Mexico. That is an impression only, inexpert and founded on too little knowledge; and my one complaint about Sean Hignett's book is that he seems unwilling or unable to offer the expert guidance on the subject of Brett's painting that I should like to have received.

An effect of this lack is to make his book seem the biography of an unimportant artist who had interesting and important friends. That may or may not be fair to Brett. Someone who knows better will have to tell us. Meanwhile, Brett's associations certainly make her a worthwhile subject, and one Hignett does justice to.

Brett's only two lovers in a physical sense seem to have been John Middleton Murry and D. H. Lawrence. It's a short list, though distinguished; and in terms of actual sexual experience it amounted to very little. It happened first with Murry, in 1923. Since Murry at this time was pursuing a variety of sexual opportunities, including Frieda on leave from Lawrence, while for the thirty-nine-year-old Brett the experience was exclusive and her first, it's not surprising she found it overwhelming and confusing. Part of the problem was Murry's unwillingness to be just an average cad. He had to be sanctimonious as well. A great deal of higher thought attached itself to the end of his penis. Brett was at a stage in her painfully slow development where she was wanting less of one and more of the other. She seems to have enjoyed the brief involvement and regretted that it didn't last.

The experience with Lawrence was much more painful. Brett alone of all his disciples followed him to New Mexico where the idyllic commune 'Rananim' was to be established around him. She and Frieda didn't get on. In fact they were to continue neighbours for decades after Lawrence's death, exchanging a sort of ritual abuse (much of it preserved in letters) rather in the way North and South Korea used to do at the 38th parallel. But Brett and Lawrence roamed the hills, mending water races, and painting. When he went to Italy in 1925 Lawrence encouraged her to follow him. She did, and during a split between the Lawrences he decided he and Brett should be lovers.

By now she doted on him. Two nights in succession Lawrence came to her bed. But the prophet of love seems not to have had much common sense in sexual matters. On both occasions he found himself impotent. He raged, blamed Brett, and with a brutality I find hard to imagine, sent her away. She never saw him again. She returned to the Lawrence ranch in New Mexico, however, and that was to be her home for the rest of her very long life. Her identity thereafter was inextricably bound up with Lawrence and the Lawrence legend.

Two hundred and twelve pages of this book deal with the first half of Brett's life up to the year of Lawrence's death. Sixty-two pages cover the second half, and many of these deal with matters relating to Lawrence. So it's difficult to see her life as other than an aspect of the biographies of figures indubitably greater. From a family famous simply by inheritance she passed to another family, that of writers and artists famous for their gifts. In both she made a place for herself, but remained awkward, difficult, something of an embarrassment and an enigma. But she survives with honour — 'a curious combination' (as a visitor to New Mexico wrote in 1929) 'of timidity and sheer grit'.

FRANK SARGESON:
THE REALIST AND THE SPRITE

Conversation in a Train and Other Critical Writing by Frank Sargeson, selected and edited by Kevin Cunningham (1983)

Frank Sargeson (1903–82) was honoured during his lifetime as the first New Zealand fiction writer to stay in New Zealand and to make a literary life his profession, with no compromises. The fact that he was often short of money only enhanced his standing as an exemplary figure. He was probably more important to other writers than to readers, many of whom found his fidelity to the realities of post-colonial society bleak and unrewarding. The fact that as a young man he qualified as a lawyer was important. It meant that his rejection of what he would have called bourgeois living in favour of a bohemian and literary life was a positive choice. Likewise his single pilgrimage, in 1927, to England and Europe, and his connexions, maintained by letter, with people like E. M. Forster, John Lehmann, and William Plomer in Britain, and James Laughlin in the United States; and the publication of his work in periodicals like *Penguin New Writing* and *New Directions* and by London publishers. Everything seemed, not contrived, but arranged to make the point that he was in New Zealand because he chose to be, and not because the opportunities to be appearing on a larger stage were lacking.

He was enormously well-read, as the range of reference in these essays, reviews, radio talks, and interviews shows. His day began early with reading, and he worked his way, not once but many times, through the masters of English literature, particularly Shakespeare and the poets, as well as the great classics of European literature. The rest of his morning was given over to writing, first revising the previous day's work, and

Times Literary Supplement, April 1985.

then adding at least one new page. A page a day was what he required of himself when writing his longer fictions. After that the day was spent growing vegetables, doing his household chores, cooking, and entertaining literary friends.

Like a number of New Zealand writers I have vivid recollections of his house in the Auckland suburb of Takapuna, and of Sargeson's hospitality. A great deal of what I find in the present volume is familiar to me from his conversation. But it has in addition an impressive lucidity, and an overview which wasn't always apparent in casual talk.

Sargeson has, in fact, two critical styles, both engaging and readable. One is a simple exposition, taking his readers by the hand and leading them through an often complex argument to reach a desired conclusion. The other is more typical of his conversation; and it hadn't occurred to me until I read his piece on Sherwood Anderson that it was a conscious method, consciously exploited:

Anderson exploits the short, suggestive sentence. What fascinates him about words is their enormous suggestive power, and he uses them to liberate the imagination; certainly not, as some writers do, to restrict and pin it down. The defect of the method is that page by page you get the impression that you are about to receive a new revelation of life, a revelation which never quite turns up. You may feel a little disappointed at the end . . . But Anderson expects you to be susceptible to suggestion and implication, to eke out his imagination with your own.

(pp.15-16)

The literary tradition Sargeson inherited was that of Britain. But he was also aware very early in his career that colonial writers who imitated British poems and fictions invariably falsified their subject. The English novel was something established in the eighteenth century:

The robust novel with the robust hero, in Fielding and Smollett: the novel of feminine sensibility, in Richardson: adventure in Defoe: and fantasy, in Swift . . . These have had a remarkably stabilizing effect on the English novel: most English novelists write, as it were, in their shadow — or in the shadow of one or other of them. Now it would be too much to say that the New Zealand novelist has to get completely out from under the shadow of these great men — nevertheless it is true that he must endeavour to throw off their influence insofar as it may hinder him from attempting to grapple with the New Zealand scene.

(p.59)

Sargeson's task, as he saw it, was to invent a literary language drawn direct from, and representing, his New Zealand subject. In this the predecessors he acknowledged were Mark Twain in America and Henry Lawson in Australia. Though there were New Zealand writers older than himself whose work he admired (he mentions in particular Jane Mander and William Satchell) there was none who had done this job with any kind of completeness.

So the emphasis, as with all literatures emerging from the falsities of a colonial phase, is on representation, a true record; and Sargeson's early stories, which are probably still his best known, made him seem supremely the realist writer, the recorder of rough, down-to-earth, monosyllabic Kiwi verities. That view even of the early work is only partly correct. There is a great deal of contrivance in the apparent artlessness of the record; and as he got older Sargeson grew less and less content with the notion that literature was primarily a representation of the real. Reality was where you began. But 'if the local writer can see his environment with sufficient intensity' that intensity will create 'a reality of its own' (p.155). What was then brought into being was 'a work of art . . . a self-contained world'.

In this faith in the power of literary art to transform even the starkest and most basic colonial reality and to create from it a world of beauty and significance, Sargeson's great example was Olive Schreiner's *The Story of an African Farm.*

Sargeson was, I think, somewhat ambivalent about the New Zealand writers who saw him as their mentor and whose work his own was said to have made possible. Like him they sprang from a puritanical society, rebelled against it, and represented it truthfully and critically in their work. George Eliot was the 'large and formidable ghost' (p.75) Sargeson saw haunting the pages of the first World's Classic volume of New Zealand short stories, and although he had the highest regard for her ('there is no Victorian novel that quite compares with *Middlemarch*', p.73), he sympathized also with the aesthete rebellion of Ruskin and Swinburne against her and her kind. In Sargeson, as well as the responsible realist, there was also a witty and anarchic sprite who wished to be done with mundane truth and morals.

The realist and the sprite are present in different parts of this collection, and sometimes together on the same page. Presiding over them there is a patient, humane, intelligent expositor, the voice of an enquiring mind with a strong compulsion to share its findings.

I took up these essays, excellently edited and introduced by Kevin Cunningham, thinking they would hold little that was new for me. I found it hard to put them down. They renewed my respect for the man. And they reminded me that it is still possible to write criticism which is a pleasure to read — if only you have the talent.

BOOKERED

1: Keri Hulme's *the bone people*

Great excitement has attended the publication of this novel in New
Zealand. At the present date nothing I have seen written about *the bone
people* could be described as 'critical'. It has been received with acclamation.
The *New Zealand Listener* gave it not one review but two — both by
women, one Maori, one Pakeha (European). As far as I can recall both
were direct addresses to the author. They told her she had spoken for
us all, or for all women, or all Maoris; but it was impossible to guess
what kind of novel was being reviewed. The book's first printing sold
out at once. Its publisher, Spiral, a 'feminist collective', reprinted and
again it sold out. Now it is to be reissued by a commercial publisher,
Hodder and Stoughton. Foreign rights are being negotiated. It has won
the New Zealand Book Award for fiction, and also a one-off award
called the Pegasus Prize for Maori Literature, about which I will have
more to say. Television, which in New Zealand is usually uninterested
in the literary scene, has turned its cameras on Keri Hulme. From being
unknown to all but a few, she has probably become one of the best-
known New Zealand writers. Bits of mythology have begun to form
around the book, abetted by an introduction in which the author says
three publishers 'turned it down' before Spiral accepted it.

Criticism is always a dialogue. One seldom has the chance to speak
first, and what the critic says is always partly in answer to what has
been said already. In the case of Keri Hulme's novel 'what has been
said' is largely a babble of excited voices in public places. *The bone people*

Ariel, October 1985 (i.e. this appeared before *the bone people* won the Booker Prize). Reprinted
in *Contemporary Literary Criticism*, 39, 1986.

touches a number of currently, or fashionably, sensitive nerves. New Zealand intellectual life, limping along in the wake of the world, has been lately lacerating itself into consciousness that racism and sexism exist. Where they don't exist, zealots nonetheless find them. Keri Hulme, a woman and, let's say for the moment, a Maori, her novel published by a 'feminist collective' after being 'turned down' by three others — this is the stuff for those zealots! As in the case of most books which take off publicly like rockets, a lot of the energy has nothing to do with the quality of the work. It is, however, the quality of the work that will determine what future the book is to have.

For the record let it be said first that of the four who were offered the novel before Spiral saw it, one was a feminist publisher who thought it insufficiently feminist for her list; another was a woman publisher who thought the book needed more work before it was ready for publication; and the remaining two were commercial publishers who were anxious about the novel's length and its prospects in the market-place. The latter two deny having 'turned it down'. They wanted more work done on it. From a purely commercial point of view it could be said they made a mistake in not accepting the book as it was when the author declined to make cuts and revisions. From the literary point of view I think the author made a mistake in rejecting all advice about how the typescript might be edited and improved.

It should also be said that Spiral received a government grant which made the publication possible, and that this was on the recommendation of the Literary Fund Advisory Committee, consisting at that time of five men and one woman. Spiral then produced a book as badly edited, printed, and proof-read as any I have seen, mismanaged its finances, and had to ask for a further grant before a reprint could be done. The Literary Fund Advisory Committee, which had never been in doubt about Keri Hulme's talent or that her book deserved support, bent its rules a little to make a second grant possible.

If *the bone people* is not in any very obvious way a 'feminist' novel, in what sense is it a Maori novel? The question arises especially because of the Pegasus Award mentioned above. Every year (or second year?) the Mobil company chooses a country to which this literary award shall be made. The prize on this occasion was to be US$4000, a visit to the United States valued at US$6000, and a guarantee of publication there. For 1984 the company chose New Zealand and decided, after consultation with government and other officials, that the prize should be offered for a novel or autobiography by a Maori, written in the past decade, in English or in Maori. It is hard to see the inclusion of the Maori language as much more than a gesture (and in fact at least one of the judges knew no Maori). If any modern literary writing has been done in the Maori language, next to none has been published, and that is likely to continue to be the case. For the present, anyway, all Maori writers of any consequence write in English; and probably few of them know more than a little of the Maori language. The works entered had thus to be considered 'Maori' not in language, or in form, but by virtue of the racial antecedents of the authors.

The award raised the question of the usefulness, and even the honesty, of what is called 'affirmative action' in favour of groups disadvantaged by history. Maori writers now sell at least as well as, often better than, the most successful Pakeha writers. They compete successfully for government grants and literary awards. Why then a special award for a Maori writer? If the intention had been to promote traditional Maori culture, surely the language ought to have been Maori. And if not Maori language, then at least the form required would need to have been one of those belonging to an oral tradition — poetry, songs, laments, or some re-telling of local myth or legend. If the intention was simply to help a Maori writer, even then it is hard to see why poetry should have been excluded, since poetry is something which exists in the Maori tradition, while the novel, obviously, is not. And finally, what is 'a Maori writer'? Of Keri Hulme's eight great-grand-parents one only was Maori. Hulme was not brought up speaking Maori, though like many Pakeha New Zealanders she has acquired some in adult life. She claims to identify with the Maori part of her inheritance — not a disadvantageous identification at the present time; but it seems to me that some essential Maori elements in her novel are unconvincing. Her uses of Maori language and mythology strike me as willed, self-conscious, not inevitable, not entirely authentic. Insofar as she is an observer of things outside herself, Hulme has observed Maoris and identified with them. If that is what constitutes a 'Maori' writer, however, then Pakeha writers like James K. Baxter and Roderick Finlayson (to name two obvious cases) could be said to have been more successfully 'Maori' than Keri Hulme.

The bone people, I would be inclined to argue, is a novel by a Pakeha which has won an award intended for a Maori. The fault is not Keri Hulme's. It is in the conception of such an award, which is thoroughly confused, and is in any case patronizing, suggesting that Maori writers can't compete openly with Europeans. It doesn't surprise me that Witi Ihimaera refused to enter his work for the Pegasus award.

The bone people is a novel about violence. It is also about love and about identity. The love and the violence have a common source. All three of the main characters, a woman, a man, and a child, could be described as violent, though the propensity exhibits itself in different ways. All three are strong characters. All three, but especially the woman and the child, are sharply portrayed. They form a close unit. What is interesting about the novel is that their bonds exist outside biology. It is the biological pattern imitated. The man's own wife and child have died. The boy he acts as father to comes as from nowhere, born out of the sea. And although a bond like sexual love grows between the man and the woman, there is no physical contact. That, I think, is the imaginative strength of the work — that it creates a sexual union where no sex occurs, creates parental love where there are no physical parents, creates the stress and fusion of a family where there is no actual family.

Interviews with Keri Hulme have shown how closely her central character, Kerewin Holmes, is based on herself. Both the novelist and her character describe themselves as sexless, sexually drawn neither to male nor female, 'neuter'.

I spent a considerable amount of time when I was, o, adolescent, wondering why I was different, whether there were other people like me. Why, when everyone else was fascinated by their developing sexual nature, I couldn't give a damn. I've never been attracted to men. Or women. Or anything else. It's difficult to explain, and nobody has ever believed it when I have tried to explain, but while I have an apparently normal female body, I don't have any sexual urge or appetite. I think I am a neuter. (p.276)

This is Kerewin Holmes speaking. Most of it, almost word for word, Keri Hulme has said of herself in a television interview.

Many — perhaps most — works of fiction are fuelled by sexual energy. Here is a novel fuelled by its lack. What for most of us would be merely the domestic subject is for Keri Hulme, I think, the equivalent of romance — the realm of the unattainable. I mean this in no derogatory sense. Whatever confusions of motive and propulsion there may have been in responses to this book (and I think it is worthwhile attempting to unravel some of them), it is not for nothing that there has been so much excitement. *The bone people* is at the core a work of great simplicity and power.

The narrative creates a simple pattern. The three principal characters are drawn slowly together to form a strong unit, though one in which negative forces are working. A catastrophe occurs which blows them apart. Each, alone, is driven by circumstances, through pain and suffering, to the edge of destruction. Each of the two adults has been partly to blame for the catastrophe, and each is saved from death by the intervention of what appears to be a force from the lower echelons of the Divine. At the end the three come together again, purged, and certain of their need for one another.

To recognize this pattern in which are mixed, not always successfully, a remorseless realism with elements of the mythical, the magical and the mystical, one must stand off at some distance from the novel. Seen from a nearer point of focus it is likely to be described in sociological terms. Joe Gillayley loves his adopted child dearly, but is subject to pressures he cannot quite recognize or control. He drinks, beats the child, and finally very nearly kills him.

Simon, the child of unknown parentage, survivor of a wreck, with the marks still on him of beatings previous to those inflicted by Joe, never speaks, but is able to write and signal messages, and to communicate his love, his rages, and his intelligence. His love for Joe is almost unwavering, despite the beatings. Simon is a major fictional character, the most complete, convincing, and fascinating of the three, and all the more remarkable in that his personality has to be conveyed to us without spoken language.

Kerewin is the isolated artist who has run out of inspiration. She lives, literally, in a tower of her own making, which (again quite literally) has to be broken down before she can paint again. The obviousness of the symbolism doesn't detract from the authenticity of the portrait. Kerewin, one feels, is bold enough and innocent enough to live by her symbols, as Yeats did when he bought a tower from Ireland's Congested Roads Board for £35 and restored it so he could write of himself 'pacing upon the battlements'. In fact Kerewin strikes me as more Irish than Maori, word-obsessed, imaginative, musical, unstable, something of a mystic, full of bluster and swagger, charm, and self-assertion. All this is shown, not from the outside, but from within, so the novel partakes of Kerewin's strengths but is not detached from her weaknesses. Like its central character, *the bone people* seems at times disarmingly, at times alarmingly, naive.

The novel is successful from the start in portraying the character of Simon and the way he insinuates himself into Kerewin's isolated life. Joe, on the other hand, strikes me as a character who is never quite perfectly formed in the novelist's imagination, and there are times when his cast of mind and turn of phrase seem to belong to Kerewin rather than to himself. The relationship between the two is less than convincing in its early stages; and though it becomes more real as the novel continues, this reader, at least, never felt entirely secure in his 'suspension of disbelief'. To give only one example: Joe is represented as physically powerful, a fairly traditional Maori male, though with more education than most. He is kind, affectionate, but with a dangerously short fuse, precarious pride, and a propensity for violence. Yet when an argument between him and Kerewin turns into a fight, Kerewin, who has learned something like kung fu during a visit to Japan, beats him effortlessly, a beating which he accepts with great good humour and with no apparent damage to his ego. That is not the only point at which the reader is likely to feel the novel has taken a dive from reality into wishful daydream.

Worse, however, is the sequence in which Joe comes close to death and then is rescued by an old Maori man who has waited his whole lifetime under semi-divine instruction to perform just this rescue, so he can pass on to the man he saves proprietorial rights over a piece of land and the talisman in which its spirit is preserved. There would be no point in recounting in detail the physical and mystical experiences which make up this section of the novel. It should be enough to say that I found it, read either as Maori lore or as fiction, almost totally spurious. There is a parallel set of events in which Kerewin, who appears to be dying of cancer, is saved by the intervention of an old woman and a magical, or simply herbal, potion.

From the first time I read letters Keri Hulme addressed to the Literary Fund Advisory Committee requesting assistance (that was more than ten years ago), I have never doubted that she has a powerful and original literary talent. I have admired some of her stories published in *Islands*. And I was sure Auckland University Press made the right decision when it accepted her collection of poems, *The Silences Between*, for publication. Her talent is abundantly clear in *the bone people*. But all the indications are that, for reasons which are not strictly literary, the achievement of this novel is going to be inflated beyond its worth. I'm glad *the bone people* has been written and published. I'm sorry it wasn't revised, decently copy-edited, and presented to better advantage. I'm sure its author will go on to better things. But I have to admit that when I stand back from the novel and reflect on it, there is, in addition to the sense of its power, which I have acknowledged, and which is probably the most important thing to be said about it, a bitter after-taste, something black and negative deeply ingrained in its imaginative fabric, which no amount of revision or editing could have eliminated, and which, for this reader at least, qualifies the feeling that the publication of this book is an occasion for celebration.

I'm not sure whether I should even attempt to explain to myself what it is constitutes that negative element, or whether it should simply be mentioned and left for other readers to confirm or deny. But I suspect it has its location in the central subject matter, and that this is something it shares (to give another point of reference) with Benjamin Britten's opera *Peter Grimes*, a work which also presents extreme violence against a child, yet demands sympathy and understanding for the man who commits it. In principle such charity is admirable. In fact, the line between charity and imaginative complicity is very fine indeed.

2: *Oscar and Lucinda*, by Peter Carey (1987)

On the basis of a good part of *Oscar and Lucinda* I could say, for what it's worth, that I am a reader capable of enjoying Peter Carey's fiction and admiring the skill with which he produces that enjoyment. In fact I would be ungrateful if I didn't report that for probably two thirds

Scripsi, April 1989.

of this novel, while conscious that I was holding certain reservations at bay until I had seen where it was taking me, I was also thinking, 'Whatever my final judgement it has to be said that Carey makes most contemporary novelists look like amateurs.' Even if I no longer want to stand by that thought, it's relevant that I had it — and had it in common with practised readers who will retain it and defend it.

My anxiety is not a fear of standing alone on the negative side. It is, rather, something that springs out of a number of uncertainties. I am quite certain that for me, and for readers of like temperament, this is a novel which destroys itself in its final hundred or so pages. What I'm not sure about is — might it have been otherwise? Or was it inevitable — inherent in the very temperament which produced the fiction as a whole? Carey can lull the senses, play upon the feelings, lead his reader on down the primrose path of narrative — but so can Steven Spielberg, who might be an appropriate person to do the movie. You may finish the novel feeling like the child enticed by candy. The candy was OK but what followed was disgusting. You may finish it chastising, not Carey, but yourself for not having grown out of sweet-flavoured enticements.

Naval ships have a method of shooting showers of metal strips — it may be foil in two senses — and turning end-on when an Exocet or other modern rocket is 'incoming'. The metal shower confuses the rocket's radar system. If a stern critic were to treat this novel as a piece of conventional historico-realist fiction it might be sunk in five minutes. Psychologically unconvincing, anachronistic, implausible, full of visible contrivance: already we have blown out its boilers, put down its communications system, and holed it at the water-line. But before anything of that kind can be said we have to get past those diversionary showers. This is not so much history as fable; not so much psychology as symbolism; not so much a novel as a bicentennial national epic; not so much fiction as meta-fiction. We are in the age of Marquez and Grass and Rushdie. Not wanting to seem old-fashioned our academic Exocet turns left, and *Oscar and Lucinda* sails on.

I am all for meta-fiction and the modern masters. And it's true that Carey plays skilfully with the nature of fiction itself, allowing the contemporary voice of someone perhaps very like himself to come and go as the source of the narrative. We know quite early in the novel that Oscar is this narrator's great-grandfather. We are teased with the possibility, the hope, and finally the expectation that it will prove that Lucinda was his great-grandmother. Carey as writer is partly a descendant of Lawrence Sterne. But the novel's meta-fictional games and devices are not nearly so strong a determinant of its quality as are the standard nineteenth-century precedents of Dickens, George Eliot, and Trollope. Of course you can argue that pastiche is a modernist technique and that it's used here with conscious intent; but the statement amounts to no more than another shower of foil. *Oscar and Lucinda* is set in nineteenth-century England and Australia, presents characters (notably two, but a host of others) which invite our imaginations to respond to them as real, tells a story, portrays a society, and stands or falls, I think, by essentially the same criteria as apply in the case of the great nineteenth-century novelists.

Two things are impressive about Carey's technique and you can't have one without the other. One is pace, the other is detail. He is able to keep the story moving at a pace that is slow without drag because he has command of so much detail. Whether from research or imagination (I suppose both) the detail seems not merely to justify the pace but to require it. The consequent sense of richness and bulk lays a hold on the reader. We have committed many waking hours to Careyland. It becomes part of our life. That's the nature of long novels. There's psychological reluctance, as with life itself, to deny or regret what has been 'lived through'.

But Careyland in *Oscar and Lucinda* is not just one place. It is partly historical reconstruction, partly mythical world, and partly a set of very up-to-date opinions. Carey is dutiful about (what else in 1988?) racism and sexism. Women and blacks are victims. That is one reasonable and well-supported historical view from the perspective of 1988; but it is not reasonable to have women and blacks of the 1850s share that perspective. Those up-to-date opinions begin to invade and undermine both the history and the myth — not because they are 'wrong' but because they are out of place. They destroy the credence on which the fiction depends. Not only Lucinda Leplastrier but her mother as well are modern women of the 1980s put into the costume of the 1850s. Of course there were early feminists; but there is a sensibility which is of our time, and these women have it. You could not even, convincingly, put them back thirty years, let alone 130.

While the women (especially) and the blacks are to a large extent the bearers of Carey's view of Australian history, Oscar is the bearer of his myth — by which I mean, I suppose, something like his personal vision of 'reality'. Oscar's background is that of Edmund Gosse, taken directly from Gosse's *Father and Son*; but unlike Gosse, Oscar Hopkins is not destined for worldly success. He is the saintly fool, possessed by the vision of bringing God to the black heathens of Australia, a mission from which the Church he serves tries to deflect him, but which, almost inadvertently, he carries out, even seeming to achieve sainthood (a discreet aureole is noticed about his head by the black woman who helps him and whom he names Mary Magdalene).

A propensity to gamble is what brings Oscar and Lucinda together. He does it to sustain himself in his mission, believing that God permits it so long as he does it for that purpose and not for pleasure. Lucinda, on the other hand, is an addict. Gambling is perhaps her substitute for those things life as a woman denies her, despite her large fortune. There seems to be an underlying notion here of gambling as something fundamental to the Australian character and history. In the end Oscar and Lucinda make a wager which ought to bring happiness to both, no matter which of them wins. In fact he wins the wager and loses his life; she loses the wager and her fortune, and wins a new life as a feminist activist which we are told about (twice) in a sentence or two, but which occurs beyond the pages of the novel.

Myth and history converge in the novel's final pages. Myth becomes history and history myth. Oscar's dream of bringing Christianity to the blacks merges (though he doesn't realize it) with Lucinda's of building something magnificent in glass. A glass church is built in prefabricated sections and transported overland to northern New South Wales. It is this hideous journey which is, I suppose, Carey's offering of a bicentennial image of Australia. It is a place of harsh male oppression, where beautiful visions come to grief, where bullies force the morally weak to inflict indignities on the good who are physically weak. It becomes finally an anal vision — Australia as the world's arsehole. As Percy Smith forces laudanum down the unwilling throat of Oscar by means of a metal funnel, 'two bullocks in the carpenter's team defecated at once'. When Oscar resolves to assert himself against his tormenter he is stopped by the sight of the overseer buggering the carpenter by the light of the campfire. In a clearing Oscar sees a man tied to a tree and flogged 'until there was a shiny red mantle on his white shoulders and brown seeping through his . . . twill trousers . . . prayer could not block out the smell of the man's shit'. The laudanum he's made addict to makes Oscar constipated so that throughout his last days he's tormented by an anal itch.

Here, not in method but in what it shows, *Oscar and Lucinda* departs from its nineteenth-century precedents. These are the harsh truths which Victorian prudery and sentimentality concealed; but the effect of the telling here is not one of liberation. The narrowness of focus, the feeling that imaginer and imagined are perilously close, produces the sense of something treacly and distasteful. Have we moved from nineteenth-century evasion to twentieth-century truth-telling; or is it merely a side-step into melodrama? There is something unsavoury about the character of the hero which invades and infects the novel as a whole.

Speculation about how a novel came about is of little use. It may be wrong; or it may be irrelevant. But my guess that the novelist began with the (essentially filmic, as in, say, *Fitzcarraldo*) idea of a glass church floating down the Bellinger River at least indicates something about the final effect of the novel, which reads as if Carey has worked backwards from that single image, asking himself how it could be brought about. Things happen, not because they are likely or psychologically plausible, but in order to push the next step forward in the long chain of causation towards that final image.

Carey's great skill in covering this trail of blatant contrivance is skill with detail — but it is of an odd kind. It doesn't seem to me that he is primarily an observer. He looks out at the world much less than he looks inward at his own evolving fantasy. I read a large part of *Oscar and Lucinda* in an eighth-floor Balmain flat which looks one way over Darling Harbour and the other over Mort Bay towards Long Nose Point — locations for more than half of what happens in the novel. Even despite this local assistance, I could seldom 'see' the events in a setting that felt real. Careyland it seems to me is less Australia than a mental landscape rich in Australian bric-à-brac but poor in observed reality.

In that world people speak and behave, and things happen, largely as they do in nineteenth-century fiction. That is the set of conventions by which the world of *Oscar and Lucinda* arranges itself. Each chapter begins with the striking of a note which rings through and controls what follows. Carey's skill in this is prodigious. He is such a virtuoso one is inclined to blame him for his lack of mistakes of tone, as if the whole were machine-made. But in order to believe in the detail one must believe in the larger design, and therein lies the problem.

Here are the opening sentences of Chapter 67:

The housekeeper at Randwick was a certain Mrs Judd who, had she not had reasons of her own for wishing to scrub the floor and black the stove and swat the flies that trapped themselves behind the orange and lilac panes of glass in the big sitting room, could have stayed at home and eaten chocolates. The Judds were wealthy members of the congregation. Mr Judd's father may or may not have been transported, but Mr Judd was the successful proprietor of a hauling business, had teams of all sorts travelling throughout the colony, owned a ship which plied the coastal trade, and a splendid mansion at Randwick itself. He was a burly man and although his hip was injured — a defect which served to tip his broad body a little to the starboard and give it the appearance of someone with an invisible chaff bag on his broad back — he still worked as hard as the men he employed. He not only had his wife in control at the vicarage of St John's, but he liked to inspect it himself from time to time. He had a possessive feeling about the building, as well he might — his donation had paid for the greater part of it and it was his taste (or his upholsterer's) which dominated its interior.

The authority of the Judds is about to be asserted over Oscar, and their strengths and limitations are present in those sentences, not only in the facts but in the tone. The tone is their own — a high moral one; but through it the author seems to smile at us, silent and despairing. This Mr Judd, lop-sided son of a convict, patron of the church because it gives him a chance to use the singing voice he is proud of, will be another tormenter of the holy fool. Here he is about to catch Oscar

and Lucinda, who have played cards for money all night, still at it at
6 a.m. The management of the scene itself is perfect. But how does
Mr Judd come to see them at that hour? The explanation is that he
has turned up with Mrs Judd in order to rake leaves clipped from the
hedge the day before. At 6 a.m?

Again and again it is this relative indifference to what is simply plausible
that makes the sentence-by-sentence perfection and the attention to detail
(those orange and lilac panes) seem all the more artificial. The whole
story, one feels, is a put-up job; and though I've seen Oscar described
as 'a great comic character', there is not, in the governing tone of the
book, a note of declared playfulness, of acknowledged extravagance (as
there is, for example in a writer like Gunter Grass) that would defuse
the feeling that what we are reading, for all the talent deployed in it,
is really a modern Victorian melodrama.

The novel comes to life and takes its firmest hold on this reader in
the relationship of the father and son (based on that of Philip Henry
and Edmund Gosse, but with an authenticity all of its own); and between
Oscar and his unlikely but convincing friend at Oxford, Wardley-Fish.
There are also wonderfully affecting moments between the two principal
characters; but here the overall determination to have a single
misunderstanding keep them apart — only just, but for ever — strains
that credulity which the underlying realism of the whole seems to require.

Carey's talent is never in doubt. And to complain of his vision, it
may be argued, is no more than a statement of personal preference for
something different. There is a sense in which his dark depiction of
Australia, like Patrick White's, is something that can't be argued with.
Australia, after all, produced them both; and the violence is there in
the history for the writer who wishes to make it the focus of his attention.
Large talents don't lie; but not even the largest sees everything. This
one seems to have grown up under a stone.

IHIMAERA: OLD WOUNDS AND ANCIENT EVILS

The Matriarch, by Witi Ihimaera (1986)

My grandmother, who was born I think about 1880, was proud of the fact that her parents were born in New Zealand. It made her, she used to say, 'a real Pig Islander'. A story she told me more than once was how my great-great-grandfather, John Flatt, a lay catechist, had fallen out with the Church Missionary Society by suggesting that its missionaries in New Zealand were acquiring too much Maori land. Twenty years ago in the British Museum I looked up evidence Flatt gave, while in London in 1837, to a Select Committee of the House of Lords looking into 'the State of the Islands of New Zealand'. I found that he had defended the acquisition of land by missionaries, saying (a familiar argument later on) that they had no other way, in that remote place, of providing a future for their children.

Of course my grandmother's story and my research may not really contradict one another. Flatt may have first defended the acquisition of land, and later thought it was becoming excessive. But at least my anecdote demonstrates something relevant to Ihimaera's novel: that family mythology likes heroes and prefers them simple. It also demonstrates that the argument over land, which is at the heart of *The Matriarch*, goes back to the beginnings of European settlement in New Zealand, and that although the Pakeha (Europeans) have progressively taken the land, they have always argued about the rights and wrongs of it. That remains true even today. Many Pakeha New Zealanders sympathize with the view (which is taught in schools) that the Maoris have been shamefully dispossessed. They join Maori land marches and protests. The present

London Review of Books, December 1986. Reprinted in *Contemporary Literary Criticism*, 46, 1988.

Government declares itself sympathetic to the Maori case, and looks to compensate where past wrongs are clearly manifest. But Pakehas go on buying Maori land. And though Maoris insist that for them the land has a spiritual value which the Pakeha does not understand, they go on selling it. Their sense of its spiritual value is always sharpest once the material value has been realized — and that has always been the case.

If the conquest had been by force of arms the history would be easier to understand. There was a period in the 1860s when wars did occur; but even then, Maoris fought against as well as with the insurgents. The Maoris were never one people; their identity was tribal, and the tribes were always warring. They had no conception of a single 'Maori nation' (a phrase Ihimaera uses frequently) nor of a single state called Aotearoa. That Maori name for New Zealand appeared first in the nineteenth century. A common adversary has forged some kind of unity — but the idea of Maori nationhood is more European and intellectual than truly Maori; just as the strongest moral arguments Maoris can summon against the Pakeha are those of a European liberal tradition. If there was one principle Maori culture always recognized it was the right of the strong over the weak.

In recent years radical young Maoris and Pakeha liberals have tended to join in an alliance the justice of whose case is seldom challenged, perhaps because in practical terms it constitutes no threat. Ihimaera's novel can be read in large part as a restatement of that case, which goes briefly as follows. The Maoris are the tangata whenua — the people of the land — and have, therefore, a moral right and precedence in Aotearoa. That right has been ignored and trampled on by the Pakeha, who have progressively, partly by force of arms, but much more by trickery, bribery, and legal and financial chicanery, dispossessed the tangata whenua of their birthright, imposing upon them a law, a culture, a religion, a system of values, an education, and a language alien to their own. Justice demands recompense and a reversal of this process.

Looked at in detail this simple image of New Zealand history as a long slow rape is at best a half truth, especially insofar as it ascribes conscious and malicious intent to the Pakeha and unwillingness to the Maori. It is also, I think, no favour to any group to foster its collective paranoia, since the film of history can't be re-run to suit the moral values of the present moment. But in broad terms it has to be accepted: we may have killed with muskets (sale of, more than use of), with European diseases, with money, with intermarriage — even with kindness. Whatever the means and the intention, and however the indigenous people may have collaborated in their own downfall, history has rolled cruelly over the Maori race. Today they are disproportionately the urban proletariat, the unemployed, the disaffected. From their 10 per cent of the population come close on 50 per cent of the inmates of New Zealand jails. Everyone

knows there is a problem which full civil rights and equality of opportunity
have not been sufficient to overcome. For that reason great importance
is now given to a revival of Maori language and culture. These, it is
thought, will bring new pride, a sense of identity, and hope. New Zealand
resounds with the rhythmic stamp of the haka, the swirl of grass skirts,
the twirl of pois, the knock of the wood-carver's hammer, and the tirelessly
repeated wail of the karanga.

It is also full of worthy Pakeha voices which sound remarkably like
those of parents in the kindergarten applauding infant work with paint
brush and Plasticene. This is a chorus I just can't bring myself to join.
However well-intentioned, it seems to me dishonest, patronizing, and
fundamentally undemocratic; and I begin to suspect that the liberal
conscience is the last and most deadly weapon in the European armoury
— deadly especially because it thinks its lethal shot is healthgiving.

I remember Witi Ihimaera as a shy, charming and handsome student
at Auckland University when I was a young lecturer in the early 1960s.
He was one of a generation of Auckland students which included David
Lange and a number of his present Cabinet. A few years later Ihimaera's
fiction began to appear. He was the first Maori writer to give an account
from the inside of tribal life and rituals. His novel *Tangi* was widely
read and admired, and it was followed by another, *Whanau*. There were
also two collections of short stories. At least one of his stories revealed
that he was under pressure to become 'political' — to lend his skill and
his mana to radical Maori protest — a pressure which at that time he
resisted. Then he announced that he was not going to write anything
more for some time — and he has stuck to that. Now, after nearly
a decade, he has produced *The Matriarch*, a 200,000 word block-buster
edited down by his publishers, I'm told, from the considerably larger
typescript first offered them. The Ihimaera of sensitive, lyrical, rather
plangent evocations is gone. In his place we have the novelist as warrior,
the novel as taiaha or mere, the reader as ally or enemy.

The matriarch of the title is Artemis Riripeta Mahana, grandmother
of the narrator, Tamatea Mahana, who closely resembles the author and
clearly draws upon some of his family history. The matriarch sees herself
as heir to two Maori power figures — Te Kooti, the rebel and religious
prophet who fought a guerilla war against the Pakeha for a number
of years and survived to be pardoned; and Wi Pere Halbert, a nineteenth-
century Maori politician who conducted from the floor of Parliament
his campaign to preserve Maori land under Maori control. The novel
moves back and forth across a great sweep of time. As the matriarch
instructs her favoured grandson, Tamatea, to whom her power will pass,
we are instructed with him in everything from the Maori creation story,
through the myth (presented as history) of the arrival of the Great Fleet
from Hawaiiki bringing the Maori to New Zealand, and in particular

of the canoe Takitimu bringing both the Maori gods and the forefathers of Tamatea's tribe. We are also given an account of Te Kooti's (probably wrongful) detention on the Chatham Islands, his escape, and his guerilla war against the settlers and the Maoris who supported them; and of the rise and fall of Wi Pere Halbert as Maori politician.

As he tells us all this Tamatea is already an adult, married, as Ihimaera was, to a Pakeha, and with two daughters; so as well as taking us back in time to history and prehistory, the narrative is going back and forth from the present to the narrator's childhood, and to the doings of the matriarch with whom he lived for some of his early years. Family and tribal rivalries are revealed. Artemis is opposed by tribes within the larger federation to which her own belongs. Her power is resented in the family. Her own husband schemes against her. Tamatea is envied, and his mana challenged. But through all vicissitudes the matriarch triumphs. She is presented as a figure of power, light, mystery, fortitude, cunning and beauty — Tamatea's protector, instructor, and friend, the source of his own skill and power.

The mixture of elements, all the way from the domestic to the divine, is as extreme as is the chronological sweep. In style the novel moves from conventional fiction, to expository prose, to rhetorical argument, to historical record (including many pages of *Hansard*). The tone swings back and forth between the grandiose and the banal. All this puts a great strain on any sense of artistic unity. But if it fails (and for me it certainly does) that is not only because of its formal inadequacies.

My quarrel with the book's 'content' can be dealt with first, and most simply, by asking what exactly it is that the matriarch achieves. She is represented as triumphant against all odds, having to call up magical forces as well as her powers as orator and as tribal and family politician to defeat her and Tamatea's enemies. What the outcome of all this effort appears to be is the protection of the mana of Tamatea. But Tamatea has little identity in the story except as its narrator, and recipient of these benefits. For that reason it is almost impossible to see him as separate from the novelist, which in turn makes the whole work appear to be a gross piece of personal mythologizing. The matriarch is great because the novelist tells us it is so; and Tamatea/Ihimaera is great because he inherits her powers.

Beyond the family and tribal rivalries we are told that 'like Te Kooti' the matriarch 'decreed war on the Pakeha' — but where in the novel does this occur? There is a protracted scene, returned to at intervals, in which she is shown claiming against opposition the right to speak on a marae, and causing some sort of public embarrassment to a Prime Minister. If anything followed from that meagre triumph the novel doesn't tell us. For the rest the matriarch's skills seem fully occupied in (for example) magically killing a tribal enemy with poisonous spiders, invoking various supernatural signs, making clouds go across the sun (and once a full-scale eclipse) to signal her anger, driving a Lagonda, and singing at moments of high drama excerpts from Verdi in the original Italian — thus invoking (I think that is the point) a parallel struggle for national unity and liberation from foreign domination.

The novel repeatedly, and in the end tiresomely, asserts the stature of the matriarch. The language ('amazing', 'breathtakingly stunning', 'an incredible beauty', 'a blinding presence', 'charismatic', 'extraordinary', 'astonishing') becomes florid as if with the effort of conjuring into being a greatness that has no foundation in fact, nor even, perhaps, in the imagination of the novelist. At no time did I really believe in the greatness of Artemis. Worse, I was never entirely persuaded that the novelist believed in it either.

The matriarch was standing with the child in front of the vault, in the place of the dead, at Waerenga A Hika. There was turmoil in her, for the slender fingers gripped the child's shoulders like talons. The vault was dark, sombre and still. It was imposing, almost defiant, and the air around it was like a slow moving river swirling into eternity. The matriarch sang, 'Tu che le vanita conoscesti del mondo,' a prayer of intercession, 'You who know the vanities of this world and enjoy in the grave profound repose. Take my tears to the throne of the Lord.' Her body had the seeds of mortality in it, blossoming like diseased flowers.

'Grandmother, what place is this?' the child asked.

The matriarch's voice was calm. It was almost a whisper on the breath, like a green kawakawa leaf suspended in the air before its twig is snapped and it falls down, down, down.

'Per me, la mia giornata a sera e giunta gia,' she sang. 'This is the place of my great-uncle, my ancestor. He was a brave and determined man. He loved me very much. He loved this land. He loved these people. He was very proud. Addio, addio bei sogni d'or illusion perduta. Il nodo si spezzo la luce s'e fatta muta. I come to his judgement and yours.'

'And mine?' the child asked.

She gripped him even tighter. 'My grandfather told me to remember that the people can rise again through me. But I must still live. Se ancor si piange in cielo, ah, il pianto mio reca appie' del Signor,' she sang in supplication. 'Have I failed, grandfather? For look at me, my wages are death.'

And she lifted her head to the place of the dead. 'Let me live,' she called. There was no answer from the vault where her grandfather lay. No sign. Only absolute and utter silence. La pace dell'avel.

Every one of these over-written passages (and they occur at intervals throughout) diminished my sense of the reality of the figure whose stature they were meant to enhance.

The Matriarch also sets out to rewrite some passages of New Zealand history from what I suppose Ihimaera would claim was a Maori point of view. So Te Kooti becomes a hero figure, and what has been known hitherto as the Matawhero Massacre is renamed the Matawhero Retaliation

— it being Te Kooti's retaliation for his wrongful detention on the Chatham Islands, and for the fact that he was hounded by the law after his escape. I don't think with hindsight anyone disputes that it would have been better if the authorities had left Te Kooti alone — though he might in any case have decided to launch an attack on the settlers. But to recount in a gloating, triumphant tone the details of the killings — skulls crushed, babies beheaded in their cradles, parents bayoneted or shot in front of children, children in front of parents — and then to make a hero figure out of the Christianity-crazed Maori who ordained, because he believed he was the Prophet come to lead his people out of Egypt, that it should happen: this seems to me intellectually puerile and imaginatively destitute. Further, the justification offered for Te Kooti's killings is followed by a tone of moral indignation ('Yes, Pakeha, you remember Matawhero. Let me remind you . . .') at the revenge taken at Ngatapu, where a number of Te Kooti's followers were shot at the top of a cliff. But the account conceals — surely deliberately — that these murders were also the work of a Maori, Te Kooti's enemy Major Ropata, whose name hardly occurs in Ihimaera's novel.

There are some rare but important moments in *The Matriarch* when the political posturing stops and the true work of fiction — to make us see — is done. The Maori sense of kinship and place intertwined, is there:

Waituhi. It was the close kinship the whanau shared with one another so that we never lived apart . . . It was the place of the heart. This place of old wooden shacks and scrub covered foothills. This place where the Waipaoa was wild in the winter and strangely menacing in the summer. This place of the painted meeting house, Rongapai, with its eaves sloping to an apex like an arrowhead thrusting at the sky. This place of people growing older, where flax and flowers grow untamed in the plots where houses once had been. This place of the village graveyard where the tribal dead sleep in the final resting of the body. This place, this Waituhi, was family. The whanau was my home. The love and affection they held for each other were the ridgepoles of my heart. The sharing and enjoying of each other were the rafters.

There are also some touching details about Maori ways — especially their lack of physical and emotional inhibition within the family. And there is one page in which something leaps out and punches me with a force nothing else in the book possesses:

It is the night of 24 September 1950. It is near the end of a very bad winter for my mother. We are living in a one-bedroom bach in Crawford Road, Kaiti, Gisborne. Our father, Te Ariki, has been away from home for two months. He has gone to a place called Mataura, in the South Island, to find work. My sisters and I are lonely for him. Our mother is, too.

The lightning flashes again. Last month our mother had to go to the hospital to have her teeth taken out. It was very painful. She wore a scarf over her face. The blood used to seep through. We thought she was dying.

The thunder booms. My father told me I had to look after the family. The rent man came last week. He lifted his fist to my mother. The electricity was cut off a few days ago. My mother bought some candles. The man from the Maori Affairs came yesterday. He was a bad man and he touched my mother. She had to fight him with her knife. E pa, please come home soon.

'There, there, Teria,' I whisper again. 'There, there, Erina.'

Yesterday when I was coming home from Kaiti School, some bigger kids jumped on me. They laughed at my clothes. They said I had nits in my hair. They made me fall on the gravel. I didn't tell my mother.

There momentarily is real life — and you might say there also is the motive and the justification for indignation, rhetoric, myth-making. But it happens almost inadvertently. The curtain closes and we are not shown it, or anything like it, again. It simply remains in the mind as a measure for all the rest — so much more direct and true and powerful than all that windy stuff about the matriarch with her spiders and her recitative.

On p.370 Ihimaera repeats Te Kooti's cry — 'We are still slaves in the land of Pharaoh'. It is strange coming from a man much honoured in his own country and now serving as New Zealand Consul in New York; but whatever the facts, in the mind it may be so. And if that is the case, freedom can only be achieved in the mind. No external power can confer it. My own view is that the kind of picking over old wounds and ancient evils that this novel represents is not the way to go about freeing the mind. The past doesn't have to be forgotten; but its rights and wrongs belong to those who lived them, not to us. There is an egotism of defeat, just as there is of victory. The sense of having been wronged can become, like alcohol, a way of life. The Irish seem to have lived for centuries off moral indignation. Is that what Ihimaera wants for his people? His proper task was the craft of fiction. He owed it to himself to write a more considered novel — one which used the language more scrupulously. Everyone would be better served by a more truthful image.

THE SURVIVAL OF ZOE

Running Backwards Over Sand, by Stephanie Dowrick (1985)

Because genuinely literary people are a minority, most publishing is not for them but for those who read a book for its subject, or its genre — what it's *about*. Fashions in subjects come and go. As they go many of the books that fed them go too, even though they may have sold in huge numbers while the fashion lasted. The books that survive do so mainly for literary reasons. The right subject may be good for sales in the short term, but good writing is more durable.

At the moment there's a fashion for books by, for and about women. Some are excellent. Many are bad and will soon be forgotten. Stephanie Dowrick is an expatriate New Zealander who as a publisher has made the most of this fashion. In partnership with Naim Attallah she founded the Women's Press in London. From feminist publisher she has now turned feminist author.

The feminism of *Running Backwards over Sand* is declared in its opening sentences: 'Here she comes, our hero. Zoe Delighty. This is her story.' Anyone who works in a university will know that linguistic and grammatical bullying by feminists is currently the most conspicuous form of sexual harassment. One thing you may not do is refer to a 'heroine'. There must only be heroes, female or male, just as there must be no actresses, only actors, female or male. So Cleopatra, or Juliet, or Brunhilde, is now a hero, to be played by an actor.

Zoe Delighty's name (we also learn this on the first page) signifies her role as a bearer of 'a vivid light'. She is some kind of torchbearer

August 1985. See my final essay, 'The New Victorians' for the provenance of this review, which is published here for the first time.

for women. This is because although she spends most of two decades suffering defeats and depressions, the author finds it possible to describe her, in the book's last word, as a survivor. What she has survived is not a war, a plague, a famine, a revolution; not even physical violence, or poverty, or illness. It is just life, with its attendant pain and discomfort. Since you and I, dear reader (female or male), are also in this sense survivors, we may be disinclined to accord Zoe the special status her author claims for her.

Zoe's life, at least as far as the novel is able to take it, might be described as hammock-shaped. At first there are ten idyllic years with her mother, her older sister, and her mother's women friends. Then the mother, Jane, dies, and the downward slope of the hammock begins. Swinish James, the father who has been good enough to leave home before Zoe was born, now insists on taking his daughters into his new family, which also happens to be Catholic. Zoe suffers at home and is expelled from school. But at a new school she discovers her own powers in a public-speaking contest. At this moment she sees the 'beacon' she is to become.

Now we jump forward in time. Zoe is a young woman. She has left New Zealand where she grew up and is living in London. She meets a German sculptor, Gabriel, becomes his lover, and follows him to Germany where he has a wife and child. Much of the remainder of this 350-page novel is taken up with their love affair and with an exhaustive attempt to explain why Gabriel won't live with Zoe, and why he finally leaves her alone in Berlin and goes to live in Frankfurt. I have to say that I didn't find this nearly as puzzling as the author does. Zoe thinks continuously and strenuously, but mostly ineptly or in clichés; and at the same time she exhibits a kind of ego-mania which would dampen the spirits of most partners (female or male).

The upward turn of the hammock begins when Zoe meets Sybilla, a German lesbian feminist from whom she learns a great deal, and with whom she has a brief affair. Zoe returns to London, shares a flat with a homosexual friend, Archie, finds work writing for a magazine, and develops her own talent as a writer. She takes courage from the example of an elderly concert pianist, Imogen Modjeska, and through her meets a young French Canadian musician, Claudia Denizet, with whom she has a passionate lesbian affair. Ahead lies her future as a writer.

All the time I was reading I found myself wanting to be kind to the author and unkind to her book. Dowrick is serious, conscientious, patient — she has worked at it. And she is a loyal New Zealander to a degree I found slightly embarrassing, but touching. She invokes Katherine Mansfield more than once; and she would probably like to think of herself in the line from Mansfield through Robin Hyde and Sylvia Ashton-Warner to Janet Frame. But what those brilliant and incisive New Zealand women had in common, in addition to their gender, was quite extraordinary talent as writers; and that is something which neither hard work nor right thinking will supply.

Skill in writing is as much knowing what to leave out as what to put in. Dowrick not only tells all; she explains all. She cajoles. She will leave nothing to the intelligence or to the imagination of her reader. And as well as over-explaining she over-writes. She forces emotion into her sentences instead of writing sentences which will draw emotion out of the reader. The reader becomes spectator rather than participant. It is a spectacle which convinced radical feminists (female and male) will enjoy insofar as the faithful are always looking to have their faith confirmed. As something like what was called agitprop in the 1930s this novel will have its following. But as fiction I don't predict for it a very long life.

CHRISTINA STEAD: MY GREAT AUSTRALIAN AUNT

Ocean of Story: The Uncollected Stories of Christina Stead, edited by R. G. Geering (1985)

In 1965, in London, I met Robie Macauley, editor of the *Kenyon Review*, who had accepted a story of mine. He asked was I related to Christina Stead. I had never heard of her. He told me she had written one of the great novels of the century, *The Man Who Loved Children*. When my story appeared someone wrote to a friend recommending it. She wrote to say how much she'd enjoyed it but asking why I was now writing as a woman. This confusion was sorted out when I found that the next issue of the *Kenyon Review* contained Christina Stead's novella 'The Puzzle-Headed Girl'. Occasionally since that time I have been sent proof copies of novels by American women, with a letter addressing me as 'Ms Stead' and asking for pre-publication comment. Names, of course, are always more significant to their bearers than to anyone else. I like to claim the major Stead as my Great Australian Aunt.

No doubt by the 1960s Stead's work was becoming known in Australia, but even there her reputation doesn't seem to have spread far outside of literary circles. It took the 1965 American re-issue (1966 in London) of *The Man Who Loved Children*, with Randall Jarrell's long introduction describing it as 'one of those books that their own age neither reads nor praises, but that the next age thinks a masterpiece', to jolt the Australian consciousness into reading Stead and re-claiming her. By that year she was sixty-two and had been publishing for more than three decades.

In 1969 she returned briefly to Australia after forty-one years away.

London Review of Books, September 1986.

On her return to London she wrote

Under the soft spotted skies of the North Sea I had forgotten the Australian splendour, the marvellous light . . . Everything was like ringing and bright fire and all sharpness. I was at dinner the other night, when someone said, 'What was Australia like?' 'It's the wonderful light, Bill,' I said to the Texan next to me. 'Yes,' he affirmed; and the Indian lady murmured, 'Yes'. Three exiles. No more was said; and the others, Londoners, did not even know what we had understood . . . When people ask, I feel like saying 'It's a brilliant country; they're a brilliant people, just at the beginning of the leaps.'

There is no objective truth (or untruth) in such statements; but there is a vast reservoir of energy in what they represent; and one can't help wondering (as also in the case of Katherine Mansfield) how much is lost when such talents expatriate themselves. It can be argued that it is all gain in that the writing gets done, and whether it would have been done without expatriation can't ever be known. Also a larger world attends to these international voices as it seldom does to the stay-at-homes. On the other hand one can see in Stead's response to Australia in 1969 that this is a writer returning to her primary subject, and correspondingly that some of the fictional subjects she derived from foreign places, though important to her intellectually, touched her less deeply. *The Man Who Loved Children* is indisputably an Australian novel which only pretends in a very perfunctory way to be set in America; and there seems still to be wide agreement that it is her best book.

Stead's double strength was that she was a roving observer (or, as she calls herself, a *listener*) who at the same time remained an Australian, never striving to become something different. She even felt her national identity was apparent physically. 'You know I'm Australian,' she told a *London Magazine* interviewer in 1970. 'I walk like an Australian, my attitude toward the British is Australian.' It's a curious conjunction of physical and mental, as if the one couldn't exist without the other. And that Australian walk appears in some of her stories, given to characters with whom she identifies. The secure sense of national identity came from her father: 'David was an Adam,' she wrote of him; 'Australia was his prolific and innocent garden.'

She was forty years away but always on the move, living (to put the places in roughly chronological order), in London, Paris, Spain, Hollywood, New York, Antwerp, Montreux, Bologna, Basle, Brussels, Lausanne, and The Hague. In 1953 she returned to London because she was, as she put it, 'losing her English'.

An Australian, then, but an expatriate; an international writer who insisted she could find subjects anywhere; and the partner of her American-born husband William Blake: these were the ways in which she identified herself. 'We never thought of having a home: home was where the other was.' When 'the other' died, but not until, she went back to Australia.

She arrived back just at the right moment to be claimed by Australia's new feminist movement, which saw in her the case of a great woman writer ignored, or even suppressed, by the literary patriarchy, her books published and then allowed to be forgotten. Feminists also found in *The Man Who Loved Children* the portrait of a patriarch male chauvinist, and in *For Love Alone* the salutary tale of how a woman falls into the trap of romantic love and then breaks out of it to find freedom.

Stead resisted all this, feeling that radical feminist criticism didn't serve her work but appropriated it for purposes of its own. She liked to acknowledge that her father and then her husband had encouraged her as a writer and had been the first to seek publishers for it; that her first publisher, Peter Davies, had fostered her talent; and that Randall Jarrell had revived interest in her work. But there was an anger beyond these particular corrections which is well remembered by those who knew her in her last years. One colleague recalls her screwing up a Women Against Rape leaflet, saying, 'They're trying to make trouble between women and men. Men are our friends.' As a leftist she believed there were battles to be fought and that women and men should fight them together. As a writer she insisted she knew and understood men better than women. And when she wrote about the relations of men and women as they had been in the past she saw, not simply the powerful and the powerless, but rather two kinds of power, one obvious and less interesting than the other, which was covert and, almost, arcane:

Some of this enchantment, foul and fair, comes from our early days when the woman in the home, so weak and ailing, often moneyless, powerless, often anxious, disturbed, wretched, with no status to speak of, no tradesunion, yet has the awful power of hunger and suck, gives life and holds off death, sets out her law, defies *their* law for our sake; from whom we obtain cure of night-terrors and the milk of paradise, a magic woman sheltering this small creature, ourselves, obliged to live in the country of the giants. Mothers and fathers can and do maim and kill; and children have their moments of fear with the kindest of parents. But the man's power is evident: the woman's is stranger.

Behind her ferocity with the feminists of those years lay her sense of fairness, her unwillingness to seem predictable or let liberal-left expectations put slogans in her mouth, and at a more personal level, simple loyalty to the memory of William Blake with whom she had lived positively for three decades. In a story in the present collection, 'Street Idyll', the meeting of two lovers is described — how they recognize one another at a distance, how they have to suppress their smiles as they get closer, their brief exchange ('I saw you as you were passing Sainsbury's' 'I saw you too, way up the hill'), their reluctance parting, though they will be together again in the evening. Only on the final page is it disclosed that they are elderly and have been married for a lifetime.

Stead was, she says

born into the ocean of story, or on its shores. I was the first child of a lively young scientist who loved his country and his zoology. My mother died — he mothered me. I went to bed early and with the light falling from the street lamp through the open slats of the venetian blind he, with one foot on the rather strange bed I had, told his tales. He meant to talk me to sleep; he talked me awake.

When her father remarried she became the story-teller to her half-brothers and sisters. She was also the disengaged observer, seeing a family of which she was part, yet which was not simply or completely her own.

Expatriation in adult life put her in much the same relation to the places that became her homes as she had occupied in relation to her father's second family. She was never where she had begun; but she was talented at adapting. And her observation, however apparently objective, was never without a sense of history or a moral principle. Few writers can generate so much indignation simply by representing without comment.

But there was something else as well as indignation — a kind of euphoria that gets into the writing especially when something awful is happening, so that at the same time that she deplores it, she seems to partake of it and relish it. In a story called 'Uncle Morgan at the Nats' Uncle Morgan plays a game in which his tiny niece is 'Granny'. Granny must prove her love by putting her hand in the fire.

Trembling and weeping the child put her hand out, felt the heat that surrounds the flame, blindly weeping, unquestioning, while Uncle Morgan, ducking his head and grinning whispered to left and right, 'She'll do it,' gleefully, 'Granny will do it!'

'Renee!' shrieked her mother and fell on the baby, pulling the poor thing from the fire.

'She touched the fire, she touched the fire,' the children shouted, jubilating, dismayed.

'Granny did not al-to-gether touch the fire, Granny let her Uncle down, Granny did not obey her Uncle,' said Morgan, in a repulsive weeping tone.

Uncle Morgan is another version of Sam Pollit of *The Man Who Loved Children* — deplorable, of course, but one of those big mad energetic presences Christina Stead loved to portray.

Her problem was perhaps that she was so naturally a writer she could write anywhere and about anything. Subjects presented themselves constantly. She had a range of styles to draw upon, from the sort of verbal expressionism of *The Salzburg Tales* — writing that draws attention to itself as writing — through to a plain workmanlike prose that offers nothing but its subject. This range of styles and subjects went together with her restless moving about Europe and America, so that she never acquired a settled reputation and identity in one place. Also it has to be acknowledged that she was a very uneven writer, better at getting an idea down while it was still hot than at working it through to a finished shape.

The present volume offers stories from the whole range of her work. The thirty-five pieces (eighteen published in her lifetime, the rest from her papers) are arranged not according to the chronology of their composition but to that of their subject matter as it can be seen to derive from Stead's life. Of course any arrangement of such disparate material was going to cause problems. The unsatisfactoriness of the present one can be simply illustrated by the fact that the first story in the book, 'The Old School', appears to have been the last thing she completed writing.

This strange mixing of early and late writing might not have mattered if R. G. Geering's 'Afterword' and notes had been more precisely informative. His difficulty was no doubt that the manuscripts don't tell a great deal, and dating even the published stories is difficult. But that he knows more than is offered here can be seen by checking *Southerly*, 1984, where some of these stories first appeared, and where Geering offered more precise information. I can see that the publishers wanted a book which would stand in its own right as fiction for the general reader, not just for the Stead specialist, but in that case there is little excuse for including pieces which are no more than clumsy drafts; nor for mixing fiction and autobiography.

In an interview published in the *Sydney Morning Herald* in 1982 Stead said she was often asked by readers and by publishers to write an autobiography and that her reply was always that she had written it in all her fiction — a statement which is true and not true. It is true in that one can see very plainly which character she identifies with, and which is modelled on her father, her step-mother, her half-brother, her husband, and so on. If one knew more, no doubt more such identifications would be possible. But the peculiarity of fiction, Stead's no less than anyone else's, is that every character draws life from its author and is by that altered, however subtly, from the original. Some of the wilder reaches of the character of Sam Pollit seem to belong more to the daughter than to the father. In becoming the character she became him more extravagantly than he could ever have been himself, revenging herself, perhaps, on the father-power he had once wielded, but at the same time enjoying it, even celebrating it.

On the other hand some of the pieces included here as fiction seem to me to belong properly in the final section, 'Biographical and Autobiographical', because the writing appears to be governed solely by 'what happened' rather than re-imagined into a life and shape of its own. And I feel that that final section belongs in some other book

— a collection which could surely be made of Stead's journalism and interviews.

If I try to abstract the qualities of the writer Christina Stead out of the range of stories offered in this collection I find that mixture of talents, all in a high degree, which prompted Angela Carter (*London Review of Books*, 16 September 1982) to insist on Stead's 'greatness', but which also explain the widespread uncertainty about what is centrally and typically 'Stead'. There is her fascination with language, at times almost for its own sake. There is her sense of history, her alertness to politics and social morality. There is her love of character — a kind of vitality that can ride over and through all worthy and proper discriminations. And then there is her impulse towards simple story-telling — not fiction as a story, but fiction as a container for many stories, one following hard upon another, as they do for example in a piece called 'I Live in You' in which the narrator runs together anecdotes told her by Peter, described in the first sentence as 'a lover, now dead'. He is not the narrator's lover specifically, but a lover at large, and one of his tales, about an undertaker, is one of those very few things you read and know you won't ever forget. Stead's genius here is not in invention; it is in finding a way of using something unspeakable that has come to her second hand.

One story in this collection, 'UNO 1945', appeared first in *Southerly* in 1962 as 'Chapter One of *I'm Dying Laughing*', a novel about the McCarthy years in the United States. Somewhere I've read that it was finished, but not to Stead's satisfaction, and she kept returning to it. This opening chapter is extraordinary because it offers what is usually fatal to fiction — dialogue in which serious political ideas are exchanged. In this case the success springs from the vividness of the characters, Emily and Stephen, husband and wife who quarrel and love one another with ferocious intensity. Instead of the characters seeming mouthpieces for ideas, ideas become aspects of character. As Stead's literary executor, R. G. Geering should see that this novel is edited by someone competent and published without delay.*

---

* It was — by Virago in 1986.

PATRICK WHITE: AUSTRALIA'S UNGRAND OLD MAN

Flaws in the Glass: A Self-Portrait by Patrick White (1981)

Matthew Arnold worried that a literary reputation in England, unconfirmed by 'the whole group of civilised nations' (by which he meant Europe), might be merely provincial. At the same time he was pretty confident about which poets Europe ought, in due course, to favour. Wordsworth was admired at home but not abroad; and since Arnold was sure Wordsworth as a poet in English ranked second only to Shakespeare and Milton, and that among European poets of the eighteenth and nineteenth centuries only Goethe was superior, he anticipated a European recognition of Wordsworth which has never come. Arnold also liked to qualify and trim the literary verdicts which Europe had already handed down. Thus Byron had been overrated; and Goethe's observations on Byron were manipulated by Arnold both to acknowledge a greatness and to set limits on it — a 'splendid personality' in poetry, but a slovenly artist and a childish intellect.

The question of home judgement and the judgement abroad arises frequently in post-colonial literatures, and the case of Patrick White illustrates its complexities. First, how 'Australian' is White? He was born in London but of parents who were both Australians of grazier stock. He returned to Australia during his first year of life and lived in Sydney until the age of thirteen. So far so good. What follows, however, though it can't deprive him of his Australianness, makes him a slightly alien figure. He is sent to an English public school, and later to Cambridge. Coming down from Cambridge, he lives a literary-bohemian life in London, and then joins the RAF during the Second World War. Is the

London Review of Books, October 1981.

man who returns to Australia to live after the war Australian? He is; but he's untypical — and the question whether the Australia he sees is the place most Australians occupy is bound to be asked from time to time.

White had published two novels before going into the RAF. His third, *The Aunt's Story*, came out in 1948 and passed relatively unnoticed. The great acclaim began with *The Tree of Man*, published in 1956. I was living in Australia when news of White's success with English and American reviewers was coming in. Along with everyone else in any way literary I read the novel, I suppose for the same reason. Success in those days meant success somewhere else. The local product, admired only at home, could never be considered quite as seriously as the work that had made its way in a larger world.

Here is a problem for the literary critic in a society emerging from its colonial phase. He can't escape from the judgements uttered abroad. If he disagrees with them (and there have always been disagreements about White), it's difficult simply to shrug them off. They loom too large. He will be tempted to attack them — even to attack the work which attracted them. I don't greatly admire A. D. Hope as a critic, and I'm sure his judgement of *The Tree of Man* was grossly unbalanced: but I think I understand the pressures which prompted him to describe it as 'pretentious and illiterate verbal sludge' when it first appeared, and then to republish that review almost twenty years later when Patrick White won the Nobel Prize. One possible view of White — unfair, no doubt, but not entirely — is that he is praised in Europe because he presents an image of Australia intelligible to the European imagination; and that he is praised in Australia because, although everyone knows how off-centre that image is, nevertheless he makes Australian literature respectable.

If the critic has his problems they are minor compared to the writer's. The critic utters his judgement and goes off to lunch. The writer has to live with it and with the indignation it engenders. Throughout *Flaws in the Glass* there are complaining references, sometimes direct, sometimes oblique, to critics, especially academics, who have failed or refused to understand White's work. That he should have made his commitment to live in Australia when he might very comfortably have lived elsewhere; and that he should have received for this little thanks and years of what looks like envious nit-picking — this, it's quite clear, seems to White a monstrous ingratitude, a further example of the great Australian nastiness.

Anyone who gives a moment's thought to it must feel some sympathy; but White's counter-punches are needless and ill-judged. To give an example: in the course of a passage claiming for himself special insights available only to those who are sexually ambivalent, he writes:

'ambivalence has given me insights into human nature, denied, I believe, to those who are unequivocally male or female — and Professor Leonie Kramer.' A footnote tells us Professor Kramer is an 'Australian academic' — no more. Why she has been singled out for this swipe is unexplained. The reason, I suppose, is that Professor Kramer wrote an unsympathetic piece about *Riders in the Chariot* in *Quadrant* in 1973. It was a very schematized and somewhat tedious exercise — but so is the novel, despite its one or two brilliantly memorable scenes. And in any case, the grumble as it stands is unintelligible. White ought to have expunged it from his book and simply visited Sydney University at night with a spray can.

White is direct, frank and unsensational about his homosexuality, which may well be a key to understanding his work and his life. He grew up in a wealthy family, comfortable, accustomed to servants (English and Scots) to whom he felt attached, undisturbed (he says) but nevertheless driven in on himself by the early recognition of his own sexual ambivalence. There seems to have been affection rather than love between him and his mother; and he records that for most of his early life places, houses and landscapes meant more to him than people.

From this protected environment he was removed to go to his English public school (Cheltenham). He hated it, felt betrayed, and longed for Australia. But on returning home he felt alien and was glad enough, after a couple of years on the land as a jackeroo, to set out again, this time for Cambridge. After Cambridge it was London, haunting the theatres and living the life of the homosexual artist on a generous allowance remitted by his father. Soon he 'moved into the comparatively sumptuous Eccleston Street duplex on the strength of an inheritance; there seemed no reason why literature should exclude pleasure and elegance'. No reason at all, I suppose; but there does seem to have been something trivial about the life White was leading in the late 1930s which gets into the prose of his account:

Joyce painted. Never a talent which threw off the influence of the Slade, she ended up teaching in loony bins. Much of her life she spent in rundown country cottages, far from a water supply and with cats for company. She had a complicated marriage, with a husband who came and went, and worse . . . I remember Betty who deplored Cambridge (with the exception of Kings, because Kings was more Oxford than Cambridge) bursting out with 'I wonder what happens to them all — such pups!' Joyce quietly suggested, 'They grow into dogs, I expect, and marry bitches.'

White's war in the North African desert was dreary on the whole, but it took him to Alexandria where, in July 1941, he met Manoly Lascaris, 'this small Greek of immense moral strength, who became the central mandala of my life's hitherto messy design'. Forty years later they are still together.

When the war ended White wanted to live in Greece. Manoly favoured

Australia, although he had never been there. The novelist wavered, and records that his decision was partly influenced by hunger. For a 'gross character' like himself, the Europe of ration-cards was intolerable. Another deciding factor was that his mother, who professed always to hate Australia, was resolved to live in England when the war ended, and the son 'knew. . . my mother and I could not live in the same hemisphere'.

He settled with Manoly on a few acres at Castle Hill just outside Sydney, where they grew vegetables, fruit and flowers, bred dogs and goats, ran a couple of cows, and were generally unsuccessful small farmers. White wrote his most famous books there (a kind of drudgery which he also describes as 'an escape'), suffered repeated asthma attacks, drank too much, raged, threw saucepans of Irish stew through the kitchen window, felt rejected by Australian critics, and was unhappy.

One is offered little more than passing glimpses of this crucial period of his life; but I suppose domesticity, homosexual or heterosexual, seldom makes substantial copy, and tends to vanish from memory almost while it is happening. In 1963, he and Manoly moved to central Sydney, a house close to Centennial Park which White has continued to enjoy. The years since have been happier, with increasing fame and frequent journeys to Greece which are recorded in detail in the section 'Journeys', making up almost a quarter of the book. Not the least of the things which strike one as odd about *Flaws in the Glass* is that it gives a much more vivid image of Greece than of Australia.

White has learned in old age to play some small part in public life, taking sides with Labor, making speeches, supporting dismissed Prime Minister Gough Whitlam against Governor-General Sir John Kerr (whom he describes as 'a rorty farting old Falstaff'), declaring himself a Republican, and writing a play with strong social overtones. But when the Nobel Prize was awarded to him in 1973 he refused to go to Stockholm to receive it, and the principal reaction recorded here is petulance at being besieged by newsmen.

One of Thomas Hardy's friends or acquaintances, a man who went by the name of Clodd, is reported to have said of him: 'He was a great writer but not a great man. There was no largeness of soul.' It seems a very old-fashioned judgement — we prefer our heroes warty these days — but one can see what Clodd meant. Even on his death-bed Hardy was dictating inept lampoons on his critics. I doubt whether the Nobel Prize, which he was disappointed not to have got, would have made any difference — and it seems to have made little to White. Close on seventy and laden with honours, he is still grumbling. I suppose there is a kind of modesty in that — a failure to take the measure of his own public success, and to recognize that negative judgements are merely an aspect of it. Perhaps, too, it takes just that kind of obsessive and discontented streak to create and sustain the alternative worlds of major fiction. But it doesn't make for impressive autobiography (it didn't in Hardy's case either). So much of White's subject matter seems trivialized here by gossip, occasional bitchiness, and even snobbery, in his anecdotes about people (Joan Sutherland, the Queen, Sidney Nolan, etc), and by a refusal to find excitement or grandeur or anything at all except dreariness in public events. The European will not learn much about Australia from this book; the non-literary person will find little about what it is like to be a writer; and the heterosexual is offered few insights into the nature of the homosexual life.

More than once White argues that homosexuality gives him an advantage as a writer since it permits him to be male or female as his characters and narrative require. This is a familiar argument, and one I have never found entirely convincing. What seems to me at least equally significant is that White's actual experience is homosexual while the most important relationships in his novels (with the exception of *The Twyborn Affair* and perhaps *The Solid Mandala*) are heterosexual. Of course the imagination ought to be able to cross that bridge, either way — but not if it is baulked by envy, resentment or a sense of inferiority. Here is how White imagines he would have been if heterosexual and male:

If an artist, probably a pompous one, preening myself in the psychic mirror for being a success . . . My unequivocal male genes would have allowed me to exploit sexuality to the full. As a father I would have been intolerant of my children, who would have hated and despised me, seeing through the great man I wasn't. I would have accepted titles, orders and expected a state funeral in accordance with a deep-seated hypocrisy I had refused to recognise.

There is a parallel passage about what he might have been if unequivocally female ('an earth mother churning out children . . . passionate, jealous, resentful . . . a whore . . . a nun'). What these passages suggest (and contrary to what he claims for the homosexual temperament) is a difficulty in imagining heterosexual experience except in terms which are either negative or melodramatic.

Australia has produced at least three major novelists since the 1930s — Christina Stead, Xavier Herbert and White. In 1975, two years after White's Nobel award, Herbert published his greatest novel, *Poor Fellow My Country*, and I remember wondering whether Australia had got its Nobel too soon. On reflection, I think it unlikely Herbert would ever have won it. Reverting to the analogy with which I began, Herbert is probably a sort of Wordsworth to White's Byron — the writer destined to be fully intelligible only within the limits of his own language and region. Australians will make their judgement on the relative importance of these writers to the development of their literature and their consciousness of themselves. But that White and Christina Stead have been able to keep the lines of literary communication to Europe open and to keep Australian voices audible in a larger literary world ought to be a matter for celebration.

White's performance as a fiction writer is uneven, and I think I can see in this autobiography some of the elements in his character which lead at times to shallowness, banality and inflation in the writing. What is disappointing about *Flaws in the Glass* is that it offers little evidence of or clue to the writer who can transform himself at times into one of the truly great magicians of the fictional mode.

EIGHT CONTEMPORARY AUSTRALIAN FICTION WRITERS

The Clairvoyant Goat & Other Stories, by Hal Porter (1981)

Every one of these stories bears, printed under its title, the monogram HP. So, it might almost be said, does every one of their sentences. I like an author's style to be distinct, but I'm mildly resistant to being nudged or having my sleeve tugged. And 'style' is not just appearance — it's the declaration of an attitude.

Most of these stories take the form of first person narration, and the narrator is very close indeed to Hal Porter. How he is in real life one doesn't know, but as he chooses to present himself in fiction he's bristling, censorious, witty, illiberal, hating sentiment, and indifferent to charity.

Does one, being of another persuasion, bristle back? It depends how much one enjoys the stories. Somewhere along the way I made a conscious decision to treat his flashes of bitchy blimpery with tolerance and condescension. Or is that a way of saying (I think it may be) that as a writer he pretty soon had the upper hand?

Everything is seen from the outside. Intimacies may be assumed to occur, deep feelings to be registered, but we are never informed of them. 'What's happening in some ill-kept room like the heart', Porter insists, 'is certain to be too coarse for public display.' So it's a world of surfaces; and Antonia Lynn's personal style as it's described in the story 'On a Blue Coast' is surely a close analogue for Porter's literary one:

It's a kind of elusiveness richly veined with the indifference they've noticed she has towards cats and babies and dogs . . . Beneath a vivid public manner and aureole of charm, she seems to conceal another self, an elusive, dodgy and disdainful Antonia. Deep inside the privacy permitted her by the rules of the game is a

Sydney Morning Herald, February 1982.

fastidious *nitouche* with her veils of non sequiturs and persiflage and pleasantries ever-ready to be distractingly fluttered in the faces of simpletons and blunderers.

This external quality, a refusal either to divulge or to respond to personal feeling, I registered at first as a limitation. By the time I'd reached p.163, where Porter acknowledged it in himself, I was so far won over by his writing as to be indifferent to negative definitions.

Yes, I am aware of a hollow and an unworth in both of us, something staring and sightless. We have blocked off, you might say, the ear's innermost chamber which alone picks up the footsteps of the pursuing shadow, the purr of the rising flood, the turning of the dark key in the dark lock. We are spiritually short-winded. Profound sympathy lies at a depth outside our range.

When you can put it as well as that you've earned the right to make your own rules. A statement of limitation is only a way of marking out the boundaries of Porter's excellence.

Not that he is equally and invariably successful. In 'The Girls with Silver Shoes', for example, all his dash and vividness are there; and by acknowledging the 'nastiness' of his subject Porter tries to stand clear of it, not to have it rub off on him. But he can't conceal that he's half in love with the snobbish Misses Fulton, and that he has taken pleasure (enough to elaborate this record of it) in their provincial revenge on a lower-bred contemporary who married wealth and a title.

As a piece of writing 'Lovers Meeting' (to take another example) is extraordinary. I don't know how I could overstate my admiration for its invention, panache, brilliance, ebullience — but all to what a curiously trivial and tasteless end!

No one would read these fictions for the 'story'. Porter trails a few fine threads of narrative, lets them go, returns to them. He's a master of the most sophisticated of fictional methods, one I think of as circumlocution — or perhaps it should be called circumambulation. The narrative revolves in time and in its preoccupations about a central point, wandering far and wide but always coming back.

Porter is also a master of place and of atmosphere. The Côte d'Azur, Rome, Malta, Tokyo, and several Australian locations — they all come up clear and fresh, rich and strange, a composite Porterland.

Like Henry Miller (Porter might detest the comparison) he has learned that to put himself, the only person he knows at all well, centre-stage gives both focus and confidence to something which remains nonetheless fiction — 'fiction' because no claim to veracity is made.

Porter is the kind who gets described as a writers' writer. That's true no doubt, but I think it misrepresents. He's a readers' writer — remembering that real readers are rare. Better than any living English-language fictionist I can think of, he demonstrates how much life there can be just in the writing, how much energy, how much pleasure.

Jimmy Brockett by Dal Stivens (1983)

When this novel first appeared, in 1951, the *Bulletin* still carried the motto 'Australia for the White Man'.

That might be one of Jimmy Brockett's mottoes. Born in the Sydney slums of the 1880s, he has an almost infallible instinct for making what he calls 'coin'. Australia is the great good place. He believes in it and he believes in himself. But there's need for a hundred million 'white men', and irrigation to support them, to keep 'the Chows' who 'breed like rabbits' from 'coming down and taking over'.

Brockett begins as a promoter (and fixer) of fights. He buys up and rents out cheap properties. He gets early into the cinema and film distribution business. He fixes horse races, and he plays games with the sharemarket. He has a 'little black book', and uses blackmail when it helps. He has fingers in Labor's political pie, and starts up his own newspaper.

Brockett tells his own story in his own native idiom. With repetitious archness he refers to himself by name (' "And what's more", I say, "Here's my cheque for two hundred quid to show you Jimmy Brockett means business." '). He thumps his chest, smokes cigars, addresses men friends as 'brother' and women as 'sister', boasts of everything from the cost of his suits to his successes with women, and calls himself 'a graduate from the school of hard knocks'. The language Stivens gives him defines the crudeness, the energy, and even the appeal of the character: 'When it came to getting things done, most of 'em had wishbone instead of backbone, and they had no more business brains than a bandicoot' (p.124). 'He was forty years old, about six-foot-three long, and so thin he could fall through a flute and never strike a note . . . I led him on, and Jerry sat there grinning like a baked possum.' (p.191) 'Monday morning saw me as busy as a magpie in a ploughed paddock . . . I'd recovered my nerve and felt able to kick the backside off an emu.'(p.214)

This momentum in the language perhaps explains why a novel I approached with a feeling of apprehension, even of ennui, in fact took hold of me, and kept hold, throughout its 250 pages. Brockett is revolting, exemplary, and fetching all at once. You groan at his successes and cheer for his enemies; yet it's his story that is being told, and he is the teller.

Technically there is one oddness in the writing. It is, throughout, first-person retrospective narrative, with occasional italicized inserts of obituary reflections written at the time of Brockett's death — these latter casting variously objective lights on Brockett's account of himself. But it's as if an earlier draft of the novel was written in continuous present tense, because the past tense, which is supposed to govern the telling, occasionally and inexplicably breaks up, slipping into present tense and back again.

Sydney Morning Herald, October 1983.

This produces puzzling sentences like 'I'd got the agreement drawn up and I expect to have no trouble at lunch today' (p.76); or 'The Mantis had been waiting daily for me to move now I have Dargan in my little black book' (p.221).

By far the most interesting conflict in the novel, and the one which probably prompted its re-issue, is that between Jimmy and his wife Sadie. Sadie is middle class, intelligent, a free spirit, and an aspiring painter. It's easy to see why she appeals to Brockett; less easy to believe in his attraction for her — though there is a sort of naive innocence about him which, together with his energy, can be seen as explaining it. Once married, however, trouble begins. The year is 1908. He expects a submissive and child-bearing wife. She declares she's tired of being a woman and being with women. 'I want to compete with men in a man's world. The only talent I have is my art. Just be patient, Jimmy, while I give it a try.'

He regards this as a whim and expects it to pass. But when she tells him she's not sure she loves him, and won't have a child until she is sure, his ego is wounded. He pressures journalists to write sympathetically of her work, but he does this in a crude and obvious way which he knows will have the reverse effect. She gets bad reviews, loses confidence, comes to heel, gives him the child he wants, and dies giving birth to it while he is entertaining himself with another woman.

The curve the narrative follows is of the rise of Brockett to power, wealth and influence, and then the gradual destruction, not of his money and property, which continue to accumulate, but of his health, his happiness, and his self-esteem. His first real defeat comes in the political field, when a man he has blackmailed at last turns the tables on him and he loses public office. His grandiose schemes for immigration and irrigation now thwarted, his sense of purpose in his own life is invested more and more in the son Sadie has given him — but there too disappointment and disaster wait.

There is a second marriage, but guilt and ill health render him impotent. The last images are of a twenty-six-stone bundle of contradictions who can still rise sometimes to the kind of inventive wickedness that has made him at once the hero and the villain of his own narrative. Asked by a lawyer why, if he dislikes his brother so much, he is leaving him anything at all (the bequest is £200, which will be deeply disappointing), Brockett replies that he has done it to ensure the brother will be there for the reading of the will — a will which concludes with the instruction that he is to be buried face-down, so that anyone who dislikes his bequests can kiss Brockett's arse.

A novel which reads as well as this one does thirty years after its first publication deserves another thirty years of life at least — and will probably have it.

Child's Play with *Eustace* and *The Prowler,* by David Malouf (1982)

David Malouf's prose is not without odd lapses (a misrelated something-or-other in the first sentence of the book puts a stream instead of a farmhouse up for sale); and on the other hand he can slip at times into 'fine writing' of the fiddly filigree kind that may set your teeth on edge. But by far the predominant effect is of precision, clarity, sharp edges, even a kind of austerity which he may have learned in part from some of the great modern Italian fiction writers, especially Alberto Moravia and Mario Soldati.

'Child's Play', the short novel which takes up most of the book, is set in Italy, where Malouf now lives, and perhaps illustrates both the advantages and disadvantages of the expatriate (or immigrant) sensibility. We see, hear, touch and smell a physical environment that is uniquely and vividly Italian. Would an Italian writer give us so sharp a sense of place? At least it would be different. Malouf's Italy is like Patrick White's Côte d'Azur or Hal Porter's Malta — a Mediterranean scene real to a point that borders on the surreal, or super-real.

But Malouf's narrator is Italian, a terrorist whose task, for no clear reason, is to gun down a great Italian man of letters. The build-up to 'the event', as it's euphemistically called, is convincing, full of tensions that give this story something of the excitement of a good thriller, with none of the thinness of texture common to that genre. What one misses is any sense of why the young man has become a killer. Is he motivated by a sense of pity for the world's victims? Of social injustice? Of history? Or by something more personal?

At one point the narrator says of himself and his associates in the terrorist gang

We are workers, technologists; young people of good health, clear of spirit, and with no grudges, no phobias, no sense of personal injustice or injury, none of those psychological or physical defects that are so dear to the hearts of journalists and so comforting to their readers . . . What we bring to the office is a steely impersonality that belongs to our role as killers.

This is one of those ideas that appeal to the intellect and on reflection must be seen as quite implausible. No one 'clear of spirit and with no grudges' becomes a willing secret killer — or not outside the bounds of those old patriotic wars we no longer have which used to render the enemy abstract and the issues simple.

Yet to go below those surfaces which Malouf so lucidly and lucently displays, to reveal (as Moravia does, for example, with his young terrorist in *The Time of Desecration*) the psychological and social springs of Brigate

Sydney Morning Herald, July 1982.

Rosse action, would require a knowledge of the Italian temperament and of the subtleties of Italian society which an immigrant, who has a foreign language as well as foreign customs to penetrate, could scarcely hope to possess.

Here I suspect is the reason why 'Child's Play' strikes one as brilliant (I'm indeed grateful to its author and glad to have read it) and yet curiously self-enclosed, almost a game, a clever exercise. This is not a fiction about Italy, or terrorism, but about fiction — about itself. The terrorist gradually comes to see himself as a mirror image of the great writer he must kill. He and his Beretta automatic are, in some sense never made clear, the logical and inevitable end towards which his victim's life and writing have been moving. He is a part of the writer's work, and its conclusion.

Again it's the intellect this appeals to, while something like common sense or common humanity rejects it as pretentious. The sense of what makes a nice pattern has replaced observation and humane intuition as the determinant of the novelist's truth.

In the two shorter fictions, 'Eustace' and 'The Prowler', the scene, vivid and exact, is more than ever peopled by shadows. Taken as a satire on the psychology of the suburbs, 'The Prowler' tells the same kind of truth (or half-truth) we might expect from a good essayist. Idea, I think, has been superimposed upon that texture of intractable, ungraspable reality which is life as we know it in our bones to be, and which we expect our best imaginative writers not to explain (do we ever quite believe the explainers?) but rather to put before us in such a way as to give us what Edmund Wilson calls 'the shock of recognition'.

The Birthday Gift, by Thomas Shapcott (1982)

This novel about twin brothers, Ben and Benno Meredith, is preceded by a note in which the author says 'This is a work of fiction . . . There is in the book no representation of any real person, either living or dead.'

Notes like that are usually written when fiction is running close enough to fact to cause anxiety. Ben Meredith is born on 21 March 1935, under the sign of Aries. So was Thomas Shapcott. The older twin, Benno, born on 20 March, is a Pisces. Shapcott's poem 'Portrait of a Younger Twin' includes the lines 'the hour that pushed us out allotted us separate stars, / two days of birth'. That note preceding the novel says 'the characters of the fiction have become themselves'. No doubt they have; but it seems they have undeniable origins in Shapcott's life. And in fact

Sydney Morning Herald, September 1982.

it was the sense that I was reading something like a personal chronicle that sent me in search of his date of birth.

Novels springing from autobiography mostly turn out more difficult than their authors expect. Things keep demanding to go in because they happened rather than because an inner artistic logic requires them. The tail of fact wants to wag the dog of fiction.

The Birthday Gift has two structures, one to deal with time, the other with personality. The time structure begins in 1941 when the twins are six, and moves forward in a succession of fixes on (in turn) 1945-6, 1947-50, 1952, and 1954, as if we are turning the pages of a family album. But between these come three sections dated 1959 when the twins are twenty-four, one married and living in Sydney, the other sorting himself out sexually in Italy — and it is to 1959 we're returned in the book's final section.

It may well be that the novel was first written simply chronologically, and then the 1959 section broken up and distributed through the sequence. If so, it was a sensible shaping device, establishing early on a feeling of moving purposefully towards a conclusion.

The Meredith twins are not identical but complementary. Ben is smaller, dark, sensitive, egotistical, Benno large, blond, affable, athletic. Ben is artistic (a composer in due course). Benno is a good, straight, no-frills Queenslander.

The birthday gift they receive at the age of six is a see-saw. Inevitably it does double duty — both plaything and symbol. When Ben is up, Benno's down, and vice versa. Or they hang suspended in fleeting and inconclusive moments of equilibrium.

In the novel's second paragraph we're told about the birth dates and the separate astral signs — Ben born in Aries, Benno in Pisces. On the second page we find them riding their trikes, Benno behaving like a ram, Ben like a fish:

Benno always barged ahead first go, then bumped as hard as he could at the end where the little brick wall held the straggly cannas in some sort of check . . . Ben preferred to weave in tidal ripples, like a fish.

This is confusing. Was there, I wondered, a misprint somewhere, a Ben for a Benno? But no. As it turns out (the Zodiacal signs return at intervals) the brothers' personalities are, or seem, contradictions of the signs. Benno, the Pisces, is a ram; Ben, the Aries, is a sinuous swimmer. If the reader is puzzled he's relieved to find that by 1952 Ben is too: 'Somehow even the stars had got them mixed up, wrong.'

But there is more than the hint of a resolution. In one of the 1959 sections Benno hears a talk in the local library about the prophecies of Nostradamus. One such refers to Arethusa, on which the lecturer comments:

'Arethusa is the abode of the water or fountain deity as well as the name of the deity itself. Or is it a pun on Ares, god of war? Or even on Aries, the zodiacal sign? Now it is interesting that the sign of Pisces, the Fish, one of the water symbols, is immediately adjacent to the sign of Aries, the Ram . . .

'You see it would be quite possible to interpret this whole prophecy in such lights to say something like: Two brothers, in a time of global unrest, will be caught in warfare; they are fighting for supremacy to a ritual throne . . .'

The 1959 sections are all called 'Arethusa'. This is the year for the twins of resolution and self-discovery.

I'm not sure what this grandiose symbolic structure adds to my understanding of the characters, and I suspect it's a case of the will trying to do the work of the imagination. Ben and Benno are two pretty ordinary chaps, living pretty ordinary lives, and it's all told in pretty ordinary prose. What's best in the novel is its regional element, the feeling it gives of Queensland tested on the senses. And of course anyone interested in Shapcott the poet will want to read it for whatever light it may cast on the writing for which he's best known.

Mr Scobie's Riddle, by Elizabeth Jolley (1983)

Comedy keeps a hold on reality; farce is a parody of it. This novel is a comedy with tragic overtones and something like a farcical sub-plot.

It concerns four inmates and the matron of an old folks' home. Three of the four, Mr Scobie of the title, Mr Hughes, and Mr Privett, seem to arrive at the home by accident when the ambulance they are travelling in crashes outside its door. All three are eighty-five, and they are soon anxious to escape.

Mr Hughes spends much time on the lavatory, calling plaintively and vainly to be helped back to bed. His favourite memory is of driving a truck loaded with bricks. The movement of the bricks made a soft noise that reminded him of 'snow in the blizzard snittering on the window panes of the attic room he . . . shared with his brothers when he was a boy in Wales'.

Mr Privett, who is the first to attempt a getaway, wants to return home to his duck and his hen, called Hep and Hildegarde, about whom he frequently breaks into curious songs and chants. His son, home after twenty-three years' absence, has succeeded in having the old house pulled down and replaced, and the old man removed into the care of a hospital.

Mr Scobie has also been tricked out of his home by greedy relatives.

Sydney Morning Herald, January 1983.

He plays classical music to himself on cassette tapes, quotes the Bible, longs for home, remembers his favourite music pupil with whom he was once and quite by accident found in compromising circumstances, and thinks of the little hill behind his home which he now regrets never having climbed.

Mr Hughes's bricks, Mr Privett's pet poultry, and Mr Scobie's hill are like flavours or essences of life carried with them into the enforced limbo of the hospital. They are victims of their families, of society at large, and of Matron Price, as is Miss Hailey, the eccentric writer in the pith helmet who looks to Mr Scobie for intellectual companionship.

Miss Hailey, formerly headmistress of a girls' school, has long since been trapped in a scandal with one of her pupils, and has signed away everything to her old friend Matron Price in whose establishment she is now condemned to spend the rest of her days. And Matron Price hopes soon to obtain a signature from Mr Scobie which will see his assets bequeathed to her.

So much for the tragi-comedy, which, for all its gusto and extravagance, tries hard to look something like life as we know it. Under it there runs the farcical sub-plot, consisting of an exchange of messages between Matron Price and Night Sister M. Shady (unregistered) by which we learn that the occupants of Room 3, among whom are Matron Price's brother, a retired Lt. Colonel of unsound mind, and Night Sister Shady's mother, Mrs Morgan, play cards for money between midnight and 4 a.m. every night in the dinette. Here Lt. Colonel Price, another of his sister's victims, loses regularly, until the ownership of the old folks' home appears to be in doubt.

The symbolism is not obtrusive but it is unmistakable. Matron Price must herself pay the price to the Shady Night Sister and the game of chance played in the hours of darkness. Why in reality she should tolerate such white-anting of her security is not a question we are invited to consider. This is a novel about death.

One by one the old men die. The deaths are recorded in a deliberately perfunctory way which matches the mixture of indifference and opportunism that has surrounded their last days. It is a view of life as bleak as that of Ben Jonson's *Volpone*, and with a similar dark gusto, as if intellect and sensibility were at war in the writer, one negative, the other affirming.

For me there is a little too much striving and ingenuity in this novel. It is lively, but perhaps over-strenuous in its determination that there should be never a dull moment and never a merely conventional one. Yet nothing can diminish the sharpness with which its five principal characters are put before us, nor the vividness with which place and circumstance are set down. The mechanics may be less than perfect, but the prose is marvellous. It's a reminder of something reassuring: a natural writer, such as Elizabeth Jolley is, can make tactical errors and still the mark of her talent is there, distinct in the writing, a direct transmission of her abundant sense of life.

The Bodysurfers, by Robert Drewe (1983)

On the cover of this book Manning Clark is quoted saying, 'These disturbing stories explore what goes on beneath the glamour and glitter of our lives . . .'.

I don't think 'explore' is quite the right word. They represent a glittering surface, and they give a sickening sense that it's brittle. What's underneath is not explored — it's only glimpsed, or hinted at. The fear is there may be nothing underneath.

The satiric mode is enormously tempting to sharp, visual, witty intelligences like Robert Drewe's. It's like a special gear, a kind of overdrive he slips easily in and out of. Along with the temptation to use it goes, no doubt, the fear of being shallow, or slick. ('I look at the mountains,' Katherine Mansfield records in her journal, 'I try to pray, and I think of something *clever*.') Drewe is not shallow — he's too accurate and detailed an observer for that — though he may sometimes leave you wondering what he finds it possible to be affirmative about. Better that lingering doubt, however, than pieties, moralism, and false comfort. The humour may be black, but it's never bitter.

The stories are loosely connected by the common denominator of the beaches which provide the settings and (perhaps) the symbolism, and by the Lang family, three generations, who appear in the foreground or background of all but two. The connexions are not forced or obvious, and not essential. Each story stands on its own. But together they lend weight to one another.

In the first story, set back in the 1940s, we see Rex Lang giving his three young children Christmas dinner in a hotel dining room after the death of his wife. In the last paragraph the children, waiting for him in the car, see through a window the hotel manageress combing his hair where his paper hat has ruffled it. Why should she not, and why should he not take comfort from it? But that window offers the motherless children a glimpse of the world of human love and deceit they must enter. Nine stories and many years later Rex Lang is dead and we are shown his grandson, floored by the discovery of a lesbian love poem in his girlfriend's handbag, reflecting that he was only just getting used

Sydney Morning Herald, December 1983.

to the idea that his parents made love to one another when he had to come to terms with the fact that they made love to other people.

In the intervening stories we have seen Rex Lang's sons in and out of beds and marriages, jealous, and occasioning jealousy. Max checks the level of the bottle of baby oil his woman friend uses for sensual massage, suspecting that she's lying when she tells him she no longer makes love to Brian, with whom she lives. His suspicion is more than confirmed. He discovers that the unseen Brian is marking the levels on the same bottle. In a later story we see Brian after the inevitable breakup, and consequent breakdown, trying and failing to regain sanity alone in a beach cottage.

David, Rex's other son, and Angela, both sophisticated, liberated academics, take sabbatical leave in California. David talks nostalgically to his three children about the birth of the protest movement in that area, 'with Joan Baez, Bob Dylan and Co.'. 'Protesting against what?' one of the children asks.

A few years on and David and Angela have parted. Now he's on a New South Wales beach with Lydia, who rubs sun-tan cream into her naked breasts. He knows he's supposed to take this calmly, and that 'ogling was out of the question'. But inwardly he's asking himself how did those nipples 'which had been used sexually to tempt him at 3.00 a.m. suddenly at 11.30 become neutral as elbows'.

By the time he's twenty David's son Paul is looking back whimsically on his father's hopes that he might grow to be a kind of heterosexual Hockney, recorder in paint of Australian surf rather than Californian pools. What have those fatherly ambitions of the seventies to do with unemployment, that lesbian love poem in his girlfriend's handbag, and the lump he has just discovered in a private place?

These are stills from an action-packed movie called, perhaps, Social Change. None of the characters can quite keep pace with the action — but out there, at least, the surf, sun, and sand remain constant.

Robert Drewe's stories are always accurate and sensitive, often comic, at moments brilliant, documents of a modern affluent malaise most of us (readers of books and review pages) inherit, or to which we aspire.

Hostages: Stories, by Fay Zwicky (1983)

In the best of these stories, 'Stopover', one that seems to say very much more than is said literally, a couple in transit between Sydney and Chicago with their two children wait at Honolulu for their onward flight. The

Sydney Morning Herald, July 1983.

airport is full of men returned from Vietnam. The children want icecreams and are refused because the call to their plane may come at any moment. The woman wishes they had never left Australia. Bloodstains on the wall of the hotel room they have spent the night in seem to her to represent America. She's troubled by the grim silence of the soldiers, the sense of horrors they must have come from, and the fact that they take no notice of the children. An Englishman talks to her about Chicago, reinforcing her fears about their destination. For a moment the children vanish and she panics. Her husband rushes off in search of them. The little girl reappears. Snatched up by her mother, sensing fear, the child fixes her eyes on the Englishman and begins to scream.

There is unusual concentration in these nine pages. Here the anxiety which in different ways is present in all Zwicky's stories is generalized. What is continuous is her sense of being 'in transit', uncertain, with the knowledge that chaos or gratuitous violence exists somewhere just out of sight, and with the sense that it might almost be a relief to have to confront it directly.

Some of Zwicky's stories locate her insecurity retrospectively in her childhood in Melbourne at the time of the Second World War — 'a Jew who has everything', as she's told, but to whom her mother says, 'They're making them into lampshades over there'. The child is asked to behave generously to a poor Jewish refugee woman. With believable adolescent contrariness she refuses, but then is consumed with secret grief for 'my innocent victim and our shared fate'. A schoolteacher is shocked when the child writes an essay romanticizing the Nizam of Hyderabad ('burnished, jewel-studded, barbaric, irresistible') — a despot who imprisons and murders his opponents. 'Surely you of all people', the teacher complains, 'should be aware that a war has just been fought to defend us all from fascism.'

The other problems, of course, have to do with love and sex. The child discovers feelings of something like romantic attachment towards Teddy, their lady-help's newest friend. She visits his flat and discovers he's living there with another woman. In another story her mother announces she's going to marry again on the very day when 'the grocer's boy unbuttoned his fly and showed me the most amazing thing'. The question is, Can women live without men? Grandmother says no. Mother says yes, but then why is she remarrying? The child is sent to stay with a friend of the family, a Miss Vizard who lives alone except for a single woman servant. Miss Vizard is surviving on her own, but the child discovers her secret — a religious mania with heavy sexual overtones.

After these childhood stories we take a leap forward to 'Stopover', and then to two stories about the breakup of a marriage — not entirely successful as fiction, but interesting because Zwicky is interesting, and because she has said in her Preface that she can't claim the usual immunity of pretending that her characters are not based on real people. The husband describes his wife as 'always looking thunderously angry about something', as someone who thinks too much, and as 'frigid'. How she sees him is less clearly stated. He seems distant, precise, controlled, as if her 'frigidity' might be the echo of some failure on his part — but these are mere notations towards a fiction that has not been written.

The last stories are less interesting. There is a piece of social realism about a young man getting married; a story about a metropolitan writer visiting West Australia. It doesn't all quite add up to a 'book'. But Zwicky the poet is there in her prose, forthright, honest, intelligent, anxious, and puzzled — the excellent woman who says of herself in one of her poems

> Heart's death old hat,
> Mine has died time and again tending experience,
> Absurd handmaiden to the absurd.

The Children Must Dance, by Tony Maniaty (1984)

Every writer must learn to live with the tricks of style in vogue when he or she came to literary consciousness. They go out of date, but whatever we do with them they remain indelibly part of our makeup. Tony Maniaty's (he was born in Brisbane in 1949) are those of the 1960s. This means among other things that clarity is avoided in favour of a rich opacity. Not only expository passages in this novel but dialogue as well are sometimes so puzzling the reader is left wondering how it is that the characters appear to understand one another.

The style is hard-boiled, oblique, world-weary, portentous — a sort of updated Graham Greene, tie-less, in sneakers and jeans. We are to read on because there's mystery, a thriller element, a degree of narrative urgency. But we are to understand that these events imply larger truths than just a solution to the mystery of whether Dr Sam Goddard, uncle to the hero Nicholas Ranse, committed suicide or was murdered. Goddard, dead on the tropical post-Portuguese-colonial island of Inhumas (somewhere 'north of Darwin') represents Ranse's childhood in Brisbane, and his death perhaps symbolizes other and larger matters as well. The writing is so like a blind boil, swollen with undischarged significance, there were times when I hesitated over such recognitions as, for example, that the dead man is Ranse's 'uncle Sam', or that his name begins with

Sydney Morning Herald, June 1984.

'God'. Were these signals the author expected me to pick up and pursue? Or was his persistent portentousness engendering parallel bad habits in his reader?

Inhumas, like Graham Greene's Haiti, has a hotel where foreigners and sophisticated locals meet, drink, and exchange laconic intelligence. At the Tropicana Ranse mixes with Aggett, a British journalist, Eduardo, the island's youthful Chief of Security, da Cunha, Minister of Information, Maria Mendonca, the sad cynical Portuguese woman whose cupidity has brought about her colonial exile, Louis Culpeper, a retired military man, and especially the sexy and enticing Teppy Zervos, his uncle's ex-mistress and the wife of an opportunist Greek businessman.

Ranse allows Teppy Zervos to seduce him, and wonders, on the grounds of no evidence apparent to this reader, whether she is his uncle's murderer. But while these questions of Dr Goddard's death preoccupy Ranse, the island's civil war continues. The revolutionary Fragas are the Government; but in the countryside the counter-revolutionary Livres are gaining ground.

Dr Goddard's house on Inhumas, Ranse discovers, is like a replica of the one he occupied in Brisbane when he lived as a comfortable academic scientist and brought up his orphaned nephew. Ranse now reads his uncle's diaries, looking for clues to the death which has been officially described as suicide. With Eduardo and Aggett he travels into the hills in search of Goddard's grave, but they are driven back by the civil war, and the episode seems curiously without point.

The novel is studded with stylistic devices, including irritating passages where the dialogue is delivered as a play script. It is rich in atmosphere and at times the narrative is gripping. It's also hard work, at once opaque enough and pregnant enough to make any reader lacking in confidence blame himself for its author's failings. That's a negative way of acknowledging that Tony Maniaty has talent. There is a density in his writing, a texture, which I admire. He probably deserves a more generous welcome than I am giving him. He also deserves the literary equivalent of a boot in the backside for sentences like the following, which is only marginally worse than many others in the novel: 'The year was starched by heat, but they swam on a road ground smoother than any spice.'

As for that final scene in which the President's mysterious mistress, Ancora Dias, with 'perfectly conical breasts' and 'teeth like marble', emerges from a closet bearing a knife and launches herself at our hero — I think I know how it all ends, but even after careful re-readings I'm not absolutely certain.

FOUR BRITISH NOVELISTS

Innocence by Penelope Fitzgerald (1986)
The Dresden Gate by Michael Schmidt (1986)

The art of fiction is to represent. It creates a world out of fragments
and details, like the dots which, joined together, make a picture. There
may be flood or famine, but the reader enters or leaves at will, and
with complete immunity. Some nagging part of the mind, both in reader
and writer, usually insists that the world a novel creates should have
significance beyond, itself. But that it should seem real is always more
compelling than that it should seem significant. Or to put it another
way, nothing seems quite so significant as the sense that something real
has been plucked out of the continuum and set down.

What is real, however, only exists for us in the act of perception
— our own or someone else's. For something to be perceived there must
be a perceiving mind. Whatever burden the novelist's sentences carry
by way of 'meaning', they must be his or her sentences and no one else's
— as distinct as a face or a fingerprint.

Finally, there is the element of narrative. Forster said, 'Oh dear yes,
I'm afraid the novel tells a story.' No doubt he was right to sigh about
the artificialities which a beginning, a middle and an end impose upon
our sense of what life is like. Often the detail seems real when the design
does not. But the art of fiction is also the art of narrative — not necessarily
of one large narrative, but certainly of many small ones, like the steel
rods which invisibly hold the concrete together. Long stories, like long
poems, are really aggregations of short ones.

Penelope Fitzgerald's *Innocence* is set in Florence. The principal characters

London Review of Books, October 1986.

are Italian. She knows quite a lot about Italian society; but more important, she has somehow got inside her Italian characters, so that when a young Englishwoman appears on the scene she seems really a foreigner and not, as one might expect, the focus of the novel's consciousness.

Innocence is a novel which imposes its own slow pace on the reader. Probably that means one has a sense that nothing we are told is insignificant. It has, not opacity, but density. It is a book that never seems to settle back, as so much currently admired fiction does, into a conventional exercise, fiction as a pastiche of itself, a comfortable armchair for the somnolent reviewer.

The time is 1955. Centre-stage are a young doctor, Salvatore Rossi, and a young woman just out of school, Chiara Ridolfi. They fall quite violently in love, and marry. There is some deft movement back and forward in time, giving us their respective backgrounds. Chiara is heir to a house of faded nobility. Salvatore is the son of a village communist. He has resolved when very young to have nothing to do with politics. Nevertheless he is enraged to find himself helplessly in love with the Ridolfi scion — and Fitzgerald clearly enjoys doing characters whose impatience borders on passion and whose passion compels anti-social behaviour. Chiara's English school-friend, a young woman known as Barney, is another character in that mould. Compulsive and overbearing, she falls in love with Chiara's taciturn cousin, Cesare, who runs the family winery — and tells him so, offering to marry him. It looks as if the novel is heading for a parallel pairing; but disconcertingly Cesare doesn't respond, except to indicate that he knows Barney loves him. By one hint only (and Fitzgerald requires us to read attentively) it is signalled that Cesare, though sympathetic to Barney, is in love with Chiara. This in turn explains his otherwise inexplicable behaviour at the dramatic climax.

But there is an older story than the one we are being told. In the late sixteenth century the Count Ridolfi was a midget. He married a midget and they produced a midget daughter. To save the child from a sense of inadequacy they employed only midgets. She was to be protected from the world of full-sized people. They acquired for her a midget companion, whom she loved — but then at some point in childhood the companion put on what is called these days a 'growth spurt'. What should be done about it? The midget daughter, believing her companion's size to be a misfortune, suggested she should be blinded so she would not see what 'ordinary' people looked like, and cut off at the knees so that her deformity would not be excessive.

We are told all this in the opening pages. But what happened? It is not until late in the novel that one of the Ridolfi houses is more or less requisitioned by the Italian Tourist Board. For a tourist brochure a version of the sixteenth-century story more palatable than the real one is invented, telling how the companion child escaped over the wall. By that, and the fact that a communist novelist wants to make a film about how a 'child of the people' was mutilated by corrupt aristocrats, we acquire — obliquely, because it is not directly stated — an answer to the question which those opening pages has left us with.

But are the Ridolfi cruel mutilators of the people? They are represented in fact as vague, well-intentioned and inconsequential. Chiara's Aunt Mad runs an asylum for homeless old women and orphaned babies, her idea being that the old women will enjoy looking after the babies. They do, but won't later give them up, hiding them in cupboards and washing baskets. Even those ancient dwarf Ridolfis were absent-mindedly thinking of their daughter's happiness, and she of her companion's 'misfortune', when they agreed to the removal of her eyes and lower legs. The 'innocence' of the title belongs as much to the Ridolfi as to 'the people'. In both it is a quality to be feared.

There is of course something bizarre about all this. Fitzgerald's view of the world is witty and arcane. But do the two parts of the story — the sixteenth century and the twentieth — join? They do, I think; but the link is made with the subtlest of strokes.

What is it that especially fascinates Fitzgerald in her two central characters? It is partly just their human uniqueness; but there is an 'idea' there as well, and I think it is that these Italians are not free (are less free, even, than Britons) of their past. Though Salvatore has in effect renounced the family politics, he is still 'a child of the people'. And though Chiara's family is in hopeless decline, she cannot help being a Ridolfi. They fall in love as human individuals; but they bring with them into marriage their respective histories. In a state of paranoia as the climax of the story approaches, Salvatore is thinking about Chiara: 'But he would hardly have thought it possible that at nineteen — even though she loved him, which of course gave her an unfair advantage — she would have known how to cut down a grown man.' *Cut down.* The phrase occurs so casually it would be easy not to notice it; but it is surely not there by accident — and it makes the link between the old story and the modern one. Is the explosive Salvatore another victim of the Ridolfi 'innocence'? Or of his own? Or need there be no victim at all?

The novel ends one way, but goes so close to ending another, it seems to offer two opposite answers to its own implied questions. In effect it asks questions rather than answering them. It is a book of strange, muted power and intelligence.

Michael Schmidt doesn't make entry to *The Dresden Gate* easy. For quite some time I was totally confused about how the various characters related one to another. And I never understood how these people with Spanish names in an unspecified South or Central American country looked to Paris as their city of origin. Nor was I absolutely sure about when

it was all supposed to be happening. The jacket reveals that it is set
in Mexico in the early twentieth century at the outbreak of the Mexican
Revolution. I was glad of that information, but I think I should have
had it from the novel. I recognize the problem. Explanatory writing
can stop a novel in its tracks. It can destroy an atmosphere. Still I think
a little professional cunning would have found a way around the problem.

But the novel soon establishes its own reality — something clearly
based on a history and a geography, but holding itself apart from them
as well. Perhaps that too is a problem. How far are the events to be
seen simply as representation, and how far are they meant to be symbolic,
or allegorical — to speak politically but at large? This is a question
which even the end of the novel did not answer for me.

One other complaint. It is not first person narrative, but the central
consciousness is that of a boy. He begins as an infant and is about seventeen
when the novel ends — but he never acquires a name. Throughout, he
is 'he' or 'the boy'. This is a conscious stratagem, and again it seems
to push the novel beyond realism towards allegory. But I found it awkward
and obtrusive, especially since everyone else in the novel has a name.

The boy is the son of Don Raoul and Paula. Paula is an heiress, and
though her family have disowned her because of her marriage, they have
provided the money with which Don Raoul has bought a huge and derelict
sugar estate, El Encantada. Paula has followed her husband from Europe
out to the estate, bringing with her his intellectual brother Alex, and
a cousin, Thérèse. Alex is in love with Paula, and Thérèse with Alex.
Two years after the boy is born Paula escapes back to Europe, never
to return. For some years the boy is looked after by Thérèse and a peasant
girl. As he grows older Alex becomes his tutor, while Thérèse withdraws
into solitariness and silence. A companion is found for the boy among
the children of the peons who work on the estate; but when companionship
turns into friendship they are cruelly separated.

As the novel goes on the estate declines, Don Raoul grows more than
ever aloof from his son, and the boy's mentor Alex succumbs gradually
to tuberculosis. The boy's obsession is with his mother who deserted
him and whom he is said to resemble; but no one will talk to him about
her. In his middle teens he is sent on a religious retreat, and his manner
suggests to the brothers who run the monastery that he might have a
vocation. After weeks of careful consideration he goes to confession,
as required, and declares that he has nothing to confess. He tries to explain
that to invent sins for the confessional would be sinful, but he is sent
home in disgrace.

Alex dies, followed at once by Thérèse. The father is now prepared
for the son he has ignored to become co-*patron* of the estate, but the
boy, seeming to belong to no one, neither to his parents, nor to his
country, nor to Europe, nor to God, sinks into a depression so extreme

that it brings him near to death. When he begins to recover he goes out night after night and learns the topography of the cane fields in darkness, wishing that he could belong to the land, like a peon:

He prayed that his blood might run thicker and his skin turn dark . . .
Was he not born here? Was he not abandoned? He was an orphan and the land should claim him . . . How could he become wholly of the land? Kneeling there in his black hat and coat, he felt as pain the blondness of his hair, the blueness of his eyes.

He decides to kill his father and make the estate serve those who work on it. But before he can carry out this plan revolution sweeps across the land. Don Raoul is shot, and in the last scene the boy is in an upstairs room of the hacienda with the crowd waiting below. Is he to go down shouting 'Long Live the Revolution!'?

He would descend with them into the burning courtyard of his house and offer them his hand. They would surely welcome him among them.
Or he would sit quite still at the window, staring north to El Abanice and the mine whose circling walls still looked to him like a castle, suspended above the rustling cane, and turning up his eyes take in that blue, that cooling distance.
He had a choice: he could go down, he could sit still.

This ending characterizes for me an ambiguity in the novel. If I understand it (and I'm not absolutely sure I do) the point is that the boy can be *of* the new land, but only if he renounces Europe (the mine walls in the second alternative still look 'like a castle') and becomes one with the people. In this the boy has become a symbol of the post-colonial consciousness — something with which I ought to be able to identify. But I am bothered by a feeling that the real situation does not in fact support the general point it is supposed to make. In real terms the statement 'He had a choice' is untrue; or if true, of no consequence. Whatever the boy does, the peons who have just killed his father will kill him. It is, I suppose, possible the novelist intends us to understand that. The colonist's dream of becoming 'one with the land' is a piece of false romanticism. If that is the case the point is lost for lack of clarity.

My problem thoughout was that I enjoyed the novel at its realist level, which is rich in detail and strong in the impressions it leaves; and I was correspondingly irritated when I felt the real was being marshalled and trimmed to make an abstract point. I found, for example, the solitariness and silence of the characters, which served the novel at a symbolic level, too extreme and prolonged to be believed. Symbolism, if that was what it was, undermined the fictional world on which it depended.

This novel is put together in spare, evocative, brooding sentences, sombre, but sombrely lyrical. I admired the prose and I enjoyed the story.

229

But even there something felt wrong. The writing is, I think, repetitious. Its cadences, beautiful in their way, are endlessly the same. It needed some relief, some variation of tone, an occasional lift, even a laugh, if only for contrast.

But it remains true that *The Dresden Gate* is more interesting than most novels one reads — the work of a real writer, a poet, who draws on unusual knowledge.

Family and Friends, by Anita Brookner (1986)
Still Life, by A. S. Byatt (1985)

In the Thames Television run-up to the 1985 Booker Prize presentation these two novels were mentioned by Claire Tomalin, literary editor of the London *Sunday Times*, as titles that might or should have made the short-list. Anita Brookner won the 1984 prize with *Hotel du Lac*. *Still Life* is the sequel to A. S. Byatt's *The Virgin in the Garden* published in 1978 and since re-issued as a King Penguin.

Brookner was Slade Professor of Art History at Cambridge and is now Professor at the Courtauld Institute in London. Finding the annual three-month vacation empty and intolerable she has taken to writing a novel each summer to fill the gap. There are now five, and she has a distinct and growing reputation. Just prior to her 1984 Booker Prize win the *Literary Review* ran an interview with her in which she contradicted the interviewer when he referred to her as a successful woman. She brushed aside her brilliant academic career now augmented by a literary one. Success, she said, meant doing well what you wanted to do. And in her case, the interviewer asked, what was that? She would like, Brookner answered, to have married and had six sons.

There was possibly an element of deliberate coat-trailing in that — rejection of feminist appropriation, and consequent misreading, of her work. But anyone who has read her novels will recognize the authentic Brookner note of gloomy candour, and will accept that she was stating, as it seemed to her, a simple emotional truth. It is a candour I admire and applaud; but my admiration is tinged with the recognition that a person of her temperament who had married and had six sons would almost certainly be lamenting that she had not become an art historian and novelist.

Brookner's novels have usually been about an intelligent woman, her unsatisfactory relations with other people (including men), her consequent

New Zealand Listener, March 1986.

loneliness, and the stratagems for survival by which she lives. They are elegant, if rather elderly, in language, well-structured, and everywhere informed by Brookner's cool clear intelligence. Women in like situations often find them compulsively readable (there is a relation, I suppose, to Jean Rhys). I respect them but I find them hard going — depressing, and alien to my sense of the world and of human resourcefulness.

Family and Friends is at least superficially something new. It is about a European (possibly Jewish?) family living in Britain. The lives of four children are surveyed, in a curiously timeless present-tense narrative, from childhood through to middle age. The two who least care about the mother's love get it; the two who want and deserve it get only her respect and her trust. The two who do their duty are defeated in love and in almost everything; the prodigals earn independence at least, and even a measure of happiness. The effect is rather like reading a fable; or perhaps a classic German novel in translation. So much is offered in summary it seems like the scenario for a huge family saga, saved from vulgarity by being boiled down to a sort of witty essence.

But it is Brookner's insistence that virtue and the life force must always be at odds, and that of the two the life force must always win, that I find so daunting. Can't they at least sometimes coincide? If she were swashbuckling and celebratory about it, one might feel her novels were perverse but pleasurable. I can see that writing sentences like 'the good live unhappily ever after' does great things for her summer vacation. Reading them didn't do a lot for mine.

A. S. Byatt, like Brookner, has been an academic as well as a writer (she recently resigned her lectureship at University College London to write full time). Unlike Brookner she has also had four children, and since she is another very subjective writer, the unlikeness is reflected in the fiction.

Byatt's novels have a great deal of intellectual and literary super-structure, which I suspect she thinks is essential to serious writing but which is really just superstructure. But in *Still Life* it has been much more successfully absorbed into the fiction than was the case with *The Virgin in the Garden*. The new novel continues the story of the Potter sisters, Stephanie and Frederica, brilliant, bookish, independent-minded daughters of a Yorkshire schoolmaster against whom both have rebelled and yet whose liberal-humanist values and world-view they both inherit and defend.

It is the mid 1950s, and the two sisters are dividing between them the world of female possibility as it then appeared. Stephanie has married a clergyman, Daniel Orton, and in the course of the novel brings forth (in good strong detail) two children. Though she doesn't share her husband's faith, she knows she could do his job better than he does it because she is a natural teacher. Daniel is solid, incorruptible, loving and unlovely, and there is a kind of dark inevitability about this curious misalliance.

In addition to her children, Stephanie has responsibility for her young brother, Marcus, after his involvement (described in the previous novel) with a deranged homosexual schoolmaster; and also for her terrible old Yorkshire mum-in-law, and for a number of parish waifs and strays.

Frederica is at Cambridge getting academic and sexual learning in about equal measure. She is forthright and clever — and one believes in her cleverness, because the dialogue tends to crackle when she is present. But Frederica is not going to be content with a life of either/or. She is going to want both. In a crucial passage at the end of Chapter 16 she considers two women at Cambridge neither of whose case she wants to be hers. One is her tutor, 'a formidable woman with a rasping tongue'; the other is a student sent down for secretly marrying a Sardinian restaurant proprietor. The first has 'sacrificed too much for the life of the mind'; the second has had it taken away from her.

So Frederica too, in a traditional way, is looking for a man, and seems to be finding him in the person of the sexually compelling young banker, Nigel Reivers. What we are to understand, however, is that she will have him without the loss of her career, and without the traditional self-effacement accepted by her sister.

All of this is, of course, convincing and true. It records a piece of social history and a shift in our notion of the role of women during those post-war years. But by means of a dramatic climax which is both surprising and powerful, and which it would be wrong for a reviewer to reveal, the novelist seems almost to overstate her case. Stephanie represents female altruism; and that altruism is turned into a synonym for self-destruction.

Yet the novel itself, if it doesn't contradict the novelist, does at least, quietly and unemphatically, make a counterstatement. For all the stated importance (and what novel-reader is going to question it?) of 'the life of the mind', it is the domestic scenes, especially those involving Stephanie's babies, which live most vividly in the novel; and it is the self-effacing Stephanie who remains the stronger, more solid, more durable presence of the two sisters.

If I have made any of this sound banal or over-familiar in summary it is not so in Byatt's writing of it. Now and then her strong prose fails in what modern literary theorists call 'foregrounding'. We slip out of a literary gear into an expository one, and the illusion sags. And there are one or two occasions when Byatt tries a modern meta-fictional device, entering the novel in her own persona and even commenting on her own performance. These moments are so alien to the mode she is writing in they fail completely.

But this novel is large enough to carry its own mistakes; and if I was uncertain about the meaning of the climax I was certainly moved by it. I finished *Still Life* with pleasure, with admiration, and with something like awe at its intelligence, its sustained seriousness, its density, its accuracy of observation, above all its lack of all sham and cant and its consequent moral authority. I agree with Claire Tomalin — the absence of this novel from the 1985 short-list is one of those puzzles for which the Booker Prize is famous. It deserves to be there. It would have made a worthy winner.

FRANÇOISE, HÉLAS!

The Still Storm by Françoise Sagan (1984)

Looking back the early 1950s seems a time when new young literary talents announced themselves and reputations were made overnight. In England there were novels like Kingsley Amis's *Lucky Jim* and John Wain's *Hurry On Down*, and there was Colin Wilson's critical study *The Outsider*. In France there was Françoise Sagan with *Bonjour Tristesse*. They were all welcomed enthusiastically. Their first books sold in enormous numbers. And all of them settled down to become pretty humdrum writers whose sales never again rose to such dizzy heights.

Sagan was only nineteen when *Bonjour Tristesse* appeared. I remember it dimly as a novel about a young woman's affair with an older man. I think it had a good deal of charm and elegance, and some local colour when the couple take a holiday in Nice.

Sagan has gone on, like all the rest of them. She's described in Larousse as the author of novels 'dedicated especially to the psychology of love in the contemporary world'.

In her new novel, *The Still Storm*, she's still concerned with 'the psychology of love', but the setting is no longer contemporary. She still writes with cool French elegance. The 'psychology' seems distinctly French too — romantic, passionate, wishful, literary, and unreal.

The story is told in the first person by an aging man who is recalling the one great and unrequited love of his life. In some of the early pages there is a dreariness where his present circumstances and imminent death seem to invade and stultify the writing; and the whole thing is so heavily upholstered with Gallic passion, I found myself detached and only mildly

Sydney Morning Herald, April 1985.

interested. Sagan writes herself into the story with such conviction, however, I was carried along, at least through the middle chapters, against my better judgement. I didn't believe a word of it; but I was prepared to suspend my disbelief.

The time is the 1830s, the place a small town in Aquitaine. The narrator, Nicholas Lomont, falls in love with the beautiful, honourable and aristocratic Flora de Margelesse, who, in her turn, falls in love with the ploughboy poet, Gildas Caussinade. Nicholas watches hopelessly while Flora, who remains his dear friend, conducts her affair with the young poet. But like half the males in the book, Nicholas, while loving (I suppose) the soul of Flora, is drawn to the body of the wickedly captivating and sexually inventive chambermaid, Martha.

There is an all-night ball, rather like a French farce played in slow motion and as tragedy, during which characters keep discovering one another in compromising situations, usually involving hyperactive Martha. This leads to two morning-after duels, one between Nicholas and an arrogant aristocrat, Norbert de Choiseux, the other between Gildas and Norbert's arrogant brother Henry. This dual duel, which looks like being part of the plot mechanics, in fact turns out to be largely irrelevant, since both Gildas and Nicholas survive. Nicholas, however, has been saved by Martha who, despite her busy night, contrives to shoot his opponent dead from behind a bush.

Martha then destroys the marriage of Gildas and Flora, Gildas kills himself, Flora goes mad, Martha inherits several huge fortunes, and Nicholas lives to tell the tale, much later and more or less on his death-bed.

In the last couple of pages, as if abashed by her own fantasies, Sagan tries to cast a certain historical symbolism back over the course the narrative has taken. We are told that Martha continued bringing about disasters and inheriting money, which she always gave to the poor. By this means she seems designed to represent the spirit of the French Revolution, the commoner of the 1830s still battling it out with the class which was supposed to have disappeared in 1789.

In the last paragraph she is discovered dead on the barricades of a later revolution, shot through the heart and 'smiling with an air of great gentleness'.

A NEW NEW ZEALAND FICTION?

The New Fiction, edited and introduced by Michael Morrissey (1985)

I

Of the 300-odd pages of this anthology the first seventy are taken up by Michael Morrissey's introduction. I have heard him criticized for this, and it does seem excessive. But it makes a distinct kind of book. The introduction is an argument about the nature of fiction and what is possible, or desirable, or likely to prove durable, at the present moment — fiction in general, and fiction in New Zealand. Since the chosen writers serve partly as illustrations to the argument, it is possible to read the book in two ways — as a collection of 'stories', or as a thesis on the nature of modern fiction. In Morrissey's defence it can also be said that although he doesn't write with notable economy, he is at least lucid and intelligible.

By 'the new fiction' Morrissey means varieties of non-realist fiction. But the word 'new' suggests a dimension of time; so examples of this kind of writing which are not 'new' in the sense of recently arrived are excluded with the editor's regret. My own 'A Fitting Tribute' and B. F. Babington's 'The Tutored Mind', both published in 1964, are mentioned as too early to be 'new', though not realist enough, apparently, to be 'old'.

More puzzling is a note which includes Janet Frame with Alan Loney and Tony Green as writers who 'were invited to submit material but for various reasons had none available'. Why an invitation when most other writers included appear to be represented by previously published work? We all know Loney's and Green's status as major and minor gurus of what Loney (or is it Roger Horrocks?) calls 'the fast track' — but were they both to turn themselves into fiction writers overnight on that account? And since it is said elsewhere that Janet Frame has been 'writing new fiction all her life', why should it have been necessary to ask for something unpublished just for this anthology?

Among other writers whose absence is regretted because 'their work lies outside the oeuvres of this anthology' (is my French failing or does Morrissey not know the meaning of 'oeuvre'?), Michael Henderson, and even more, Michael Gifkins, seem so pre-eminently to lie within its scope I find their exclusion incomprehensible. I don't know whether either will regret it — a good sailor doesn't necessarily relish being assigned to a leaking ship. But either Morrissey is confused, or he is not giving his reasons for his decisions.

Finally there is the exclusion of Maurice Duggan, not only from the anthology but from the discussion. Duggan began in the realist tradition which Morrissey so dislikes, but he didn't end there. And if nothing else of Duggan's quite belongs, 'The Magsman Miscellany' (first published 1975) surely does.

I suspect these inconsistencies in the selection may spring from Morrissey's desire not only to show to advantage a mode of fiction he favours, but also to be seen as its champion. That word 'new' together with the definite article is the clue: 'the new fiction'. How new would it seem if the anthology included work by established figures like Frame? And how well would what is represented here stand up if it had to be measured alongside a story like 'The Magsman Miscellany'? For me there is not a single fiction here as enjoyable as the Duggan story, nor one as teasingly expansive in what it seems to say about truth and fiction, and how they relate, and what that relation implies about 'reality'. It was Duggan's posthumous message to New Zealand writers and readers. Morrissey's failure to use it, or even to talk about it, seems to me a major flaw.

II

There is a case to be made against the realist tradition in New Zealand fiction; but not, surely, if it implies that such writing should not have occurred or that it must not happen again. That part of Morrissey's introduction which addresses itself to this subject is an irritating mixture of half-truths, overstatement, vituperation, and things which need saying and are occasionally well said. Morrissey refuses to name the perpetrators of the fiction he dislikes, even exempting Sargeson from responsibility for the damage done by his (unnamed) 'imitators'. This good form, or politeness, or evasion, has the unbalancing effect of permitting Morrissey to sound off extravagantly. Since no writer or work is named, the contempt can be extreme. But no writer worth talking about deserves such scorn.

It is true I think that writers like Sargeson, John Mulgan, Bill Pearson, and Maurice Gee (Janet Frame too, though she is no realist) exemplify one face of puritan moralizing while condemning another. It is true that the range of New Zealand fiction has been narrow and (a point Morrissey doesn't quite make but lies somewhere behind his complaints) has been too easily content with fictional conventions, not seeming at all sophisticated, or questioning, in the matter of how truth and fiction relate. But what kind of escape from these constrictions does 'the new fiction' offer? It may only be a matter of running out of one cage to find yourself in another, even smaller. Even the dullest of realist stories offers at least (in Mulgan's phrase) 'a report on experience'. To read an average collection of traditional New Zealand stories may not be a mind-expanding experience; but it could not be as boring as reading in sequence through Morrissey's anthology. The traditional story might be like an old steam train chugging wearily through a familiar landscape, but at least there are windows, a view, and the certainty that you won't end where you began. I don't mean that all, or even most, of Morrissey's writers are boring; only that there is a sameness about what they do, and a sense, not of expansion, but of constriction, when they are read one after another in sequence.

One source of this sameness is that it is very difficult to signal that fiction is not to be read as a record of 'reality' except by comedy, or by devices, or by a tone, which are comic in effect; and just as the older conventions could be repetitiously 'serious', so there is a sameness in levity which can be quite as irritating. There is also, cumulatively, a feeling of abstraction about a succession of stories which insist on being 'unreal' — because they become then mental exercises instead of records. It has to be a very interesting mind indeed before its exercises are worth watching. On the other hand good observation almost justifies itself even if it doesn't alone constitute an art.

By this I don't mean to imply that the old realist tradition in fiction seems to me good enough for all purposes. It doesn't — and in the fiction-writing I have done I have found myself again and again driven beyond it. But if realism fails it seems to me it fails in surrendering the real — the truth — the actual. One goes beyond realism in order to get nearer to reality, not to dispense with it.

By this measure one could argue that Wystan Curnow, one of the most theoretically kosher and sophisticated of the writers represented here, is not, as Morrissey (and possibly Wystan Curnow himself) would argue, moving away from the realist tradition. He is, rather, insisting on a more rigorous form of it. The persona is not, so far as I can see, distinguishable from the writer. The voice is his. The places and events are 'real'. The facts are facts. There is no 'story'. It's all true, real, actual. What then makes this fiction rather than a report? The art (where

Curnow succeeds, which isn't always) is in the language, and in the tone, and the pace. Words and phrases are picked out, like specimens, or picked off, like targets. At its best this writing evokes my admiration and a certain pleasure, limited by the limits of my patience. But I part company with this author in what I want from fiction. I want it to be as complex and as self-conscious as need be to stay alive and fresh as an art in 1985. But I don't want it to stop doing what it has always done — telling stories, and seeming to convey some truth broader than its immediate subject. Wystan Curnow will have none of such falseness. Not only are his fictions all true — there is no manipulation towards a story, a conclusion, a point. So a traditional New Zealand realism becomes super-realism; and the traditional puritanism is simply transferred from the action of the story into the realm of aesthetics.

More than twenty years ago I was reading Jorge Luis Borges, whose name comes up from time to time in Morrissey's introduction, and whose influence can be felt on a number of the writers represented.* What seemed to be noticed about Borges at that time (and I suppose is still noticed) was the sophisticated games his stories played, questioning fiction itself, and hence the nature of reality. What went unremarked was that even in the most intellectual of his stories Borges structured the material very skilfully as narrative. He was a natural story-teller. Later he went on to write straight gaucho stories like 'The Intruder' — a kind that could have come out of the *Decameron* or the *Thousand and One Nights*. This was received as the subtlest trick of all: Borges *pretending* to write stories straight. How could you tell the difference between someone telling such stories straight, and Borges pretending to? I agree the full context of his fiction made the distinction almost a real one. But that didn't alter the fact that to tell it either way, tongue in cheek or otherwise, with or without inverted commas, required precisely the same skills.

I am not wanting to deride the avant garde in fiction. But it seems worth pointing out that where it succeeds it often uses what it may be thought to repudiate. Just as the avant garde poem which breaks with traditional metrical form may require a more rather than a less precise ear in the musical disposition of line and phrase, so fiction which breaks with the established conventions of representation may need a more rather than a less highly developed sense of narrative sequence. And by narrative sequence I mean an instinct for arousing a new interest/anticipation/expectation/appetite in the very act of satisfying one previously aroused. This narrative skill is something a writer has or lacks. It is not something you can *choose* to have. Look closely at Wordsworth's contribution to the *Lyrical Ballads* and you will see that though his skills as a poet flag from time to time, his talent as a story-teller never does. Similarly it

* See 'Auckland Diary'.

could be argued that for all the newness of the fiction Morrissey offers here, narrative skill, however it may be disguised, is still a very important element in the disposition of material.

III

But there are other ways of coming at fiction. One is to say that it is a more or less pure product of the mind of the writer. I think Henry James says or implies this in one of his introductions. It means a fiction may succeed or fail on its own terms, but either way it will reveal the quality of mind and sensibility of its author. From this point of view a fiction by a Henry James or a William Faulkner which fails in some way will still be more satisfying, or interesting, and of course more durable, than one which succeeds but is written by a lesser writer. And in fiction of the kind offered in this anthology, where there is much less than usual that is immediately graspable as 'story', the quality of the mind of the writer is what one is left with often as the clearest impression.

It is a difference in the quality of mind that makes Malcolm Fraser's or John Barnett's fictions superior to Gary Langford's for example. Langford is determinedly 'funny', at about the level of a student review. Barnett and Fraser achieve varieties of wit, because they are concerned not to create dislocations but to discover them. In the surreal as much as in the realist mode, observation — *noticing* — serves better than invention.

Morrissey is fluently entertaining, out of a kind of cheerfulness and confidence (over-confidence at times). Ian Wedde and David Eggleton are alike, and different from Barnett and Fraser, in displaying a headlong energy, momentum, gusto (a word I've found myself using before in writing of Wedde). They are dynamic writers, moving through a landscape which is at once real and surreal, whereas Barnett and Fraser, or equally Ted Jenner and Chris Else, seem to sit still while the world moves around them, assuming strange shapes. All these qualities in the writing reflect a mind, a sensibility, even a personality. *'Le style, c'est l'homme.'*

IV

This year (1985) an M.A. class in Auckland has been meeting once a week on the subject of critical theory. To end the course the class was invited to read a story by Russell Haley and come prepared to discuss it. Why Haley? Partly it was a courtesy extended to the person who was the Department's Writer in Residence. But I think it was also because Haley's writing, like a lot of the fiction in Morrissey's anthology, suits current theoretical approaches to literature. A fiction which is deliberately 'open', which sets out to make the reader insecure and to frustrate any momentary sense we may have that the ground has stopped shaking under our feet, leaves much more space in which the post-structuralist critic can operate, 'deconstruct', 'over-read', do cartwheels, take off his clothes at the picnic. This wonderful freedom which the newest critics claim even as they carve into works which seem loudly to protest at what is being done to them, is actually licensed by texts like Haley's.

But before our new fictionists begin celebrating that their time has come they should consider what this development means. Alex Calder (editor of *And*) declared at one of these seminars that the text did not matter — it was 'what we do with it' that was important. For the post-structuralist critic any stubborn anchoring in what most of us still choose to call 'the real world' is a nuisance; and any inhibiting authorial circumscription likewise. The author has no authority, and neither has the text, which is whatever the reader, elevating himself by declaration of independence to the status of critic, cares to make of it.

This new freedom is sometimes (as in Simon During's article in *And*, 'Towards a Revision of Local Critical Habits') presented as a revolt against the authority of the university, but it is nothing of the sort. It is a revolt by the university against the authority of literature. The academic worm has turned.

So there was also recently a seminar given in the Auckland University Sociology Department on New Zealand Literature by Senior Lecturer in English, Dr Jonathan Lamb, who has never taught in that field and who began by disarmingly acknowledging that he had read very little of the stuff. Why burden yourself with reading if the texts are unimportant? Theory is something more easily run up when unencumbered by facts — just as I suppose the fictional tap flows more freely if it is uninhibited by the need to be plausible. One text by Yorkshireman Haley, set in a dubious Barbados or Kandahar, might be enough for another Yorkshireman, Lamb, to run up a whole course under the heading 'New Zealand Literature — Theoretical Approaches'.

I don't mean to be provincial. All our Yorkshiremen should be welcome and gainfully employed. But there is something naive about the way 'theory' has become the new Internationalism of New Zealand literature. It is Roger Horrocks's mental exercycle. It unstops Leigh Davis's most oracular fluencies. It makes the eyes of Michael Morrissey's introduction shine.

V

'*Le style, c'est l'homme.*' But what about *la femme*? There are not many of them in Morrissey's anthology, not because he wanted it that way, but because very few are interested in the surreal, or in writing which makes language predominate over subject, or in any mode which elevates formal considerations above those of reference, meaning, and purpose. As Morrissey puts it, it is male writers 'who most willingly disengage themselves from social comment and self-analysis and give their work over to formal concerns and wilful experimentation'.

This distinction between male and female writers has a parallel in criticism. Where young men students at the moment tend to be interested in theory, the young women are interested in feminism. Not that feminist criticism is without elements of theory. But feminist interests in literature tend always towards realism, moralism, and witness. Fiction becomes a means by which a woman discovers herself and by which she speaks for the 'submerged population' (to make off with a phrase of Frank O'Connor's) of her sisters. It's true that Keri Hulme is probably the strongest writer represented in this anthology — but she doesn't quite belong in it; and I've heard Morrissey say she is only there because he despaired of finding women writers of consequence who were doing work which fitted his notion of 'the new fiction'.

But it would be wrong to suggest that this anthology represents male fiction in New Zealand at the moment — just as it would be wrong to say that a doctrinaire feminist novel like Stephanie Dowrick's *Running Backwards over Sand* is representative of women's writing. I don't think consciousness of theory, nor of gender, ever liberated anyone into better fiction. You may find your way through fiction to either; but to begin there is like deciding what your 'discovery' should be before you have made it. For that reason I think either approach is likely to produce work peripheral rather than central — not to be condemned for that reason, but assigning itself to a marginal place in whatever it is we mean by 'literature'.

That is where I think Morrissey's anthology places itself — on the margins. It is certainly of interest. It is unlikely to have wide appeal. And it is unlikely to lead to any major development in the future — in fact already one has the feeling of looking back at a range of experimentation that is beginning to seem dated. These pieces, as I see them, are mostly minor offshoots from the major stem of fiction. But they arouse interesting questions about fiction itself. And the fact that that kind of questioning has gone on, and has carried into practice, should mean that fewer writers will feel free to sink back thoughtlessly into the old conventions of representation, as if ' "Pass me the butter," said Margery' was a secure, unambiguous and necessarily meaningful mode of discourse.

THREE

ARGUING WITH THE ZEITGEIST

TEACHING ENGLISH

Before I say anything about reading literary works, just a word about first learning to read, because there are principles to be drawn from it which apply at every stage.

The first is that the appetite for reading is most directly and effectively aroused by being read *to*.

And second (related to that): In all reading that has any literary element — which isn't purely informational — the ear is more important than the eye.

There's an apparent contradiction here. The eye is the instrument of apprehension. It takes in the signal. In what I would call 'good reading' (as distinct from plundering a text for its 'content') those marks on the page, apprehended visually, are translated into actual or imagined sound, which in turn is translated into meaning. The sound of the words is part of the linguistic texture. It communicates all kinds of subtle things like tone and emotion which are distinct from literal meaning.

Many people do learn to translate the visual sign directly into literal meaning. I suspect these people, though often highly intelligent, are less well-equipped for literary reading than the predominantly aural reader.

So good readers are often slow readers. Speed-reading techniques designed to teach you to skim a text visually snapping up facts along the way can be useful for specific tasks; but they're damaging if they become your sole method of reading.

So (to return to my original point) if you want a child to learn to read; if you want to facilitate the learning process — you read to it. You read things that are interesting and exciting. You read with expression.

An address to the annual conference of the National Association of Teachers of English in Christchurch, May 1982.

You make a ritual of it. You arouse in the child the feeling that in those marks on paper there is a magic which an adult can unlock and release into the air. They represent a kind of freedom — an alternative world. The child will want free access to that world — so the child will want to learn to read.

For the health of our community parents ought to be told that simple fact. It's as important as anything currently told them in ante-natal classes.

Because this principle applies at every level, right through to university (where the reading of poems and the performance of plays can be so beneficial), every teacher of English should develop skills in reading aloud, projecting the voice, picking up the rhythms of prose fiction or of poetry. Something of the actor is important. I'm not talking about what used to be called 'elocution'. It's not a matter of getting rid of your New Zealand accent, or your Midlands accent, or your New York accent, or your Oxford accent. It's a matter of speaking out clearly, fitting your native accent to the music of the poem, putting it to the service of the rises and falls, the natural run of sentences, and to the excitement of the action if it's a story you're reading.

Good choices in what you read are important, and the right choice is not necessarily the worthy one. Stories are sometimes written these days specifically to convey information and to mould correct social attitudes. Often they're tedious as narrative and badly composed. These are our equivalents of those boring moral tales the Victorians inflicted on our great-grandparents.

Poems and fiction that really do suit children are often good across a very wide spectrum of ages and (still thinking of reading aloud to them) abilities. Seven-year-olds should listen spellbound to *Treasure Island*; but so should twelve-year-olds, or seventeen-year-olds — or adults.

A lot of poetry is very complex and too difficult for children; but a lot of the greatest poetry in the language could be put across I suspect at almost any level. I think you could rivet the attention of children of almost any age with a reading of Coleridge's 'Kubla Khan' — from infant classes right through to university. At each level they would get something different — more or less complex depending on the age and linguistic ability of the child. And if a great deal — nearly all of it — passed some children by, for those of high ability you would have unlocked a sense of the marvellous range and possibility and power hidden in the language that comes unthinking out of our mouths every day. Suddenly the word is seen to be like the atom — a reservoir of power and possibility.

> In Xanadu did Kubla Khan
> A stately pleasure dome decree,
> Where Alph the sacred river ran
> Through caverns measureless to man

Down to a sunless sea.
So twice five miles of fertile ground
With walls and towers were girdled round,
And there were gardens bright with sinuous rills
Where blossomed many an incense-bearing tree;
And there were forests ancient as the hills,
Enfolding sunny spots of greenery.

By the time you've got all the way through to the damsel with a dulcimer, language has asserted a power more absolute than a simple consideration of what it 'means' can account for. This is the powerhouse teachers of English used to hold the keys to. What I'm here to accuse you of is handing in your keys.

And to ask why you've done it.

But I will come to that. First I want to remind you that it isn't just poetry of the past that has this power and this instantaneous effect. There probably isn't an English teacher in New Zealand who would think T. S. Eliot appropriate to any but the most advanced and sophisticated pupils. But I suspect there are passages in Eliot that would have the same instantaneous effect as I'm saying 'Kubla Khan' would have on a very wide range of children of all ages.

'This music crept by me upon the waters'
And along the Strand up Queen Victoria Street
O City city I can sometimes hear
Beside a public bar in Lower Thames Street
The pleasant whining of a mandoline
And a clatter and a chatter from within
Where fishmen lounge at noon: where the walls
Of Magnus Martyr hold
Inexplicable splendour of Ionian white and gold.

That's from *The Waste Land*. And what about this from 'Ash Wednesday'?

From the wide window towards the granite shore
The white sails still fly seaward, seaward flying
Unbroken wings.
And the lost heart stiffens and rejoices
In the lost lilac and the lost sea voices
And the weak spirit quickens to rebel
For the bent golden-rod and the lost sea smell
Quickens to recover
The cry of the quail and the whirling plover
And the blind eye creates
The empty forms between the ivory gates
And smell renews the salt savour of the sandy earth.

If you hesitate and wonder for example whether your pupils will

247

understand what the words 'inexplicable splendour' mean, or what 'Ionian' means, and so settle for something easier, I think you're giving in to needless worries. A strong context explains words — or if it doesn't explain them, it gives them a kind of magical force and authority. 'Ionian' — of course! Ionian white and gold, whatever it might be, is clearly more remarkable, more marvellous, than *ordinary* white and gold, which would have about it no 'inexplicable splendour'.

Trust poetry. Don't buy off the ghost of the past with little funny bits of Roger McGough and Sam Hunt. Give them the real stuff. Live dangerously!

As well as discovering his or her own powers as a performer a teacher of English needs to discover them among pupils or students. Shakespeare is written to be spoken and acted. One of the greatest follies committed by university English Departments during the past four or five decades has been to study the text of Shakespeare cold on the page. The result has been more and more extravagantly tenuous readings, elevating secondary nuances to primary consideration and neglecting the primary rhetorical force of passages — that force which immediately reasserts itself when the play is treated as it was written, as a text for performance.

Shakespeare (since I've mentioned him) is the richest single resource of that power of language — the English language — the one you and I are employed to teach. But I won't embark on the pros and cons of Shakespeare in school. I'm glad he was there when I was there. And my only other comment is that of course teachers in London schools have a great advantage because they can take senior pupils of appropriate ability to any number of first-rate productions of the plays.

In the area of what's taught under the heading of literature two radical changes have occurred since I was at school. One I positively welcome; the other I don't greatly regret. The one I welcome is that pupils now read New Zealand literature; the one I regret a little but not too much is that no effort seems to be made to teach even advanced pupils the basic historical outlines of the development of English literature. Since the universities have also largely given up the effort to teach literary history as such, we can hardly complain if the schools have dropped it altogether.

The study of our own literature is essential to the establishment of intellectual freedom and imaginative independence; and it's important in helping us to recognize how literature relates to reality in other places. I don't think a person who hasn't read some fiction and poetry reflecting the region he or she knows at first hand is properly equipped to deal with literature of a different region and society.

But I should add that I don't think the reading of New Zealand literature is enough — certainly not for our better students. Ideally they should, if they stay five years at secondary school, read some poems and stories from a number of places — from England (the parent culture), from America (the dominant culture), from Australia (our neighbour), from Europe (in translation — the broader parent culture) — and so on. A broad spread, against the background of reading from our local literature.

And finally, if we can't look any longer for much sense of literary history, they should at least have read some things from past ages. I'm talking again about the more able students of English. Surely some of them will have read some Dickens, some Mark Twain or Melville, perhaps a Sir Walter Scott or two, perhaps Fielding's *Joseph Andrews* and a couple of novels by Jane Austen; and of course a sampling of poems from past centuries — especially some from the Romantic period. All this is in addition to whatever Shakespeare it has been possible to give them.

How many of the better students will arrive at the university with this kind of background? I wish a proper survey had been done so that we knew. I suspect the answer is 'very few' — even though what I'm proposing is pretty minimal. Is there any reason why this is so? If I had to nominate a reason I wouldn't say 'television', or the change in reading habits it has brought about. I would say — airing what can't be much more than a suspicion — that the reason here in New Zealand is something that goes by the name of the New English Syllabus.

It used to be that the first three years of secondary school were the years when the reading habit was confirmed among those who were going to be readers for life. My anxiety at present is that that has changed, and that those have become the years when the reading habit is lost.

Of course I recognize that a bad syllabus won't prevent a good teacher from doing a good job; and conversely, an excellent syllabus won't turn a sow's ear into a silk purse. Nevertheless I think a system such as the New English Syllabus can gradually affect the range of possibilities offered in the classroom and affect the overall level — or the tone, if you like — of teaching in a given subject.

My recollection is that the New English Syllabus came into being in the early 1970s as a result of work done by a committee headed by a geographer, Russell Aitken, and including, I think, Charmaine Pountney and Peter Goddard. It has since taken the form of a Statement of Aims which has just been accepted by the Minister of Education. But the Statement of Aims enshrines what was fundamental in the New English Syllabus; and in particular it's constructed around the 'eight modes of language' which seem to have gone right through the schools and to have about them the finality and authority of the Ten Commandments — because, I suppose, that's the most concrete and specific part of what is otherwise a very general and unspecific document.

When a structure like the 'eight modes of language' gets widely disseminated through a group of professional people so that it becomes just a fact of life for them, it's very difficult for those people to look at it objectively or in fact to see it at all. I want to say to you very emphatically that those 'eight modes' flout common sense, are misleading, unprofessional, and have the effect of misdirecting the energies of those of you — secondary teachers — who are supposed to take notice of them.

As set out in the Statement of Aims the eight modes are divided into verbal and non-verbal modes — four of each. They're divided also into modes of receiving and modes of transmitting (to use the language of radio communication).

The verbal modes of transmission are speaking and writing.

The verbal modes of receiving are listening and reading.

No problem so far. This is 'language' as we all understand it.

Now (according to the Statement of Aims, p.5) we move to the 'non-verbal' modes.

The non-verbal modes of transmission are 'moving' and 'shaping'.

The corresponding non-verbal modes of reception are 'watching' and 'viewing'.

'Moving' is anything from a raised eyebrow to a complex mime. (It's what in earlier drafts was called 'body language'.)

'Shaping' is described as the use of 'visual effects in media such as posters, models , television and cinema'.

I will try to deal with all this calmly.

What's wrong first is that the tabulation reduces all modes to equivalence; or at least it refuses to discriminate among them. So the verbal modes, speaking and writing (with their corresponding listening and reading) lie there on the page as if they are of no more importance than what are called 'non-verbal' modes.

Second, there's nothing to suggest that the people who drew this up recognized that when you speak of 'non-verbal modes of language' you have effectively moved from literal statements into metaphorical ones. ('Body language' is a metaphor.) The whole discussion moves from one to the other as if the term 'language' retained the same kind of meaning and value in each category.

Third, 'shaping' is described as 'non-verbal', yet the reference is to things like posters, television, and cinema, all of which are heavily verbal. People *talk* on television; television plays, and movies, are *scripted*. Posters use *words*. In fact if you turn off the sound on television and just watch the images, you will much sooner lose track of what's happening than if you shut your eyes and listen. By that measure television is more verbal than visual. To segregate out those aspects of it, or of cinema, which are 'non-verbal' is artificial and misleading.

Much more could be said about this. I simply repeat — the 'eight modes' formula flouts common sense, creates confusion, and misdirects energies by reducing to apparent equality things which are not, and cannot be, equal. And what a bad advertisement for the study of language that its guidelines should be set out in language which is itself confusing! This is the kind of thing that makes one feel, 'It could only happen here — or in some other intellectual backwater.'

What was in the minds of those worthy persons who inflicted this confusion on our schools? The scientific-looking diagram with its precise and balancing numerology: not seven modes of language, or nine, or ten, but exactly eight — *the* eight modes of language: how definitive that sounds! What did they think they were doing?

They were trying to make people whose linguistic skills are minimal feel better about themselves. 'The eight modes of language' was designed — whether consciously or not — to dress up and conceal the demotion of literature in the study of English and the expulsion of linguistic excellence as a measure of success. What it says in effect is, If you can't read, don't worry — you can watch television and movies; if you can't talk much, well — there's always body language. The main thing is that you should feel good about yourself. The study of English should do nothing to damage your self-respect. And that's the message I've heard again and again at this conference.

It's well-intentioned but I think totally misguided. I don't think you can conceal from people their own linguistic ineptitude. They're made aware of it every day. The English classroom can't be a repair shop for damaged psyches, and shouldn't try to be. The attempt to make it so only damages the study of English, which in turn damages our whole society. The New English Syllabus is an example of the mess people can make when they haven't been sufficiently trained in precision and scrupulousness to do well the job they were given to do.

When I read *Macbeth* in the fifth form in the 1940s I was required to learn passages by heart and deliver them aloud. It was hardly the most sophisticated of teaching methods but at least it left something behind. I can still quote those passages. They've lain there at the back of my mind like a marvellous linguistic loam, fertilizing my sense of the possibilities and power of the English language. When children in a top-stream Auckland fifth form this year did *Macbeth* they had to get into groups and make models of the castle in which Duncan was murdered.

I mention this only because it's typical of what the N.E.S. has encouraged in recent years. Making models, setting up interviews with characters, writing newspaper editorials, painting pictures, drawing cartoons and comic strips, cutting out pictures from magazines, making dice games based on a journey in the book — these are some of the ways children are encouraged to respond to their literary reading. The English classroom has become a kind of activities room, looking more like the art room than anything else.

It's clear that those who drew up the N.E.S were concerned that while

English as it had traditionally been taught suited high-ability pupils, it didn't do much for the less able. And they were aware — as the Statement of Aims makes clear — that one's sense of self is tied up with one's sense of being able to use the language. Our social bonds are primarily linguistic — they are primarily *verbal*. Language is power. So it was felt the study of English shouldn't deprive children of their confidence. It should give them credit for what skills they have. If they can't read or talk, find something they can do, and call *that* language.

I'm not in the least unfeeling to those in our society who, either through heredity or the effects of the environment they're born into, suffer linguistic deprivation and consequent loss of social status. But you don't help the disabled by giving wheelchairs to those who can walk.

I sincerely believe that at every level, including the university, but especially the secondary level, rigour has gone out of the study of English, and with it have gone the sense of challenge, and of consequent pleasures and excitements. The able have suffered, and I can't see how the less able have profited. But above all the subject has suffered. Its reputation in the university has certainly declined during these past ten years. Too many bright kids think of English as a vague do-goodery sort of subject where you sit around and exchange pious chat; or where for some reason which is never clear you engage in manual and visual tasks in response to verbal works.

I know there are now, as there always have been, marvellous and dedicated teachers doing wonderful things and communicating enthusiasms. But the predominant drift in English studies is away from exactness, away from a disciplined use of the language, away from clarity and towards an accommodating vagueness thought somehow to be virtuous because how could anyone be harmed by it?

What then do I recommend?

First, scrap the Eight Modes of Language.

Second, push for a redrafting of the Statement of Aims in a language which is simple, direct, less abstract, with fewer pieties and a great deal more content.

Third: in the classroom I think much more attention has to be given to varying levels of ability and attainment in English. You have to take notice of the fact that some children will arrive in the third form having read more than others will have read by the time they leave the seventh. You can't cater for all those together. If I argue for segregation according to ability I'm told I'm élitist. But *nature* is élitist. Are we to respond to what nature has provided; or pretend the world is a different kind of place from what it is. No one pretends all children have equal abilities in maths, or foreign languages. Why should we pretend English is any different?

At this conference I've heard the pursuit of linguistic excellence described as a form of 'class colonialism'. I've heard Jack Shallcrass talk about 'the coercive and authoritarian society'; and Charmaine Pountney talk about 'productive rage'.

Of course we're all armchair radicals these days — or bean-bag radicals. To those people who have presided over the change in English studies in our secondary schools and who see themselves as revolutionaries I want to say that nothing is more revolutionary than good literature; nothing more truly radical than the language used with precision. If I learned radicalism anywhere I learned it from literature; and what it taught me especially (you only have to think of Dickens and Shakespeare to see the truth of this) was to question *every* piety — the liberal piety no less than the reactionary one.

AUCKLAND DIARY

I am writing a novel — a novella perhaps. Last year in London I wrote a draft. All this year it has been put aside awaiting revision. The time arrives when I'm free to go back to it and I admit to myself I'm glad to have had an excuse for ignoring it. It's difficult; probably won't ever be published. How am I to make it work? Talking to friends I remember an idea — a device for dealing with it — that came to me in my bunk on the ship returning to New Zealand from London. I describe it to them, but without conviction. It doesn't occur to me to use it.

A few days later I'm browsing in a bookshop, looking perhaps for a Sign. I pick up a book of stories by Jorge Luis Borges. I'm told he was awarded the Formentor Prize in 1961, and I buy the book. I read a story. It uses something very like the device that came to me in my bunk in the Caribbean. I glance through his prologue and find he refers to this story in conjunction with Henry James's *The Sacred Fount*. I don't understand the connexion he's making, but for me there's another: my novel began, years ago, as a short story, after I had read *The Sacred Fount*.

I have my Sign. I begin rewriting and it seems to go well. My wife and I are invited to a literary party to meet a visiting German professor. I don't catch his name — or I forget it. I talk first to Droescher, our host, a German who has lived many years in Spain before coming to Auckland. We discuss a story of mine which a Madrid magazine is to republish. I know no Spanish, and Droescher will check the translation for me. He asks me about the novel and I tell him it's going satisfactorily. Have I time for it? Yes, I have now. There's only one other job to do — an article for a British weekly in a series called 'Out of London'.

New Statesman, December 1966, in a series called 'Out of London'. A German translation of this piece appeared in *Akzente*, April 1972. The novel referred to was abandoned, or consigned to the tin trunk.

Won't that throw me out of gear? (I've spoken of 'getting into gear' for fiction.) No. I will write the article as fiction, though characters, places, and events will be actual. 'This conversation could be part of it. Your name would be "Droescher".' I see he's going to ask me how such a piece could be fiction and I stare at him, I suppose in a way which inhibits the question. Does he recognize that an answer would have to be theoretical, and that literary theory can have no place in fiction? At any rate he doesn't ask the question, and I see that I'm already controlling the actual.

The guest of honour has been talking first to one group, then another in rotation. His voice is loud and I permit myself certain prejudices about German professors. He has been for some time in the next room, still audible. He enters briskly, wheels towards me and stops. He asks my 'field' and I say, 'Modern poetry and criticism' — like that. He begins with a good straight service: Literary History and Literary Criticism. I respond with a backhand drive. Was he at the FILLM Congress on that theme in New York in 1963? He was invited, of course, but he didn't attend. Wasn't New York in August too hot? I agree it was hot. Now we are talking about a series in the *TLS* — 'The Critical Moment'. He contributed to the second issue, which I didn't read. I tell him the man who supervised my Ph.D. contributed to the first. It's the best I can do — like waving your racquet after an ace.

Our conversation becomes less academic, more serious, its substance gossip. The name of Jorge Luis Borges enters — I suppose I introduce it. The professor mentions the awarding of the Formentor Prize to Borges. He recalls long arguments about the relative merits of Borges and Beckett, resolved by a compromise — the award to be shared between them. Does he mean he has something to do with the prize? Oh yes. He is on the awarding committee.

I have been drinking red wine. A certain acceleration takes place. Does the professor understand he has been gathered into a work of fiction? His conversation becomes sharper, more pointed. I leave him at last only because I know I must myself choose the terminal moment. I cross the room and listen to Droescher talking in German to two others. I understand no word of their language but in a moment it establishes itself as a norm and I suppose I must be following it. I'm dismayed when they tell me they have been talking about carrier pigeons. They begin to sing.

My wife and I are leaving. We are talking at the door to Droescher. His wife comes to ask him to call a taxi for the professor. I offer to drive him to his hotel. In the car he tells me he would like to read some New Zealand writers. I mention some names. I also offer to send him a copy of my book . . . I pause, wondering whether 'on modern poetics' will describe it. But there's no need. 'Ah yes,' he says. 'That one. I read your book in Tubingen.'

Next morning there's an article about him in the newspaper. I learn that he left Germany in the 1930s and returned after the war, that he was a friend of Thomas Mann's, an associate of Brecht's in the Berliner Ensemble . . .

We decide to go for a picnic somewhere away from the city beaches. My young sister has stayed the night with us after minding our three-year-old, Oliver, and she decides she will come with us. I think first of the west coast — Karekare or Piha — but my wife objects. She is pregnant, and those winding unsealed roads may make her ill. We decide to cross the harbour and go north to the Mahurangi Peninsula.

We are perhaps twenty miles out of Auckland, climbing steeply, when my sister points to a road crossing a flat below. She says it leads to a newly opened beach reserve. We turn back to explore it. The reserve has been an estate — the big house is still occupied — with lines of tall plane trees in bud, flame trees, a stand of tall pines along the river. The beach itself is sheltered by bush-covered bluffs running out to sea at either end, the bush patched with yellow-gold kowhai bloom and white clematis.

There's no one in sight. We have lunch, then walk the length of the beach to the river mouth. We spend perhaps an hour on the sand, collecting shells, launching logs which float upstream with the incoming tide. The day is unusually warm for September and we regret not having brought bathing suits. Oliver builds sand castles. My sister (sixteen years old) instructs us in botany. I choose myself a manuka staff and Oliver, imitating, picks up a stick brought in by the tide. He's rightly proud of it. It's wave-worn, patterned with clear white barnacle shells.

We're returning along the beach, my sister walking with me, my wife following with the boy. There are now perhaps half a dozen people on the beach. I look up to the grass area above the sand and notice in the distance a man wearing a suit and tie. I point him out to my sister. We're amused by formal dress in this place. A moment later I see that it's the professor. I'm not surprised — merely delighted to have confirmed my power of eliciting fiction from the actual. I watch him. He's visibly alien, the European intellectual, picking his way carefully over uneven grass under pohutukawas. I'm conscious of all he brings with him — and so is he. My wife catches us up. She says, 'It's him.'

Now he has recognized us. I'm conscious of my appearance, bare-footed, gripping my staff, trousers rolled to the knee, sand in my beard, a sweater knotted by the arms round my waist. All I need is a patch over one eye and a rum barrel to lean on.

The professor waves and we go up to talk to him. The Droeschers appear. They have brought him in their car. Like us, they've never been to this place before. We all laugh, embarrassed by the extravagant coincidence. We stand in a group taking in the scene, trying to name the islands we can see, explaining to the professor that in mid summer the pohutukawas will bloom brilliant red for perhaps a fortnight, the blooms appearing first at one end of the beach, then passing in succession down the line of trees to the other, tingeing the sand red with stamens . . .

Five or ten miles on the homeward drive the boy begins to cry. He has left his stick behind. He won't be consoled — wants to go back for it. We stop at Orewa for lemonade. Two fire engines pass, sirens wailing, red lights flashing. The lemonade and the fire engines quieten him, but he remains subdued — understandably. It was a fine stick. But I'm held now, truly caught, by a clear memory of where he left it — at the bottom of the concrete steps we climbed from the sand to the grass where the professor stood waiting. I see those steps quite clearly, surmounted by urns. I know they can't exist in that place; they belong — last year at Marienbad? Yet no effort will remove them. They have taken up residence in my fiction. I see the wave-worn stick with its clear white barnacles lying just below the bottom step while the tide, dragging weed, nudging shells, advances towards it up the beach.

LONDON DIARY

Finding the sun pouring in through our London kitchen window K puts a chair in place and settles with a book. She expects the sun to rise to the left where there is plenty of sky. It doesn't. It goes off to the right and disappears behind trees. When you come from the Southern Hemisphere you're used to the idea that the seasons are reversed — summer in August, winter at Christmas. You're prepared for it before you ever cross the Equator. All the literature tells you of it — the seasons as they occur in books rather than in 'reality'; and our Christmas cards in New Zealand still sometimes show fir trees and snow. But in all the years of coming half-way around the world (I've now crossed the Equator seventeen times) I don't remember noticing this peculiar habit of the Northern sun. Because I'm not of a scientific bent it takes some hasty diagrams to convince myself that we haven't made a mistake. But of course it's true. If you imagine a stick figure in the Northern Hemisphere looking down the globe towards the sun's path around the Equator, the sun moving east to west rises at the figure's left and sets at his right hand. A corresponding figure in the Southern Hemisphere, looking north to the Equator, will see the sun rise from the right and pass over to the left — hence K's (and my) expectation in our London kitchen.

With our two teenage daughters we have rented the house for five weeks. It belongs to a couple who are taking their holiday abroad. He is a retired civil servant (knighted); she has been a tutor in literature. His study is lined with books on economics and politics; hers with books I am entirely at home with, though in rather better order and condition than mine. The house is on four floors, counting basement flat and attic bedroom. It is compact, more solid, and in most respects better appointed,

London Review of Books, October 1984.

than our own in New Zealand: but to get in and out of it we have to operate an array of keys, bolts, and locking devices, not to mention time-switches to bring light and sound on and off at strategic times when we're absent. It's a Victorian house looking out on a small square (more accurately an oval) with an enclosed garden and tall trees. We were told there is a viscount next door, and somewhere not far away a grandson of Winston Churchill. There are also crows, squirrels and a goat, which strike me more immediately and ingratiatingly. The house has its own garden, at the back, and I enjoy watering the beans and tomatoes, picking spinach and herbs and roses, and listening to the pears dropping.

This enclave of affluence sits more or less midway between the Brixton Road and the Clapham Road — hence, I suppose, the locking and timing devices. No doubt there's much to be said, and not all of it simply wishful, about working-class energies, the fruitful mixing of cultures, the melding of black and white. What strikes the visiting eye is the squalor and the distress.

Flying to London from New Zealand, you spend twenty-four hours in the air. Even with a break of two days in Los Angeles it takes most of a week before your inner time-switch stops turning you on like a 100-watt light-bulb at two or three in the morning, and plunging you into darkness in mid sentence over lunch. But it wasn't the inner time-switch that woke us a few nights after our arrival. It was a scream — or rather, screaming. It went on at length. I've never heard anything quite like it. K was out of bed and over to the window almost at once, while I lay staring at the ceiling trying to remember where I was so I could make sense of that terrifying noise. There were shouts and the sounds of chase. A black youth came into view down in the street, pursued by two white youths. He went up and over the wire fence enclosing the garden in the square, and vanished among the trees. His pursuers circled about the garden, shouting: 'Come out you black bastard.' Meanwhile, like most other occupants of the enclave, we were staggering downstairs and out to our front gate. Information passed up and down the street. A young woman had been mugged. She was unhurt, and being comforted. Audibly the police were on the way. Soon there was the sound of their boots as they raced from their squad-cars and vans. I had heard that sound last during the Springbok tour of New Zealand, when it came to represent the Enemy. It's hard to like the police, or to do without them. We were standing around now, watching their torches flashing among the trees. I admit to hoping the black youth would escape. After ten minutes or so he was caught on the far side of the square. His shouts didn't last as long as his victim's and weren't as blood-curdling, but they were full of fear, and I had no doubt a little instant justice was being meted out.

What does one come to London for? Long ago there was the sense that it was the centre of the world, but it was not 'reality'. ('Reality' was more mundane, less supercharged, less like literature and the News.) That sense passed, partly because the world changed, and partly as London acquired its own mundaneness. Now it is, I suppose, for me, a shameless culture-feast — theatre, music, galleries, but not museums, not architecture, not history. When I was a child I was always bored by museums. Later I was 'good at' history, but it was history, I now recognize, as causal narrative, as fiction, even as romance. The events we studied were removed not only in time but in space. There is a cliché about people from the New World (used most often as a way of putting Americans in their place) that we lack a proper historical sense. It may be true. The New Zealand poet Charles Brasch wrote poems looking forward to a time when we, too, would have a landscape littered with ruins. 'The plains are nameless and the cities cry for meaning,' he wailed. I think he may have been remembering New Zealand from his rooms in an Oxford college, forgetting that if there were indeed any nameless plains they were nameless only to the European settler — and not for long. As a child I used to play on the slopes of the small volcanic hills with which the Auckland isthmus is dotted — each of them about 500 feet in height, their slopes visibly terraced by what were once Maori fortifications. It was easy to imagine the far-distant tribal wars that had been fought up and down those slopes. But that was not our own past. Our European past existed only in books, and on the far side of the world. New Zealand men went away and fought in wars there, and came back and seldom talked about it, thus increasing its mystery and its romance. Certainly I feel quite remote from those serious English couples who wander into churches with guide-books, point out architectural features to one another, and murmur dates.

As a day-to-day environment London strikes even the visitor who knows it very well and feels at home in it as a city in which it is incomparably difficult and time-consuming to do even the simplest of tasks — to acquire a travel-card, for example, since one is living in SW9. First you need a photograph. The coin-operated machine at Stockwell tube station is jammed. We are told Brixton is the nearest station with a machine. There we wait with half a dozen others. Slowly it becomes clear that the machine, which shows all the signs of being in good working order, is producing photographs sometimes, not always. Two of the four of us achieve a photograph, though all four pay. Next day I try at Victoria. Again a queue, but this time success. I take the photograph to the ticket-sales counter. There are three queues — two for regular sales, one for travel-cards and red-rovers. The queues are long and move slowly. When I am close to the window the man in the next window closes, directing his queue to join ours. There is a fierce and quite wordless war going on between those who have waited in the travel-card and red-rovers queue, and those who have waited in the other and don't believe they should be sent all the way back to the tail to wait again. Meanwhile the man who has closed his window is inside the booth still, laughing and chatting with his mates. The wait is long, the tempers short, blood pressure high, though there is a corresponding sense of achievement when you finally get your ticket. It is supposed to save money. It has cost me the price of two photographs and two tube-train journeys in addition to my £4.70. Should I now phone or write to Photo-Me of Walton-on-Thames who are responsible for the machines? Of course not. I would only experience the same frustrations all over again. This is a very tedious recital, but it is truly representative. Every visitor to London has a stock of such stories. And with Thatcherism it has all got worse. With three million unemployed, post-offices, shops, cafeterias, every facility requiring a staff to serve the public seems undermanned. If you think post-office queues are long in the West End, try SW9. Are the poor not supposed to write letters? Like Marie Antoinette urging cake on the masses, the Post Office recommends long-distance phone-calls.

In New Zealand just before I left we got a Labour government into office after three terms (nine years) of National (i.e. conservative) rule. It happened convincingly, because there was complete accord between the moderate Left, represented by the present leadership of the parliamentary party (both the new PM and his deputy are lawyers) and the trade unions. Even the Socialist Unity (i.e. Communist) Party supported Labour. That accord, and the fact that it held, owes a lot to the personality and strengths of David Lange: but if the Left had split, as it has split here between socialists and SDP, we would have had yet another term of the execrable Muldoon and the yes-men he gathered around him.

In our SW9 house there is evidence that our landlord and his wife have joined the SDP. Also I notice that among the runs of periodicals they keep in the attic, the *New Statesman* was discontinued in 1983. It's easy to see how it happens. In *The Real Thing*, Tom Stoppard turns some of his best verbal fire against the kind of cant and half-truth to which the Left is prone. The mistake he makes, or the play makes, it seems to me, is confusing the cant and the cause. His playwright hero defends brilliantly and wittily his conviction that to be a writer you need, not a cause, but the skills of a writer. His adversary is permitted to put, but with no comparable eloquence, the counterstatement that to have the skills of a writer and nothing to say is not exactly a position of strength. What comfort will there be for those who attack (as Stoppard's play does) the failings of the language in which the anti-nuclear argument is put, if that argument proves nevertheless to be correct? Looked at from a long way off — I mean from New Zealand, which is as far as you can go before you start coming back the other way — it still sometimes seems a possibility, remote, but too real to be taken lightly, that the 'unreality' of Europe will one day become actual.

261

RAPALLO DIARY

I have been a few days in Rapallo where Ezra Pound spent two decades of his writing life. He had despaired of London in 1921 and moved to Paris. The Paris period lasted three or four years. Not long after Mussolini came to power Pound took up residence in Rapallo. He could hardly have chosen a more perfect place. Perfect for what, though? For beauty. For comfort. For ease of living. But for his career as a poet I think Rapallo was probably a mistake, which helps to explain the gradual decline of the Cantos into the dreariness that characterizes Cantos 50 to 70, until the shock of Italy's collapse, his brutal internment at Pisa, and the prospect of a trial and execution for treason released the opaque splendours of the Pisan sequence.

Even in October the air in Rapallo is warm, the light soft, the sea calm and clear. I once lived with my family most of a year in Menton, 100 miles along the coast on what is now the French side of the border, and Rapallo is visually and in the life of the town remarkably similar. There is the same combination of colours — yellow and orange faces of the buildings, dark red slates, green of citrus trees and palms, smoky-grey olive trees on the hills that rise behind the town, and the blue of the sea. Along the waterfront there are cafes and restaurants that are big glittering nets for tourist butterflies. One street inland the town goes noisily about its Mediterranean business. That polluted sea still yields wonderful fish which the locals are wonderfully practised at converting into delicious meals. Fruit, vegetables and poultry come into the market from the terraced farms round about. With foreign money coming in all through the year there are few signs of poverty or unemployment. A little less *propre* than its French counterpart, Rapallo probably allowed

Written in the northern autumn, 1984, and published here for the first time.

Pound room to expand, to be himself, to act out his extravagant role of poet and political philosopher, which London had denied him.

Yet the freedom of a foreign language and culture can be a trap; and the beauty and comfort of the Mediterranean can quickly pall. I'm sure Pound must have felt it closing around him. He worked against it with furious energy, sending off letters in all directions, trying to correct the Anglophone world by correspondence, but all the time losing touch with it, losing the sure sense a writer needs of being in tune with the shifts of history which are reflected in the subtle shifts a language makes even from one year to the next. Meanwhile Pound's personal life bound him more and more firmly to Rapallo. His parents followed their beloved only child to live there in retirement. Down on the waterfront he occupied with his wife Dorothy an apartment that looks out across the bay to a headland on which the most notable feature is the tower and church of Sant' Ambrogio. Up there his mistress Olga Rudge lived in a villa. Every few days Pound set off up the salita — the cobbled walking path that climbs steeply through villas and olive groves — to Olga's house. Down on the flat was one reality, up on the headland was another, and he seemed unwilling or unable to relinquish either.

During this period Pound was persuading himself that Douglas Social Credit would solve Europe's economic problems, that Mussolini was a Douglasite economist, that the Jews, with their tradition of usury, were conspiring to obstruct progress towards the creation of interest-free credit, and that there were lessons relevant to a Douglasite economic revolution to be learned from Chinese and from American history. This intellectual porridge, brewed up at cafe tables under the palm trees in the evenings, while the bats flitted over the roof tiles and the painted fishing boats brought their catch into the little harbour, went not only into the Cantos. In time it was to be served up over Rome radio in wartime broadcasts meant to persuade Americans that President Roosevelt was evil and that America's interests lay with the Axis. Pound was not mad exactly. He had simply lost contact with his language, and consequently with his sense of reality. I know there are notable examples of expatriate writers whose careers have prospered in foreign places. Silence, exile and cunning was the formula that took Joyce to Trieste. But I wonder whether Joyce's progress can't be seen as another example of a loss of contact with the living material of his art. In *Finnegans Wake* the language loses all its rights and becomes mere servant to an eccentric master.

Pound and Eliot, both expatriates, represent different kinds of snobbery. Eliot's was social, Pound's intellectual. Pound was the kind of New World expatriate who has to prove his superiority by having privileged access to, and ultimately command over, the culture from which his fellow countrymen are removed and alienated. Most of his excesses spring from that compulsion. Of the two men, Pound strikes me as the more foolish, the more generous, and the more congenial. He had none of Eliot's puritan severity; and in defeat he rediscovered the natural world — the grass growing 'bambooiform' around his Pisan tent, the ants 'staggering' in the early light, the birds like notes of music on the prison wire — while from memory he created wonderful living portraits of Old Billyum Yeats, Possum Eliot, 'Fordie', and Jim Joyce. The Pisan Cantos will never be popular poetry; but for those equipped to take what they offer they are almost incomparably rich — an entirely human and humane document, as Eliot's *Four Quartets* is not.

It took us two days to find Olga Rudge's house at Sant' Ambrogio. Asking for the Casa Sessanta got us nowhere. The name Rudge, written on a piece of paper for a local shopkeeper, produced signs of recognition and some useful direction. Finally a charming Milanese insurance agent at the gate of his holiday villa pointed it out for us. He called it the Casa Ezra Pound, and referred to Olga Rudge as Pound's secretary. He seemed not to know of another Pound household down in the town — not surprising when one reflects that Pound's daughter to Olga Rudge didn't know of it either until she was an adult. But the Milanese insurance man knew that the Casa Ezra Pound was only the upper storey of the villa. The lower had been occupied by a workshop for pressing olives. He took us up to his own house and showed us the centuries-old olive press he had been unable to remove and which he had had built into the dining room as a decorative feature. I don't think I've ever been in a more elegantly designed interior. And the view down towards San Pantale and the cliffs of Zoagli, which figure in the Cantos, was breathtaking. 'One possesses *something*', he said, opening his door to show us. As we stood out on the terrace he produced, out of season, a line of Shakespeare he was proud to be able to quote — 'Rough winds do shake the darling buds of May' — and he assured me that in Shakespeare's day 'winds' was pronounced as in 'winds the clock'.

In the Hotel Miranda on the Rapallo seafront I read J. G. Ballard's *The Empire of the Sun*. For the child Ballard the realities of war were more pressingly present than they were for Pound, locked in an intellectual landscape of his own making; though by the end of the war, when Pound made his trek north from Rome through the ruined Italian landscape to tell his daughter the truth about his private life, the collapse of his revolutionary dream had taken physical form and lay all about him.

STOCKHOLM DIARY

My grandfather, Christian Karlson, after whom I was named, was a Swede who left his country as a young man, became a seaman, and finally a sea captain and never returned. He died before I was born; and I have never been to Sweden. But I grew up in New Zealand with the myth of my grandfather, in a house full of mementoes, and with the idea that it was in some way rather superior to be Swedish. I identified romantically with that part of my inheritance. It seemed more interesting than the English, the Irish and the Scots which, in almost equal parts, account for the rest of the cocktail which is myself.

Eighteen months ago I almost got to Sweden. I was in Copenhagen, just across the water from Malmo where my grandfather grew up. But the sea between was frozen. The ferries and hydrofoils weren't running. I couldn't delay, so I looked across the ice at Sweden and returned to London.

This time I'm invited by a friend, a novelist, Lars Ardelius, so I fly direct to Stockholm. I leave London the morning the Booker short-list is announced. That evening in a bar close to the waterfront I'm hearing gossip about who might win the Nobel Prize for literature. Joseph Brodsky seems to be favoured, with Nadine Gordimer a possibility. Wole Soyinka is also mentioned. I'm told some people feel it's 'Africa's turn'; and although Gordimer might be a better writer, Soyinka is a better colour. No mention is made of Tomas Tranströmer, the Swedish poet whose English publishers advertise him as 'a hot favourite' for the Nobel Prize. I suggest that some recent Nobel Prizes have been eccentric, to say the least; and that Gunter Grass should have it. I'm told a story about Grass visiting Stock-

London Magazine, February 1987. This was written in the northern autumn of 1986. The gossip I heard was evidently sound. First Brodsky received the Nobel Prize; then in the following year, Soyinka.

265

holm, holding forth in a group of literary and academic Swedes. Beside
Grass sat a little man who said nothing and whom Grass ignored. After
the little man had left Grass was told he'd been sitting beside the chairman
of the literary sub-committee of the Swedish Academy — the, so to
speak, Anthony Thwaite of the Nobel Committee. Next day Grass was
seen walking slowly along the seafront back and forth, outside the
chairman's hotel. It's a good story; but I still insist that the Nobel Prize
for literature needs Grass more than he needs it.

The days are wonderfully sunny and bright, the sky blue, the leaves
vivid autumn colours, and in shadow the chill is astonishing. By midnight
ice has to be scraped off windscreens. I'm reminded that Stockholm is
nearer than Moscow to the Pole. In sunlight the hotels, palaces, and
churches, the great houses, museums, and theatres, are collectively grand
and imposing. Stockholm is as fine in its way as Paris, but lacking the
population, the action and density, to give it quite the feel of one of
the great capitals — though that is certainly what it once was.

On my second night I go to the home of the novelist and playwright
Per Jersild and his wife Ulla. Other novelists are there — Lars Ardelius,
Lars-Olof Franzén and Inger Alfén. Also Magareta Rye, a publisher with
the Swedish Writers' Co-operative. The wine is Spanish, not French,
because I come from New Zealand. I miss the point of this, and when
asked whether I drink French wine, I say yes. It's only then I realize
the Spanish wine is connected with the bombing of the *Rainbow Warrior*
and the continued French nuclear testing in the Pacific. The truth is
that though I felt strongly about the one, and continue to feel strongly
about the other, it has never occurred to me not to drink any French
wine that happened to be put in front of me. It seems the Swedish quarter
of my gene pool has failed an essential test. And it's the same when
the talk gets around to the question of guilt. They agree there has been
a relaxation in recent years, but nevertheless guilt is part of the Swedish
character. I have to admit I don't feel it often — certainly I'm not regular
and dependable in my guilts.

But there is something uniform in every aspect of this occasion —
the furniture, the look of the room and the people and the pictures on
the wall, the very casual but just perceptible formality, the way things
are laid out down to the smallest detail, the look of food on a plate
— all of which strikes me as foreign to my experience but not alien
to my temperament. It's a particular style — spare but not spartan, orderly,
visual — quite distinct, it seems to me, from the richness and multiplicity,
the heavy texture and tendency to cross threads and crosscurrents, that
belong to the Anglo-Saxon tradition.

My bedside reading at the moment is Michael Moorcock's lively *Letters
from Hollywood* — an odd choice you might think, but I like random
conjunctions by which each thing observed seems sharper. So a New

Zealander lies in bed in the Hotel Tegnérlunden while outside red and gold leaves shower down over a tidy Stockholm square, reading a Londoner writing about California. Not that Moorcock, though I find him entertaining, is entirely to my taste. For some reason it seems to me terribly English that he should, for example, go on at such length explaining that the common preference for San Francisco over Los Angeles is a form of snobbery and that Los Angeles is really superior. He sends out currently fashionable signals that he deplores male chauvinism, while revealing the hell his ex-wives' trans-Atlantic phone calls and cries for help are making of his life, and even resolving at one point to be more *careful* about whom he marries next. The life he decribes, awash with booze and lived largely on credit, is what used to be called Bohemian when I was young. I think even then it seemed to me messy; it certainly does now. I try (turning it all around the other way for a moment) to see the Swedes as Moorcock might see them — strenous, finicky, lugubrious, maddeningly precise in their discriminations — and certainly preferring San Francisco to Los Angeles! This is still the puritan north, and I suppose even its sexual libertarianism is only an aspect of rationality. (If it's rational to indulge, let's do it!) Nevertheless my preference is for order. There's a point at which I find it difficult to distinguish between an aesthetic response and a moral one. I feel vaguely that that might be deplorable; at least it's something in oneself to be watched. But it's so.

In the Stockholm National Gallery there is an exhibition of nineteenth-century American painting. I'm surprised at how thrilling some of it seems — not because it is (or isn't) 'great art', but because of the vividness with which it conveys a sense of the Dream of the New World Coming True. There is one by a painter whose name is Cole, showing an overpowering landscape of mountain, river, forest, and plain. In the foreground a single figure rides, dwarfed yet heroic. Cole has given his painting the title, 'Here Pass I the White Mountain'. How much history there is packed into that inversion! In Stockholm's Moderna Muséet there is an exhibition by a modern American photographer. His subject is almost exclusively young drug addicts, a world of dismal seediness and self-destruction. For the exhibition poster, which is all over town, the Swedes with conscientious explicitness have chosen a photograph showing a well-endowed young man, naked and semi-erect, watching a naked young woman shooting up. What became of the American Dream? Has it all gone sour? Or would Michael Moorcock, who pops uppers and downers according to need and knows about good and inferior cocaine, argue that the wide horizons and the sense that everything is possible survive in the extravagances of Los Angeles, and even in the drug culture itself about which he writes with the weary, superior tone of an old connoisseur?

On the evening after the supper at Per and Ulla Jersild's I meet Lars Ardelius in the Piano Bar of the Grand Hotel — the one that has been housing the negotiators at the East-West Arms Limitation Talks just successfully concluded. The late afternoon sun pours through big windows that look out on to the waterfront and across to the medieval town. Lars, who until now has been casual in his dress, is sitting at a window wearing a linen jacket in grey and turquoise stripes with a matching tie, drinking a daiquiri and a glass of lager. After drinks we go on to the Opera House where we occupy the Director's box in the centre of the circle. The opera is *Cosi fan Tutti*, sung in Swedish; and it begins, with the young soldiers making their wager about their respective fiancées' fidelity, against a background of projected scenes explicitly pornographic. Like the poster for the exhibition of photographs, this takes one by surprise, and seems conscientious rather than liberated. The singing is excellent, the opera puzzling and slightly distasteful, as it always is, I suppose because the women are cajoled and tricked into infidelity and then blamed for it.

Supper after the opera is at the Restaurant KB, whose insignia shows an angel and a devil with locked arms drinking a toast. KB stands for Konstnärsbaren — artists' bar — and it takes pride in the writers and painters of note who have traditionally met there. Again the feeling is peculiarly foreign — panelled walls and upholstered furniture, waiters in bow ties and black waistcoats, a feeling almost of having wandered into the set of a play of the 1890s, where serious social issues are to be hammered out. I enjoy the food, especially the local things, like the red lingonberry sauce with the beef, and a dessert of yellow sweet-sour berries called hjortron, very expensive because rare (gathered by countrywomen on the moors) served with home-made ice cream.

A group of actors come in from the local theatre. Lars receives hugs and there are introductions. A theatre critic and his wife come over. While the wife talks to Lars in Swedish the critic tells me about the sixty-seat theatre Lars has built at his summer-house on an island, where a number of successful plays (including one by Per Jersild) have had their first airing. Over the years since Lars first made the island his summer retreat, numbers of Stockholm writers, film-makers, and politicians have followed his example.

The conversation turns to New Zealand's anti-nuclear policy. David Lange is a popular figure. I have in my bag a xerox of an article from the *Atlantic Monthly* about what the writer calls New Zealand's anti-Americanism, given me, I think probably as a reproach, by the New Zealand High Commissioner in London because my first novel, *Smith's Dream*, written at the height of the Vietnam War, is cited as early evidence of this trend. The same article says New Zealanders are not used to their country being newsworthy and are consequently pleased when David Lange's name is mentioned favourably. I think the word naive is used. It is certainly implied. All of that is in the back of my mind when I hear Lange praised. Having lived most of one's adult life seeing New

Zealand represented abroad by Prime Ministers like Sidney Holland who seemed of low intelligence, or Keith Holyoake who was a pompous ass, or Rob Muldoon who was an articulate bully with no clear purpose except to stay in the top job, it would be difficult not to take pleasure in the present change. And if one's convictions are firmly anti-nuclear, as mine are, the pleasure is so much the greater. If that is naive, then I am naive, and Sweden is a congenial place to visit because it contains so many who are of like mind.

On the Sunday morning I go for a walk in search of the place where Olof Palme was shot, which I know is somewhere not far from my hotel. The place, on a street called Sveavägen, is not marked by anything except the flowers and cards and scrawled notes dropped there by visitors and passers-by. The flowers are pushed into a pile to allow pedestrians to pass on either side; but on Sunday there are few people about. At the end of an alley off the main street I can see the steps up which the gunman ran after shooting Palme who was walking home with his wife from a cinema on a Friday evening. Across the street in Adolf Fredricks Kyrka a bell is tolling for Sunday morning service. Palme is buried in the churchyard. As yet there is no headstone or memorial — only flowers and notes dropped there, as on the pavement, by visitors.

In Scandinavian countries there are many stories which begin 'There was a Swede, a Dane and a Norwegian', more or less exactly parallel to the stories I heard as a child which began 'There was an Englishman, a Scotsman and an Irishman'. I remember hearing in Denmark that if these stories are told by a Swede or a Dane, the Norwegian, like the Irishman in the stories I used to hear, is always the fool. 'Yes and if they're told by us, it's the same,' a Norwegian added cheerfully. I'm told in Stockholm that Danes regard Swedes as rather stiff and formal, not easy, relaxed mixers. What strikes me about them is something like frankness and directness. It has something to do with eye contact. In London (you notice it especially on the tube) eye contact is avoided. If it occurs inadvertently it causes embarrassment; if deliberately, that usually signals aggression. If Swedes are interested in a stranger, they look — neither furtively nor aggressively. Not only that, but women and men seem equal. In Anglo-Saxon countries a man is freer to look at a woman he admires than she is to look at him. When I mention this and say I can't see that in Sweden such a difference exists, I'm told it doesn't and the fact that it doesn't causes misunderstandings especially with visiting Spanish and Italian males, who imagine that beautiful blondes are signalling sexual interest in them at every turn.

One of the pleasures of a Scandinavian hotel is the breakfast. A variety of things, all more to my taste than the English cooked breakfast, are laid out and you help yourself to whatever takes your fancy. You can begin with orange juice and muesli and yoghurt. Then there is a heavy black bread (or lighter breads if you prefer), and dishes of salted uncooked herrings, caviare, small meat balls, sliced salami, hard-boiled eggs, slices of cheese, and raw tomato and green pepper; also the most wonderful jams, heavy with real fruit; and of course strong coffee. If the high cost of everything is chewing through your kronor, and you're planning to spend the day sight-seeing, you can eat a good breakfast and bag yourself a lunch as well. I remember finding a strange machine in our house when I was child which I was told was a coffee grinder. At that time, partly because the war was on, and partly I suppose because New Zealand was still a tea-drinking outpost of Empire, no one I knew drank real coffee. There was a sort of bottled essence called coffee-and-chicory which my mother and grandmother drank in the mornings. The old coffee grinder was a relic of the time when my grandfather was alive. Beans had to be obtained for him; and also salted herrings for his breakfast. In Stockholm I eat, of course, the salted herrings and the black bread, and drink strong coffee.

Everywhere I go socially English is spoken although I'm the only English speaker. I'm embarrassed by this, but the Swedes are realists. If 99 per cent of those who visit your country, and 99. 999 per cent of those who don't, know nothing of your language; and if your population is eight million — there's no choice. You learn at least a second language — preferably the one most widely spoken — and you practise it whenever you can. It's a nice question to try to balance the linguistic isolation of Sweden against the geographical isolation of New Zealand. Personally, I would rather inherit a language which is international and live at the perimeter. On the other hand I would like (but I mightn't like it if I did!) to inherit a culture as rich and tight and stable as Sweden's seems to be. If there is anything more than romantic myth-making in my notion that Sweden continues in my genes, that has to be balanced against the powerful determining fact of the language in which I came to consciousness. It is often said that Britain and the United States are two nations divided by a common language — but is that saying more than that family relationships are as likely to be warring as affectionate? Linguistic kinship is powerful because so much of the way the mind works is determined by the language which is its instrument. I talked recently to a very distinguished writer and critic who teaches at the Sorbonne and who is bilingual in English and French, having spoken both as an infant. She told me that when she writes in French she feels herself to be using a dead language, its bounds are so fixed and its vocabulary so limited, lacking the fine shades of English. Any Paris concierge, if roused, will let fly with impressive fluency and eloquence, not because, as Anglophones are inclined to suppose, they are all brilliant, and natural orators, but because French rhetoric is a repetitious formula. Speakers of French and English are truly foreign to one another in a way that

English and Americans are not. The dislikes and differences between the latter can be enormous; but the common ground is more significant — as General de Gaulle perfectly well knew when he kept Britain out of the European Community. When France and America woo one another it is like a very stagey public flirtation which everyone knows will never go near the bedroom. And that in turn is why it makes perfectly good sense for David Lange, or Neil Kinnock, to reject American nuclear demands, deplore American foreign policy, and still insist that they see themselves as part of the family, preserving the traditional alliances. I have hated American foreign policy for most of my adult life; but so have millions of loyal Americans.

The point about the isolation of the Swedish language is made back here in London, after my return from Stockholm, at a reading by Swedish poets at the Hayward Gallery, accompanying the marvellous exhibition of turn-of-the-century Scandinavian paintings, Dreams of a Summer Night. The poets read at a lectern against the background of a large painting by Bergh of a man and woman standing on a wooden verandah looking out over a landscape of trees and lake water with the late evening midsummer light coming at them almost horizontally. Tomas Tranströmer reads one of his poems in Swedish and a translation is read by Dannie Abse, who introduces the poets. But towards the end the translation begins to sound strange and Tranströmer becomes agitated. He jumps up to explain that the last page Abse has read belongs to a different poem. The pages of translations have somehow got wrongly stapled together. Of course it might have happened with any language, but it seems much less likely if the language had been one more widely known.

I'm sure Tranströmer deserves his pre-eminence among the Swedish poets. But the one who catches my imagination most strongly on this occasion is Lars Forssell; and he reads a poem which I take as a warning to someone of my temperament. It is about a chameleon who believes the leaf is green because he is on it, and green is his colour at the moment; that the roof is red because he once basked there — and so on. We don't want to go under to our environment and so we invent explanatory myths, large and small, by which we preserve some sense, if not of dominance, at least of self. But then if there were no problems — if one were perfectly well adjusted — what occasion would there be for writing anything at all?

LUDWIG AND JACK: A SHORT ESSAY ON THE RELATION OF STYLE AND CONTENT

Jack Kerouac: After a while you get to learn it can't always be like that but at first you think it can go on for ever. So there I am in the back of the pick-up with Allen and Neil and we're goin somewhere I don't know where but we're passing round that bottle of bad brandy tryin to keep out of the cold. There's a pile of snow in the tray with us and it's been standing like that all day parked outside the RCMP while we got ourselves bailed so it's frozen hard and we're too far gone on the brandy to try shovelling. Red Lane's driving and the road surface is like glass — there's been maybe a bit of a thaw with the sun very bright that afternoon and now it's frozen again and you just need to touch the brake and you're into a spin. Fuck we're shouting at that Canuck Red Lane to step on it and get us there wherever the hell it is but Red isn't getting any of the brandy so he keeps his foot steady. And maybe Countessa who's inside the cab with him is telling him to take it easy and stay alive but I doubt it, that wasn't Countessa's way. She was a sad beautiful lay with eyes like a jersey calf and an arm like a pin cushion. And her dog had to go with her in the cab — she didn't trust him with us out on the tray with the brandy — so that's how the five of us, six if you count the dog we called Foster after Foster Dulles, we went out from 100th street down the hill and up and over the high-level bridge to some place out of town where Neil had a friend . . .

Ludwig Wittgenstein: I am glad you mention the bridge. In my time too when I was offered a post at Edmonton they called it the 'high level bridge'. I used to wonder why not the 'high bridge'. It is high, we have to suppose in absolute terms — high for a bridge. High as bridges go

Rambling Jack, August 1986.

the world over. But then there is a question of other bridges in the
town and it seems safe to assume that this one is distinguished from
the others by its altitude, because all bridges must be 'level' in its other
sense, namely horizontal. So why 'high level'? You know we have 'high-
level discussions' these days. Even 'top-level'. But this cannot be the
meaning of 'high level' when it is attached to 'bridge'. We cannot have
in that sense a 'high level' of bridge except perhaps — if you will excuse
the pun — among card players. Yet I persist in the feeling that this
is not just a tautology . . .

Jack Kerouac: You probably know, Ludwig, that Bob Kroetsch has a scene
in one of his books where he fucks a girl standing up and they're on
that bridge in the snow at twenty below. Well maybe he did, all sorts
of impossible great things happened in those sad beautiful days. I remember
Allen waving his dick around in some pretty kooky places but they used
to say the wind-chill factor up there put it down to God knows fifty
or seventy below and I can't see a hard-on lasting as long as it would
take to unbutton your flies. Allen used to say that bridge was the most
beautiful in the world because it was the saddest and the ugliest . . .

Ludwig Wittgenstein: This of course brings us to the heart of the problem.
Perhaps not the same problem, but related, and possibly more interesting.
We know, or we think we know, so exactly what we mean when we
say that the bridge in question is ugly; and I agree with your friend
Mr Ginsberg. In that simple sense it is ugly. But so much is called up
when we make such a judgement. Let us suppose for a moment that
up-river a tribe of Indians has persisted undiscovered since the arrival
of the European. Now we have to suppose that all at once, for some
reason we don't need to speculate about, they set off travelling down-
river over the ice — let us say to avoid some natural disaster, because
you would not expect them to travel ordinarily in such weather. So
at just the moment when you and your friends are passing over the bridge
away from the town centre — or equally it might be at the moment
when Mr Kroetsch, or the character in his book, is engaging with his
lady-friend in the act you cast doubt upon (and let me say by way of
parenthesis that I agree with your doubts) — at just this (or that) moment
our Indians arrive at a bend in the river. They look up and see the
bridge. Do they think it is ugly, it is beautiful? Of course they do not.
They are struck dumb with amazement. They have never seen such a
thing. Perhaps they pray to their gods, or reach for a magic talisman,
as a modern Catholic might cross himself or go down on his knees to
say a Hail Mary. You see my point I am sure. To say something is
ugly or beautiful we in fact conjure up a whole tradition, a whole history.
Our own experience of bridges, real bridges, bridges seen in books and

movies, together with our knowledge, however slight, of modern engineering and construction — all of this comes inevitably into play. To the Indian there is nothing of that to draw upon. His senses you might argue are assaulted by the thing itself, without a context . . .

Jack Kerouac: Yeah well that's true, Ludwig. It's gonna be a shock. And they used to say those Injuns before they got all blotchy with the booze had eyes that could pick the nits out of your hair at a hundred yards. I remember one of our all-night drinking sessions and smoking too — it was some kind of hash, or maybe it was when we were on cactus down in the desert — anyway it was Neil was telling us how those redskin males had to be able to see all the stars in the Pleiades before they could get their whatever it was like a licence for huntin bears. And we were screwing up our eyes, it was one of those clear desert nights but we couldn't even find the fuckin Pleiades. And Allen said how the fuck would you know whether the young Injun could see the stars — he might be just bullshitting. If he knew how many stars he was supposed to see and he said he could see them, you'd have to give him his licence. But it's pretty well-known they had good eyes so I'm pickin the first Injun round the bend's gonna be able to tell us whether Bob Kroetsch was lying or not. I mean what did he see up there — was it a good stiff hard-on or a limp rag? Was it high level or wasn't it? . . .

Ludwig Wittgenstein (laughs): Uck, uck, uck . . .

Jack Kerouac: But for Christ's sake it didn't matter to us that night. Bob, or that character of his, the one in the book — he could have been up to his ears in it I don't reckon any of us on the back of Red's pick-up would have seen. We were too cold, and too boozy. And then Allen threw up all over that heap of frozen snow — he couldn't get his head over the side quick enough, and Neil and I jumped up shouting at him to keep his lousy puke to himself. And *crunch*, the pick-up swivels on the ice, the front fender crumples against the side of the bridge and one headlight gets knocked out. We never worked out how it happened. Maybe it was because Allen threw up and that made us start shouting. Red couldn't remember afterwards because he'd banged his head on the windshield . . .

Ludwig Wittgenstein: Of course we say 'because' in these circumstances but it is never clear that by 'because' we mean a cause has been precisely stated. There may be a 'why' to such an event which is not quite the same, I suspect, as a 'cause'. It has been said often enough that if something is said to have been 'caused' by something else this is only a matter of concomitance. We all argue a little naively around this point, often when secretly or overtly we want to place blame. You tell Mr Ginsberg if he hadn't vomited, or if he had vomited over the side of the truck, you and your friend would not have jumped up shouting and the driver would not have been distracted. And perhaps Mr Ginsberg argues (just for the sake of *my* argument, you understand) that he is sure at that moment Mr Kroetsch's character and his young lady were on the bridge engaging in something which by any standards must be considered remarkable in such weather, and certainly likely to take the attention of your driver. The driver, however, can confirm neither of these 'cause' arguments, 'because', he says (another 'cause' supplied, you notice) he banged his head. None of these explanations, by the way, takes into account my Indians who may have been whooping or shrieking at their first sight of a high level bridge. Let us say for the sake of argument that all of these events occurred simultaneously. Are the Indians whooping at the bridge, or the vomit, or the car-crash, or at Mr Kroetsch's character's feat at (so to speak) one hundred above and forty below?

Jack Kerouac: Yeah well to be honest with you Ludwig I don't remember the redskins that night but I can believe you. Anything was possible in those sad beautiful times. We didn't even have to get ourselves towed. The pick-up engine was still running so Red takes us straight to a little house not far from the bridge where he has a friend who has a few bottles of this and a few bottles of that and she won't mind us spreading ourselves around her floor in this weather and after crumpling a fender. And Red he's telling us how he first picked Countessa up off the streets when she was doing a square night's work for a square night's pay — and that was every night — a regular whore with a regular beat before she started to get sad and go downhill. We were a weird generation — 'I've seen the best of my generation', that's Allen's sad beautiful line and it's true. And now Red Lane's dead and so's Countessa . . .

Ludwig Wittgenstein: Which brings us to another kind of problem. Philosophically speaking . . .

POSTSCRIPT:
THE NEW VICTORIANS

My last collection of literary essays and reviews, *In the Glass Case*, dealt only with New Zealand writers and writing. Over fifteen or more years I had deliberately chosen New Zealand subjects to write about with the idea of aggregating just such a collection as it finally became. To do this I had declined opportunities to write about internationally known poets — offers from publishers and editors which followed on the publication in England and America of my book *The New Poetic*. It was my (in retrospect, rather solemn) notion that a mature literature needed a mature criticism; that the discussion of New Zealand writing thus far had been mainly low-key and unsophisticated, or where excellent, random. Although there seemed to be an idea prevalent in New Zealand (one which perhaps persists) that it is not possible, or proper, to combine the roles of writer and critic, I had grown up in the time of the dominance of T. S. Eliot who always insisted on the conjunction of creative and critical faculties and the necessity that in the writer of consequence they must develop together.

So the publication of *In the Glass Case* was an occasion for me of some moment. Since that time I have continued to publish poetry, fiction, and criticism — three collections of new poems, two novels, a book on Pound and the Modernist movement, and the essays, lectures, and reviews from which those in this book have been selected. But it wasn't until I came to make the selection that I recognized the degree to which, in my occasional writing, I have turned away from New Zealand. I have, in the current jargon, let the market dictate. I have left the university. When invited abroad to lecture, I have gone. When asked to write for

Written for this collection of essays in August 1988, and published in *Metro*, February 1989.

a journal that pays better than New Zealand journals, I have done it. My subject remains the same — modern literature in general, but only New Zealand literature as occasions present themselves, and no longer with any ambition to offer a comprehensive view.

The year when In the Glass Case was published, 1981, was also the year of the Springbok tour which split New Zealand down the middle and made it feel like a country experiencing civil war. On the one side were those who were, or seemed, or claimed to be, politically, ethically, ethnically, intellectually and internationally aware; on the other, those who didn't care too much about, or for, awareness of those various kinds, but who enjoyed a good game of rugby. There was a wonderful camaraderie and unity of purpose among those who opposed the tour. It reminded me of the headiest days of my involvement in protest against the Vietnam War; and I remain convinced it was right, and proud to have been part of it. But in the intervening years I have discovered how tenuous the bond is that holds such groups together; or perhaps (more to the point) how incapable I am — except in rare moments of crisis when the need for action supersedes the desire to get things right in words — of standing together with any group. In the seven or eight years since the Springbok tour it seems to me the discussion of serious issues in New Zealand has been jargonized to a degree I find intolerable. That in itself is something to be expected from time to time in the public arena. One looks then to literature — to writers, historians, schoolteachers, sophisticated readers, the universities — to protect the language, to 'keep clean the tools of thought', to resist the slogans and the intellectual short-cuts. In New Zealand it isn't happening. Our literary community, which when it had almost no public status used to be so resolute in its criticism of our society, is becoming the handmaiden of political and sociological myth-making. Moralism rules. Good writing — the notion of accurate observation, truth to experience and to the facts, the right words in the right order — is relatively unimportant.

I had my first clear sense of this when I was invited by the late Peter Smart to address a conference of the National Association of Teachers of English in 1982. I took this as an occasion to criticize what was then called the New English Syllabus. I didn't expect everyone to agree with me — only to listen. The reader will be able to judge whether what I said was offensive, or imprudent. To me, as a teacher of English in a university and the parent of school-age children, it seemed at least a reasonable point of view based on observation, experience, and serious reflection.

I have never met such hostility from an audience. I believed that in arguing for more rigour in the teaching of English language and literature I was doing my duty as a writer and a professor; but I found myself cast in the role of savager of the poor, the semi-literate, the underprivileged, the Maori. I don't record this in order to complain, nor looking for sympathy. I record it as a measure (one of many) of the state of the nation. If our teachers of English will not rally to the defence of language and literature against a bureaucracy which wants to see them only as tools of the social services, who remains to protect them?

Feminism has grown as a force in New Zealand during these years, and I know that to argue, even reasonably, with a moral crusade is inevitably to cause insult. I have never wanted to defend inequalities based on gender. I have never thought the woman's place was in the home, nor the man's in the workforce, unless each wants it that way. I have always been out of sympathy with what appears to be a socially engendered notion that males not only are less sensitive than females, but that they ought to be. In my fiction (with the exception perhaps of *Smith's Dream*) there have always been 'feminine' elements (my first two long stories, 'A Race Apart' and 'A Fitting Tribute' had female first-person narrators) which make it closer in style and tone and manner to the Mansfield–Ashton-Warner–Frame line of development than to that of Mulgan–Sargeson–Shadbolt–Gee. But I have found myself resisting the rhetoric of the Women's Movement which strikes me more and more as an unpleasant combination of moralist busy-bodying and political manipulation. History is retold to suit the purposes of the teller; and if part of it is history one has lived through, one simply rebels at the misrepresentation.

A radical change is occurring in our social organization, chiefly, I suppose, because effective birth control has freed women from constraints which, though social in effect, were biological in origin. Even if I feel — and I do — that there is some loss (and I mean loss both to women and men) as well as great gain in the changes, I wouldn't want to resist them in the least. What I resist, and what many good strong independent women resist, is the rewriting of history, shifting Marxist class terminology into the area of gender, making men simply oppressors and women oppressed, and bringing that forward as a 'fact' into the present. At present the suicide rate among young males in New Zealand is four times that among females; the rate of male admission to mental institutions is also higher — but we are told that females are oppressed. Clearly liberals — those good people with whom I went to the barricades in 1981 — are selective in the use they make of statistics. The huge disproportion of Maoris in our jails is said to be (and no doubt is, at least in part) a sign that they are oppressed and disadvantaged. No one offers the even greater disproportion of males over females in jail as a sign that males are oppressed and disadvantaged. I am not saying this is so — only that statistics are being used, or ignored, according to their convenience.

The Women's Movement has had a powerful effect on the literary scene, and on the use of English. No young person will now believe

278

that the generic 'he' was ever sexually neutral — though you will find it as often in Virginia Woolf and Katherine Mansfield as in male writers — and it survives in sayings like 'He who hesitates is lost'. My own response to feminist demands for 'non-sexist' language was at first to ignore them. I felt that as a writer I had to defend my own sense of style against any and every encroachment. But as time has gone by the complainants have brought about what they said was the case all along. By insisting that the generic 'he' is not neuter but masculine, they have made it so; and so for a male writer to go on using it becomes a defiant act which may seem to signal all kinds of irrelevant and untrue things about himself — that he doesn't care about rape, beats his wife, thinks women inferior, and so on. I have therefore struggled (shall I say?) *manfully* to avoid saying 'The writer will find that he . . .'. It continues to be difficult; and for reasons which are still not clear to me, but have everything to do with English grammar and nothing to do with gender, I found it impossible and gave up the attempt in the essay 'Poetry' which opens the book.

But other dictates, such as the comic-strip list put out recently by Radio New Zealand for non-sexist language, take no account of tone or subtleties of context and are best ignored. For example, 'poetess' has always had pejorative overtones, and I can't recall anyone writing seriously about a woman poet and using that term. On the other hand 'actress' has no such negative implications; nor has 'heroine'. They signal difference of course, and the difference is gender — no more than that. Cleopatra is not only the heroine of Shakespeare's play; she is also the dominant character — and consequently it's more significant to know who is the leading actress in any production of *Antony and Cleopatra* than to know who is the leading actor. The idea that Cleopatra is one 'hero' and Antony another, and that both are played on the modern stage by 'actors', is misleading and confusing. It is one of the follies of our time that it should be enshrined in a directive from a government agency.

Yeats says 'an intellectual hatred is the worst'. One saw it a few years back when a group of feminists assaulted Mervyn Thompson, playwright and lecturer in drama in the Auckland University English Department, tied him to a tree, threatened him with castration, daubed 'rapist' on his car, and ran off when disturbed. Notices were put about the campus declaring that Thompson was a rapist; and his plays were subsequently picketed by students and boycotted by more than one theatre group. The action against him seemed to have been taken in imitation of a feminist play, *Setting the Table*, by Renée Taylor (as she then was — she later shed the patronymic and became Renée), where women take similar action against a man they believe to be a rapist. Thompson, a strong feminist sympathizer, had put on a second production of the play in the English Department, and I remember arguing with him that he

279

should not have. The play was agitprop — weak dramatically because, unlike apparently doctrinaire plays by Shaw or Brecht, it nowhere generated the sense that there was, or could be, a counterstatement. It asked its audience to applaud vigilante action, and of course radical feminists loved it — but so would old Southern red-necks have loved a play justifying the lynching of Blacks (who were also usually declared to be rapists). Thompson thus became the victim of a propaganda he had given support to; and in all he has said and written about this subject since, I'm not sure that that is an irony he has fully apprehended.

I'm sure Thompson has never raped anyone; but interviewed on television he looked hang-dog and said there might have been an occasion when he had been 'insensitive', putting his own sexual interests ahead of those of his partner of the time. Watching, I felt that a dominant moralism (as distinct from morality) was beginning to dictate the behaviour of everyone in public life. Nothing was allowed to be a true and simple expression of human sexuality and the male psyche. The intellectual community was being corrupted by a childish desire to be 'good', and could only be made healthy if enough people forgot about 'goodness' (pleasing Mummy and Daddy) and thought instead about authenticity. This feeling — which continues — probably lies beneath the surface, but I hope visibly, elsewhere in this collection.

For me the Mervyn Thompson episode had a strange aftermath when I was asked to review Stephanie Dowrick's novel, *Running Backwards over Sand*. The editor who asked me to do it was a woman, and I had had excellent relations with her and with her newspaper. I didn't admire the novel but I wrote as charitably as critical honesty would permit. After a long silence I was paid; but when a review of the novel appeared it was by someone else — a woman, who also thought it weak, and said so. When I asked why this had happened the editor wrote to me

Now the awkward bit: I didn't use your review of the Stephanie Dowrick book. When I sent it to you, I didn't know there had been difficulties between radical feminists and academics in New Zealand, though I have since heard the full story of your colleague being tied to a tree.

Because the novel took such a strongly feminist position, I thought your review could be seen as displaying enough lack of sympathy for this position to make a fair review difficult. I am not arguing that this is indeed so: I am just saying that it could seem so. In the event I sent the book to _____ _____ to review, and she clearly didn't like it any better than you did.

So the paper was prepared to pay twice to have a bad novel reviewed. Ten days later the editor wrote to me

If it is any consolation over the Dowrick book, I agree with your judgement on its literary merits. Or at least I do over the relatively small part I was able to struggle through. I thought it was like walking through treacle, rather than backwards over sand, though that too.

That is much more severe than anything I had said; yet this editor felt she could not use my review.

Women writers continue to insist they are neglected or unfairly treated by the patriarchy which once ruled the literary roost. A common story is that of the woman in late-flowering middle age whose creativity was held back in her younger days by domestic responsibility. We have heard this with varying degrees of emphasis from many women writers in New Zealand. I have never doubted that what they say is true. I only wonder about the husbands of those years whose creativity was not merely held back — it was crushed altogether — by the parallel necessity to earn a living to support wife and family.

There was an odd reversal of roles at the recent Wattie Award occasion when Stevan Eldred-Grigg, who received the second prize for his novel *Oracles and Miracles*, declared that he was a writer and a 'mother', and that they were two of the worst-paid occupations. They are, of course; and I have always believed that home minders of small children should be properly paid by the state. But I felt Eldred-Grigg exactly repeated the common omission of his female counterparts of past years when he failed to mention that he is supported by a wife who is a medical practitioner. In being simultaneously house-person, child-minder, and writer, he is repeating the pattern by which, for example, Fiona Kidman and Marilyn Duckworth in New Zealand, or Margaret Drabble and A. S. Byatt in England, began their literary careers. Of course most writers, female and male, who are serious would like to be at it full time. It is economics, not gender, which makes that preference so difficult to achieve. But at least it is arguable (I would say demonstrable) that under the old dispensation there was a better chance of a woman writing novels while being a housewife than there was of a man while holding down a full-time job.

In an interview in the *New Zealand Listener* Lauris Edmond said the fact her poetry had had little serious critical attention made her feel that there was a submerged male critical prejudice working against it — a refusal to take it seriously because it was by a woman and about female experience. This is a good example of the bind a broadly feminist programme has inflicted on women writers. Conscientious editors look for women to write about women and before long women writers begin to feel slighted by men. But many men who might want to find occasion to write about women are inhibited, first because they have been told they are inadequate to the task, and second because any negative comment they may feel inclined to make will be a sign of male chauvinism and insensitivity. Yet to write only about male writers might suggest that you are still part of the 'old boy network'. From this critical impasse male academics escape into the safehouse of critical theory, while their female counterparts put themselves into the 'women's studies' enclosure.

Literary apartheid rules, and the result is boredom all round. Fortunately there are signs of a new young generation who are ready to rebel against it.

Within a few weeks of the interview referred to above, Edmond published in the same journal a poem called 'The Lecture'. It went as follows:

> I am just going downstairs to where
> I shall tell them lies. Up here
> at the window the maple trees' shadow
>
> fingers the indigo dusk and the fireflies
> carry their tiny cargoes of light
> up, down, right to the ground, then
>
> almost over the high branches again
> riding their currents of bark-scented dark
> with an unquestioning poise
>
> giving off sparks from a wholesome
> summer travail. I could watch them
> all night; what I cannot do
>
> is burn at the small purifying fires
> of their industry. I shall go soon,
> persons are waiting to hear what I claim
>
> that I know. I will talk down, say
> 'in respect of', offer insights, despising
> both them and myself, but thinking:
>
> 'up there in the quiet room
> where the fireflies are to be seen
> at work in their luminous trees
>
> there is my truth, my candour, my courage
> there I too can shine with the natural
> intermittent light of myself'
>
> and then I shall go on holding forth.

It's a poem about truth and lying. It claims truth for the poem as distinct from the public 'prose' voice that will give the lecture downstairs. This is bad in itself. The insights of poetry and prose may be different in kind; there is no reason why they should not both be truthful to the best of the writer's ability.

> I will talk down, say
> 'in respect of', offer insights, despising
> both them and myself.

Is it her own insights she will despise, or her audience? The grammar doesn't permit us to be quite sure, but she probably means her audience, since they are despised in tandem with herself. But to her *other* audience, the one for the poem, she offers a different, honest self — one which responds sensitively to nature and whose natural place is 'up here' where 'the maple trees' shadow / fingers the indigo dusk'.

The success or otherwise of the poem depends on its convincing us that here, though not downstairs, she is being truthful. It is of course very difficult to be truthful about yourself. You need a clear head and a steady hand. Subjective truth is what the Women's Movement has claimed women writers are best at. But in Edmond's poem I think we are offered an inadvertent snapshot of a woman deceiving herself.

Anyone who has given lectures must surely see through the poem to what lies behind it — *fear*. You are about to go in front of an audience. At the last minute you feel you have nothing worthwhile to say. You tell yourself it doesn't matter. It's just something to be got through. Your 'real' self is something truer and finer than the self you must project to survive the coming exposure. How better protect yourself against possible failure than by believing that behind the false public face resides a sensitive poetic person who responds to the beauty of fireflies? But this 'poetic' person when you commit it to paper may be just another public mask. Why, after all, should Edmond write 'I shall' (three times) when in conversation, being a New Zealander, she would say 'I will' — yet also inconsistently slip once into 'I will'? Because, I think, she is not being authentic. She is adopting a false voice, and her language betrays her. She exaggerates her own fault (I don't believe she would really 'tell them lies', or say 'in respect of') — but only in order to claim for herself as *poet* 'truth . . . candour . . . courage'.

In the poem you can see Edmond's skills as a writer. She is sensitive. She uses the language intelligently and economically. The cadences are beautiful, the fireflies finely observed. But some kind of rigour is lacking and so the whole effect is 'poetic' in the bad sense. 'Truth . . . candour . . . courage' are precisely what is lacking.

This is what I would say of it if the poem were by a man. Should I not say it because its author is a woman? But this poet has complained of being slighted by male critics. It seems to me the Women's Movement as it operates in the literary sphere has to decide which it wants — to be patronized, or to be treated as equals.

The other great issue of the day is that of race. We used to think in New Zealand we had no racial problem. We were wrong. We thought we had found a formula for a satisfactory mixing of races — and it may be that we have done as well as any nation and better than most. There has always been a degree of accord between Maori and Pakeha — a fund of goodwill on both sides and the wish to resolve differences.

There are also clear conflicts of interest. It's good for the health of the nation that these conflicts should be brought out into the open. No one should fear plain speaking. No one should believe he/she has a monopoly on truth or virtue.

I am not a social engineer, nor a politician. My professional concern is literature and language; but I believe they are of immense consequence to everything else. My proper function as I see it — as poet, fiction writer, essayist, reviewer — is to represent truthfully. Sometimes poetry and fiction have strange oblique ways of getting at 'reality'. Expository prose goes at it more directly. But if I am not one way or another putting truthful images in front of those who read me, then by my own standard I fail.

I have to ask myself why three or four references to Maori issues and Maori writing in this collection have negative overtones. It will be said I am racist, or at least anti-Maori. I will have to live with that, although I know it to be untrue. In fact each statement is specific and its context explains it. I am upholding a long and honourable tradition of Western literature — specifically literature in the English language. It is a tradition which gathers within itself a whole civilization — its spirit, its values, its historical record, its imaginative triumphs, its linguistic riches, its experiments with form. It is the flag I sail under — European literature, literature in English, as it exists historically and as it has been transmuted by these people, Pakeha and Maori, in this place, during these 150 years. If someone tells me another culture has another way of expressing itself and a different judgement to make of mine, I don't doubt or reject that. I simply say that is not my culture, and to pretend it is would be false. When I see Albert Wendt quoted as saying that New Zealand came out of the South Pacific, and must be returned to the South Pacific, I say to myself that New Zealand is not just a geographic location — it is also the minds of all its inhabitants, their languages, their histories, and what they inherit and produce. Time never simply 'returns' a country or a people to their past. The South Pacific has changed. It has been Europeanized. That's why Albert Wendt writes novels (a European form) and writes them in English.

Of course Maori elements have entered and will enter Pakeha writing. But the Pakeha element is not one half of a dual culture. It is a single culture absorbing relatively small amounts from the other. Maori culture is another single culture which has absorbed very large European elements. Understandably the time has come when it wants to recover something of its separateness. I know, and claim to speak for, one of these cultures. I respect the other's separateness. I don't — can't by the standards of my own culture — believe they are equal, either in their influence upon our lives as New Zealanders or in their significance in the modern world. A great deal of falsity it seems to me comes from pretending that they are equal in their power to influence the lives of either race — or that they ought to be equal.

The problem with the Treaty of Waitangi is that it was a pact between Maori tribes and the British Crown of 1840. It took no account of New Zealanders who were neither English nor Maori, because at that time there were none. Pakeha New Zealanders — the 'native born' as Keith Sinclair calls us in his book on New Zealand national identity — were not a party to the treaty, and I think for that reason do not feel responsible for it or in sympathy with its present-day consequences. One may feel, as many liberal-minded Pakehas do, that that is wrong; but if I'm right that it is a fact, and if that fact is not recognized, then it's hard to see how we can even begin to understand one another.

I think what I have done when the race question has impinged on literary matters is to say some things which I believe are not peculiar to me — are in fact in the minds of many Pakehas — but which are said only in private between (so to speak) consenting adults. In this I'm sure it is thought I am making trouble. My belief however (and of course I may be mistaken) is that worse trouble — confusion, misunderstanding — springs from the Pakeha disinclination to speak out frankly.

Recently in my bleaker moments I have thought that a small country like New Zealand can suffer a collective derangement without anyone articulate and confident noticing and saying it is happening. I have heard Allen Curnow say in conversation that we are subject to waves of intellectual fashion which strike us after they have abated at source, and there is not, here, the conservative inertia that operates as a safety drag mechanism in larger, longer-established societies. Feminism and anti-racism have hit us late, hard and together. Worthy in themselves, they can generate a kind of moral fervour which destroys both the sense of history and all thought of future consequences. In Britain the *London Review of Books* has for months run a correspondence and a series of reviews around the question of whether 'anti anti-racism' is a defensible position. Many have argued that it is at the present time; that such a position does not mean a defence of racism, but on the contrary believes that the programme of 'anti-racism' is itself, or has become, discriminatory. It's not my wish to go through the complications of that argument, but only to say that it's a sign of the health of the British intellectual community (which New Zealanders often affect to despise) that such a debate can be carried on at a high level in a liberal paper; and that no such thing is imaginable in this country. New Zealand children seem to sprout from the green grass, snatch a golden pen that comes down to them in a ray of moral white light, and in the absence of any sense of history begin scribbling in the *Listener* that it is wrong not to treat women and Maoris as equals. That is the climate in which we have to debate complex and delicate issues.

This gloomy and oppressive feeling about our intellectual life has reached a high point in recent months, culminating in the Wattie Award presentations for 1988. But first and (though improbably) not unconnected, we had Telethon. The money from Telethon was to go to help the victims of, and to prevent, domestic violence and sexual abuse. The advertising for it was extensive and included, for example, a picture of four girl babies with the caption ONE OF THESE WILL BE SCARRED FOR LIFE. Another showed a father at the door of his little daughter's bedroom, with a caption to the effect that some little girls 'fear the goodnight kiss'.

Recently an article in the *Listener* by Emily Flynn analysed in detail the false statistics on which the whole campaign was based. Depending on how broadly sexual assault is interpreted it can be claimed that one in four females will experience it — but to reach that statistic you have to include very minor examples, and cases which happen only once in a lifetime and leave no lasting effect. To arrive at the slogan that one in four females will be 'scarred for life' was a monstrous misrepresentation of the facts. Flynn also showed that the natural father — quite contrary to the idea put about — is the male least likely to sexually assault a female child. She showed how sets of statistics had been misused and wrongly combined to produce the desired picture. She also traced a lot of the misinformation to a source in the research of Miriam Saphira whose book on the subject is currently part of a package put out by the Education Department.

There has been no visible response to Flynn's article. It could not be contested so it was ignored. Those who foster myths for purposes they conceive to be moral do not want their work impeded by facts.

You might ask why this should be my concern. I see it as mine because it is a question of scrupulousness in language. Actions follow words and if the words are untrue the action will be misplaced and damaging. I worry about New Zealand's future because I can't see enough evidence of concern that the words people utter in public places and commit to paper should be honestly used and precisely related to facts. And teachers of English at every level who ought to be the guardians of that concern are frequently among the chief promoters of misuse.

And so we come to the Goodman Fielder Wattie Awards — New Zealand's most lavish, widely publicized and prestigious book prizes. In recent years the three judges have usually included a Maori, a woman, and a man. One has had the impression (possibly unfair) that the Maori has been there to see to Maori interests, the woman to see to women's interests, and the man to demonstrate that a modern white male can be trusted to yield priority to women and Maoris. The criterion which requires that one third of the (so to speak) 'marks' should go to 'impact on the community', and one third for book production and presentation, has meant that the literary element has not figured strongly in the judging.

has meant that the literary element has not figured strongly in the judging. All three of this year's award-winning writers were Ph.D.s in history. Claudia Orange's book on the Treaty of Waitangi took first prize. Eldred-Grigg's fiction based on oral history came second. Jock Phillips's *A Man's Country?*, challenging male stereotypes in New Zealand history, came third. What they have in common is that none of them manages — or, perhaps, even tries — to enter the past imaginatively; or where imagination is present, it is exercised selectively and with a clear purpose. Each is in its way a bullying book, remaking the past in terms of a set of proselytizing ideas which belong to the 1980s. A truthful picture of the past is not the point or object of the exercise. Rather, the past is ransacked to provide illustrations in support of a position in our current debates about either racism or sexism.

I grew up at a time when we all knew — those of us who were educated young 'intellectuals' — about how sanctimonious and moralizing the Victorian age had been, and how long its effects lingered in colonial New Zealand. But all that was being put behind us. We were to be free of it. On the Wattie occasion I felt that after all these years we hadn't put it behind us at all. This was a room full of moral self-satisfaction, full of 'good' rather than authentic behaviour. A modest, truthful, well-written history like Russell Stone's biography of John Logan Campbell didn't deserve to rate below Jock Phillips's one-sided 'study'. A novel like Maurice Gee's *Prowlers* belonged among the prize-winners, and will probably outlast them all.

But the final indignity offered to the state of literature in New Zealand was the special prize awarded to the book rated fourth — *What's Wrong with Bottoms?* — a picture book with text designed to alert children to the possibility of sexual assault and advise them what they might do if it happens. This special award for a special little book got a special round of applause. I knew at that moment how far I and my country had drifted apart.

REFERENCES

Stendhal's Mirror and Yeats's Looking-Glass

1. *Articulate Energy*, London, 1955, p.124.
2. *Ah, Sweet Dancer: W. B. Yeats–Margot Ruddock: A Correspondence*, ed. Roger McHugh, London, 1970, p.81.
3. Yvor Winters, *The Poetry of W. B Yeats*, Denver, 1960.
4. W. H. Auden, 'Petition', in *Collected Shorter Poems 1930-44*, London, 1950, p.120.
5. 'Put on' must mean 'take on', 'assume', 'acquire'. Yvor Winters says the question implies she did put on his *power*, and he asks, 'In what sense? She was quite simply overpowered.' Richard Ellmann (Yeats: *The Man and the Masks*, London, 1949, p.246) says the poem is asking, 'Could power and knowledge ever exist together in this world?' Helen Vendler (*Yeats's Vision and the Later Plays*, Cambridge, Mass., 1963, p.107) says the poem is asking 'whether a special knowledge attaches to the conferred power of artistic creation'.
6. In an earlier version of the poem Yeats had the line 'Did nothing pass before her in the air?'
7. *The Letters of W. B Yeats*, ed. Allan Wade, London, 1954, p.721.
8. Richard Ellmann, *The Identity of Yeats*, London, 1954, p. 225.
9. A. Norman Jeffares, *Commentary on the Collected Poems of W. B. Yeats*, London, 1968, p.299.
10. 'Here is a fragment of my last curse on old age. It means that even the greatest men are owls, scarecrows, by the time their fame has come.' (This is followed by a quotation of a version of stanza 6.) *The Letters of W. B. Yeats*, p.719.

Yeats the European

1. Thomas R. Whitaker, *Swan and Shadow*, Chapel Hill, N.C., 1964, pp.222-32.
2. The stanza describing the incident is there from the earliest remaining drafts of the poem. See Curtis Bradford, *Yeats at Work*, Carbondale, 1965, pp.64-80.
3. *The Letters of W. B. Yeats*, ed. Allan Wade, London, 1954, p.680.
4. *W. B. Yeats*, New York, 1970, p.356.
5. See Grattan Freyer, *W. B. Yeats and the Anti-Democratic Tradition*, Dublin, 1981, p.70.

6. *The Letters of W. B. Yeats*, p.668.
7. See Elizabeth Cullingford, *Yeats, Ireland and Facism*, London, 1984, Chap. 6. Cullingford, p.87, quotes a MS in which Yeats admits he hopes for a German defeat. She explains in some detail why in the context of Irish politics Yeats could not declare this openly.
8. Cullingford, p.118.
9. Richard Ellmann, *The Man and the Masks*, London, 1961, p.249.
10. See Bloom and Whitaker, for example; also George Unterecker, *A Reader's Guide to W. B. Yeats*, p.182: 'For 1919 had brought the end of the First World War and, for the Irish, a time of what seemed deliberate reprisals on England's part for the nationalistic efforts that had gained strength while English attention was focussed on Germany. The Black and Tans and the Auxiliaries were recklessly used to frighten the Irish into submission.'
11. By Roy Foster, Yeats's current official biographer; and by Professor A. N. Jeffares.
12. Even if Yeats had noticed this problem when he changed the title in 1928, he might have found it difficult to correct. Simply substituting 'five years ago' would have deprived the line of a syllable.
13. *The Letters of W. B. Yeats*, p.656.
14. *The Oxford Book of Modern Verse, 1892-1935*, ed. W. B. Yeats, Oxford, 1936, Introduction, xxxiv.

Eliot, Arnold and the English Poetic Tradition

1. *The Use of Poetry and Use of Criticism*, 1933, p.129.
2. 'Literature as Knowledge', *Essays of Four Decades*, 1968, p.76.
3. 'Thomas Gray', *Essays in Criticism Second Series*, 1888; repr. 1960, pp. 54, 56-7.
4. *The Six Chief Lives from Johnson's 'Lives of the Poets'*, ed. with a Preface by Matthew Arnold, 1881, Preface, p. xx.
5. 'Milton', *Essays in Criticism Second Series*, p. 38.
6. 'Wordsworth', op. cit., pp. 88, 91, 93, etc.
7. 'The Metaphysical Poets' (1921), *Selected Essays*, 1951, pp. 286, 287, 288.
8. 'The Metaphysical Poets', *Homage to John Dryden*, 1924, p.30 and *Selected Essays*, p.288. An interesting textual confusion arises from this emendation. In his second essay on Milton (*On Poetry and Poets*, 1957, p.152) Eliot quotes himself as having written 'in an essay on Dryden' that the dissociation of sensibility was 'due to' Milton and Dryden. He appears to have quoted himself from Tillyard's book on Milton, thus mistaking the essay from which the quotation comes, and overlooking his own later emendation.
9. 'Andrew Marvell' (1921), *Selected Essays*, p.293.
10. Ibid., p. 301.
11. 'Milton' (1936), *On Poetry and Poets*, p.142.
12. *Homage to John Dryden*, p.9.
13. 'Andrew Marvell', *Selected Essays*, p.302.
14. Ibid., p.296.
15. Ibid., p.301.
16. 'Poetry in the 18th Century' (1930), *The Pelican Guide to English Literature 4: From Dryden to Johnson*, ed. Boris Ford, 1963, p.275.
17. 'John Dryden' (1921), *Selected Essays*, p.309.
18. Ibid., p.305.
19. Ibid., pp.314-15.
20. Ibid., p.316.
21. 'Andrew Marvell' *Selected Essays*, p.297.
22. 'The Study of Poetry', *Essays in Criticism Second Series*, pp.22, 24.
23. 'Milton' (1936), *On Poetry and Poets*, p.141.
24. 'Milton', *Essays in Criticism Second Series*, p.38.

25. *Mixed Essays* (1879), 1903 ed., p.267.
26. Ibid., p.244.
27. Ibid., p.249.
28. Ibid., p.261.
29. Ibid., p.264.
30. Ibid., pp.265, 266.
31. 'Milton', *Essays in Criticism Second Series*, p. 37.
32. Ibid., p. 40.
33. 'Milton' (1947), *On Poetry and Poets*, p. 158.
34. The obvious case is Collins who, like Joseph Warton, liked to make this distinction. In 'Ode on the Poetical Character' Collins imagines Milton 'From *Waller's* Myrtle Shades retreating', Waller exemplifying the smooth versifying tradition that reached its peak in Dryden and Pope. (Here again we can see a poet offering a view of literary history to justify his own practice.)
35. 'Eliot's Dark Embryo', *The New Poetic*, 1964.
36. 'Milton' (1947), *On Poetry and Poets*, p.160.
37. 'Mr. Gray to Mr. West', *Gray's Poems, Letters and Essays*, with an introduction by John Drinkwater, 1955, p.136.
38. *The Works of Samuel Johnson* . . . in twelve volumes, 1806, xi, *The Lives of the Poets*, p.323.
39. ' . . . through all his greater works there prevails an uniform peculiarity of *Diction* . . . far removed from common use . . .' Ibid., xii, p.157.
40. *The Rambler* No, 168, *The Yale Edition of the Works of Samuel Johnson*, v, p.126.
41. *The Lyrical Ballads* 1798-1805, with an introduction and notes by George Sampson, 1965, p.5.
42. Ibid., p.17.
43. 'Wordsworth', *Essays in Criticism Second Series*, p.93.
44. *Selected Essays*, pp.309–10.
45. Gray, 'The Bard'.
46. 'Andrew Marvell', *Selected Essays*, p.303.
47. 'Observations', *The Egoist*, May 1918.
48. E.g. from 'Shakespeare and the Stoicism of Seneca': 'In truth neither Shakespeare nor Dante [*as poets*, the context implies] did any real thinking — that was not their job . . . The poet makes poetry, the metaphysician makes metaphysics, the bee makes honey, the spider secretes a filament; you can hardly say that any of these agents believes: he merely does', *Selected Essays*, pp.136 and 138; and from 'Arnold and Pater': 'The theory . . . of "art for art's sake" is still valid in so far as it can be taken as an exhortation to the artist to stick to his job . . . The right practice of "art for art's sake" was the devotion of Flaubert or Henry James.' *Selected Essays*, pp.442-3.
49. In 'Arnold and Pater' (1930).
50. See the quotations under note 48 above. And consider also the following from *The Use of Poetry and Use of Criticism*, p.151: 'The chief use of the "meaning" of a poem, in the ordinary sense, may be . . . to satisfy one habit of the reader, to keep his mind diverted and quiet, while the poem does its work upon him . . . This is a normal situation of which I approve.'
51. In *The New Poetic*.
52. 'The Urban Apocalypse', in *Eliot in His Time: Essays on the Occasion of the Fiftieth Anniversary of 'The Waste Land'*, ed. A. Walton Litz, 1973.
53. Ibid., p.34.
54. Ibid., pp.41-2.
55. Ibid., p.48.
56. Ibid., p.46.
57. Sir James G. Frazer, *The Golden Bough*, abridged edition, 1923, p.1.

Auden's 'Spain'

1. *The Poet's Tongue*, ed. W. H. Auden & John Garrett, 1935. Compare the lines in Auden's 'August for the people . . . '
    What better than your strict and adult pen
    Can warn us . . .
    Make action urgent and its nature clear.
2. John Mander, *The Writer and Commitment*, 1961, p.67.
3. Auden's statement (in his foreword to *Collected Shorter Poems 1927-57*) that the stanza equates 'goodness with success' seems to me incorrect. That 'History' 'cannot help or pardon' the defeated is merely a statement of fact. 'History' is here 'the future'. It cannot 'help' the defeated. And *if* their defeat was a result of their inertia, it has no power to pardon — to undo the punishment. That is not to say that the fault is 'unpardonable'.
4. *The Review*, Nos 11-12, 1964 (?), p.46.
5. Mander, p.70, and Frederick Grubb, *A Vision of Reality*, 1965, p.163.
6. 'Looking Back on the Spanish War', *Collected Essays*, 1961, p.217.
7. Stephen Spender, *World Within World*, 1951, p.247.
8. Mander, p.27.
9. *The Crowning Privilege*, p.130.
10. *The Review*, Nos 11-12, 1964 (?), p.51.
11. Hugh D. Ford, *A Poet's War*, 1965, p.288.
12. Spender, p.247.
13. Monroe K. Spears, *The Poetry of W. H Auden*, 1963, p.177.
14. Ford, p.288.
15. Julian Symons, *Critical Occasions*, 1966, p.210.
16. Mander, for example; and Julian Symons, *The Thirties*, 1960, p.124.
17. Ford, p.288.
18. 'Looking Back on the Spanish War', *Collected Essays*, p.217.
19. Ford, p.207.
20. *I Believe* (a collection of essays by 'eminent men and women of our time'), 1940, pp.30-31.
21. 'Inside the Whale', *Collected Essays*, p.145.
22. Certainly on the subject of revisions Auden has been monstrously treated by J. W. Beach (*The Making of the Auden Canon*, 1957), a writer who seems to lack any sense of style, and who proceeds on the assumption that leftist politics and Christianity are *necessarily* opposed.
23. E. P. Thompson argues that it is. (*Out of Apathy*, ed. E. P. Thompson, p.195.)
24. Winter 1965, p.207.
25. Edgell Rickword frowned predictably and doctrinairely on this line describing it as 'emotionally irresponsible'. He called it 'an extraordinary example of what used to be accepted as the aloofness proper to the intellectual, in one who has recently been to Spain'. *New Verse*, Nos 26-27, 1937.
26. Orwell's attack (in his essay 'Inside the Whale') on the line about 'necessary murder' is unjustified. There is nothing to suggest 'murder' in the ordinary sense of the word. One feels Orwell is straining so hard to present himself as the senior in experience that he has lost sight of the poem.

Les Murray: Authentic Oz

1. 'Eric Rolls and the Golden Disobedience', *Persistence in Folly*, Sydney, 1984, p.152.
2. *The Peasant Mandarin: Prose Pieces*, St Lucia, Qld, 1978, pp.172-184.

At Home With the Poets

1. Text of a talk on editing the Penguin by Ian Wedde, distributed by Penguin Books, Auckland, p.4.
2. Chapman, 'Fiction and the Social Pattern', *Landfall*, 7, March 1953; and Baxter, *The Fire and the Anvil*, 1955.

Katherine Mansfield and T. S. Eliot: A Double Centenary

1. The reference here is to Mansfield's 'The Child-Who-Was-Tired' which clearly owes more than it should to Chekhov's story 'Spat' khochetsia'. There is a very full appendix on this in Claire Tomalin's *Katherine Mansfield: A Secret Life*, London, 1987, pp.261-72.
2. Peter Ackroyd, *T.S. Eliot*, London, 1984, p. 20.
3. That Mansfield contracted gonorrhoea is not new; that without it she would have been much less likely to succumb to tuberculosis, is.
4. *Old Friends*, London, 1956, pp.121-22.
5. *The Collected Letters of Katherine Mansfield Volume One 1903-1917*, Oxford, 1984, ed. Vincent O'Sullivan and Margaret Scott, p.312. The moon in Eliot's 'Conversation Galante' is described as 'an old battered lantern hung aloft'.
6. Foreword by T. S. Eliot to *Katherine Mansfield and Other Literary Studies*, John Middleton Murry, London, 1959, p.ix. Eliot's reviewing for the *Athenaeum* led in turn to work for the *TLS*.
7. *The Collected Letters of Katherine Mansfield Volume Two 1918-1919*, Oxford, 1987, ed. Vincent O'Sullivan with Margaret Scott, p.318.
8. *Collected Letters Volume Two*, p.334.
9. *Journal of Katherine Mansfield*, London, 1954, ed. John Middleton Murry, p.124.
10. *Collected Letters Volume Two*, p.356.
11. Eliot had in fact published two reviews of the same book, *Ben Jonson*, by Gregory Smith, one, signed, in the *Athenaeum*, the other unsigned in the *TLS*. These two were later cleverly cobbled together to form the famous essay on Jonson which appeared in *The Sacred Wood* and later in *Selected Essays*. It was only in following up the Mansfield comment that I discovered this double source for what has always been read as a single essay.
12. *Katherine Mansfield's Letters to John Middleton Murry 1913-1922*, ed. John Middleton Murry, London, 1954, p.398.
13. See *Novels & Novelists*, Katherine Mansfield, ed. John Middleton Murry, London, 1930, p.103.
14. See *Novels & Novelists*, p.282.
15. I have to thank Margaret Scott, joint editor of the Mansfield *Collected Letters*, for supplying me with texts of these two letters and four others which refer to Eliot.
16. Letter to Violet Schiff, October 1921. Copy from Margaret Scott.
17. Details of Mansfield's writing during this period are traced on pp.43-45 of my *In the Glass Case: Essays on New Zealand Literature*, Auckland, 1981. The stages of the composition of *The Waste Land* are followed through in detail in Chapter Four of my *Pound, Yeats, Eliot & the Modernist Movement*, London, 1986, and also in the appendix to that book. In a footnote on pp.339-40 of his second biography of Mansfield (1980), Antony Alpers disagrees with my dating the writing of 'A Married Man's Story' as not May 1918, but the autumn of 1921. His footnote is clearly a hasty one, based on my report of a letter from Murry to Sydney Schiff, not on his own reading of it. When I reprinted my Mansfield essay in *In the Glass Case* (it first appeared in *The New Review*, 1977), I considered Alpers's footnote (see *In the Glass Case*, p.280, note 37) and stuck to my guns. When Alpers came to put together an edition of

Mansfield's stories in chronological order, he changed his ground and accepted that 'A Married Man's Story' belongs to 1921, but without any acknowledgement that he had previously argued for the earlier dating.

18. *34 Short Stories*, Katherine Mansfield, selected by Elizabeth Bowen, London, 1957, p.15. The same view of Mansfield's originality and historical importance in the development of modern fiction is found in Frank O'Connor's *The Lonely Voice*, London, 1963, and in T. O. Beachcroft's *The Modest Art*, London, 1968. All three are themselves story writers.

19. *The Diary of Virginia Woolf Volume II: 1920-1924*, ed. Anne Olivier Bell assisted by Andrew McNeillie, London, 1978, p.227.

20. Letter to Violet Schiff, August 1922. Copy from Margaret Scott.

21. Copy from Margaret Scott.

22. *The Letters of T. S. Eliot Volume I 1898-1922*, ed. Valerie Eliot, London, 1988, p.389.

23. *Letters Vol. I*, p.588.

24. *Letters Vol. I*, p.592.

25. Tomalin, p.240-41, and Ackroyd, p.142. It appears Tomalin is referring to an occasion in 1922, and Ackroyd to one in 1926 — but this may be only a result of an ambiguity in Ackroyd's note.

26. *After Strange Gods, A Primer of Modern Heresy*, London, 1933, pp.35-38.

27. 'I threw down Bliss with the exclamation "She's done for!" Indeed I don't see how much faith in her as woman or writer can survive that sort of story.' *The Diary of Virginia Woolf Volume I: 1915-1919*, ed. Anne Olivier Bell, London, 1977, p.179. One could argue that this merely illustrates the jealousy of Mansfield's writing which Woolf later acknowledged, but I think it is more than that. The problem with 'Bliss' is that it uses satire but applies it selectively. We seem to be asked to take Bertha Young, if not on her own terms, at least sympathetically and seriously. But does she deserve less stringency than the Norman Knights or Eddie Warren? Isn't she quite as silly as they? Or conversely, why should the story's charity not have been extended to humanizing them? And then there is an inexcusable, but so far as I know unremarked, error of fact, of a kind which often signals that a writer's imagination is not fully engaged: the story occurs in the spring (the pear tree in blossom is an important symbol), but Bertha arrives home with a load of late summer or autumn fruit, including grapes and pears — something quite impossible before the era of airfreighting.

28. 'K. M.' by Ottoline Morrell, in *Dear Lady Ginger: An Exchange of Letters between Lady Ottoline Morrell and D'Arcy Cresswell*, ed. Helen Shaw, Auckland, 1983, p.120.

29. *The Use of Poetry and the Use of Criticism*, London, 1933, p.69.

30. Lyndall Gordon, *Eliot's New Life*, Oxford, 1988, p. 13.

INDEX

294